PENGUIN BOOKS

MARRIED FOR BETTER, NOT WORSE

Gary B. Lundberg is a licensed marriage and family therapist in private practice and is a clinical member of the American Association for Marriage and Family Therapy. Joy Saunders Lundberg is a writer, speaker, and award-winning lyricist. Their previous book, *I Don't Have to Make Everything All Better,* shows how validating communication techniques can help others help themselves. Together they present seminars, workshops, and keynote addresses thoughout the country and cohost a weekly radio show on relationships called *Morning Break with the Lundbergs.*

Married for Better, Not Worse

THE FOURTEEN SECRETS
TO A HAPPY MARRIAGE

Gary and Joy Lundberg

PENGUIN BOOKS

PENGUIN BOOKS

Published by the Penguin Group

Penguin Putnam Inc., 375 Hudson Street, New York, New York, 10014, U.S.A.

Penguin Books Ltd, 80 Strand, London WC2R 0RL, England

Penguin Books Australia Ltd, 250 Camberwell Road,
Camberwell, Victoria 3124, Australia

Penguin Books Canada Ltd, 10 Alcorn Avenue,
Toronto, Ontario, Canada M4V 3B2

Penguin Books India (P) Ltd, 11 Community Centre
Panchsheel Park, New Delhi – 110 017 India

Penguin Books (N.Z.) Ltd, Cnr Rosedale and Airborne Roads,
Albany, Auckland, New Zealand

Penguin Books (South Africa) (Pty) Ltd, 24 Sturdee Avenue,
Rosebank, Johannesburg 2196, South Africa

Penguin Books Ltd, Registered Offices:
Harmondsworth, Middlesex, England

First published in the United States of America by Viking,
a member of Penguin Putnam Inc. 2001
Published in Penguin Books 2002

1   3   5   7   9   10   8   6   4   2

Grateful acknowledgment is made for permission to use the following copyrighted material:
Excerpt from selection by W. M. Bova from *Check Mates.* Reprinted with permission from
Reader's Digest, September 1990. Copyright © 1990 by The Reader's Digest Assn., Inc.
The Lockhorns cartoon. By permission of Wm. Hoest Enterprises.
Arlo & Janice and *For Better or Worse* cartoons. Reproduced by permission
of Newspaper Enterprise Association, Inc.
Excerpt from *Dear Abby* column by Abigail Van Buren. © 2000 Universal Press Syndicate.
Reprinted with permission. All rights reserved.

THE LIBRARY OF CONGRESS HAS CATALOGED THE HARDCOVER EDITION AS FOLLOWS:
Lundberg, Gary B.
Married for better, not worse : the fourteen secrets to a happy marriage / Gary and Joy Lundberg.
p.   cm.
Includes bibliographical references.
ISBN 0-670-89983-6 (hc.)
ISBN 0 14 20.0087 6 (pbk.)
1. Marriage.   2. Communication in marriage.   I. Lundberg, Joy Saunders.   II. Title.
HQ734 .L82   2001
306.81—dc21   00-047741

Printed in the United States of America
Set in Bembo / Designed by Cindy LaBreacht

Contents

Acknowledgments

Many people have given freely of their time to assist us in making this book a reality. We are filled with gratitude at their goodness and willingness to join in this effort to help marriages be fulfilling and happy. Their wisdom and experiences have been invaluable and we couldn't have done it without them. So we say:

(1) Thank you to the many couples and individuals who responded to our survey and gave us permission to share their experiences. Some had serious struggles they were dealing with and others were in deeply rewarding marriage relationships. Each shed light on ways to find joy in marriage.

(2) Thank you to the following who critiqued our original manuscript and gave us great suggestions and enthusiastic encouragement: Ken Atchity (our fabulous agent), Tracy Taylor (our dedicated assistant), Dr. Thomas and Marilou Myers, Ester Rasband, Shawna Powelson, Janice Kapp Perry, Lynne Christy, Jan Godfrey, Dr. Virgil Kovalenko, Elaine Rapier, Dan and Deb Christensen, David Dodge, Dr. Lynn Jay and Elaine Lundberg, and Don and Jonia Lundberg (our brothers and their wives).

(3) Thank you to those who have assisted in the editing process: Al Christy for his insights and professional tips during the early stages of the manuscript, Jessica Kipp for her kind calls and assistance in working with us, and our editor,

associate publisher at Viking Penguin, Jane von Mehren—the one person we cannot thank enough. Jane is a master editor in every sense of the word. Her editing skills always amaze us. She has the ability to bring out the best in us and make us look better than we are. She's priceless!

(4) Thanks to our parents: Lynne and Elese Lundberg and Clarence and Opal Saunders for giving us beautiful examples of holding on to marriage and showing us how to make it work.

(5) Thanks to our children and their spouses: Mike and Hyun, Lynda and George, Carol and Kim, John and Rose, and Paul and Amy for being so open and willing to share their marriage ups and downs with us. Their critiques and ideas were extemely valuable.

(6) Now last and most important, we say thank you to a loving Heavenly Father whom we turned to daily for help in writing this book. If it ends up being a blessing to our readers, we give the glory to Him.

Introduction

*A successful marriage requires falling in love
many times, always with the same person.*
—MIGNON MCLAUGHLIN

Most people are on a search for happiness. When asked "What do you want?" most of us answer, "I want to be happy." And for most of us happiness includes being married to our best friend and having children, a home, and a good job. That happiness is enhanced when you share it with a mate is a truism Americans live by: At least 90 percent of the U.S. adult population marries at least once. Even those who divorce seem to retain the desire for a spouse since a high percentage of them remarry.

There is so much hope and excitement as a couple starts out their married life. Together they are ready to face whatever life brings. As we travel throughout the country for our seminars and workshops, it is a pleasure to visit those who are holding on to each other and finding happiness in their mutual strength. Couples growing old together, enjoying children, grandchildren, and even great-grandchildren, is such a stabilizing force in human relations. The challenge is for couples of all ages to be jointly committed to this goal.

Today, 50 percent of the couples who marry end up divorcing. When there are problems, the belief seems to be that "this marriage must be wrong and I will find a better life with someone else." And yet is that always, even often, true?

In an article entitled "D-I-V-O-R-C-E Does Not Spell Relief"[1] Lois Glenn Carlton recounts her experiences looking back from the vantage point of her third marriage. She begins, "After having survived two divorces, neither of which were my fault, of course, I look back on that part of my life with the wisdom of a retired pit-bull. It was tough, hard to let go of, and the scars are still healing." Her first marriage, at age sixteen, lasted two years, with one child. Her second marriage lasted fifteen years and saw the birth of "five more children, a much larger waistline, [and] an ulcer . . ." With the passage of time, she has a different perspective:

> Fourteen years after that divorce, I came upon a few letters I received from my ex-husband before the divorce. I saw things in those letters I had been too hurt or bitter to see then. I saw his pain, anger, and fear and knew it was time for some forgiveness. I wrote him and apologized for my part. I received a phone call in return. It helped and I can only hope our children will someday forgive us for the pain we selfishly inflicted on them.
>
> Did I learn anything from these experiences? I learned that no one is perfect. There is no white knight in shining armor to pluck me from a fate worse than death and carry me off to a romantic forever. I learned divorce does not necessarily end the relationship. There are always birthdays, holidays, illnesses, and other occasions that will bring the estranged couples together, like it or not. Meeting in court to haggle over child support is another popular rendezvous. I believe divorce should be an absolute last resort. I am not speaking of spouse or child abuse, that needs immediate help and counseling. But for the largest percentage of couples, being out of commitment is the root problem . . . Divorce may

bring temporary relief, but it is just temporary. Having a new mate is exciting in the getting-to-know-you stages, but since people aren't perfect you will soon have a new set of personality clashes. When the romantic dust settles, and the starry eyes focus, if you have not squared away the old insecurities and upgraded a poor self-image, the old buttons are easily pushed . . .

No one can make me happy, and no matter how much my mates loves me, it soon gets tiresome for him to be constantly reassuring me. Living on compliments is like an addiction. One is never enough and leads to searching outside the home when the source dries up. Happiness is a state of mind and mostly has to do with how you feel about yourself. And how you feel about yourself is your responsibility, not his . . . I've been married almost fourteen years this time, but I'll probably never have a golden anniversary partly because I'll be too old. And most all my children have eloped because they can't figure out how to work one father and two stepfathers and stepmothers into the [wedding receiving] line . . . So how do I spell relief? I know for sure it isn't D-I-V-O-R-C-E . . . [It] always ends up spelled L-O-V-E.

At a recent workshop, one divorced man, who has been dating divorced women, told us, "In most cases I hear them say, 'I acted too hastily. I wish I would have stayed married to my husband.'" It seems that many people learn only in retrospect. When the hard times come, our faith and trust in the marriage get replaced by hurt, anger, and blame. Then comes the demand for a divorce. Why is this scene repeated time and again in homes as well as in therapy and ecclesiastical and law offices throughout the world? There is so much pain and confusion, so many lives torn apart, so many lifelong scars inflicted on so many—so much wasted time, energy, and resources.

For several years we have been presenting seminars based on the principles in our book *I Don't Have to Make Everything All Better,* and a few years ago we were asked by a church group to create a two-day marriage retreat, addressing issues not covered in the book as well as teaching how our validation principles work within the marital relationship. Since then we have presented many marriage retreats and workshops and have found that they are helping couples find greater happiness in their marriages and, in some cases, saving troubled marriages.

One young married woman told us, "Your marriage seminar has made a huge difference in our marriage. I begged my husband to go with me and he drug his feet all the way. Then you began and he really got into it. It was down-to-earth information that we both could relate to. It's amazing how it has helped us. We're having so much more fun being married to each other now."

Two years ago a couple contemplating divorce came to one of our retreats as a last resort. They had put their house up for sale and were on the path to divorce. After the retreat they took their house off the market and began working on putting their marriage back together. Now they have built a new home and are working at building a happy life. At another retreat a couple attended soon after the husband confessed having an affair. They didn't know if their marriage could survive, but by the end of the last session they had decided that they wanted to work to save their relationship. Today, two years later, they are still together and succeeding at it.

It is our experiences with the marriage retreats and workshops we have presented, along with years of clinical practice, that form the basis of this book. In addition, we bring the experience of more than forty years of private practice as marriage partners and parents of five children as well as more than twenty years as business partners. Through the years, we have forged a strong belief in marriage and learned a great deal about how to preserve it.

To add to our understanding of the issues that arise in a marriage, we sent a survey to four hundred people in different parts of the United States. They were asked to describe the things they had experienced or observed that make a marriage miserable. Discovering the miseries opens a way to suggest some resolutions. We are grateful to the large number of people who responded and for their openness in what they shared. Their insights helped guide us to formulate this book. We have liberally illustrated our fourteen principles with actual and combined experiences from clients, from the survey, and from interviews and conversations with others. (All names and identifying details have been changed to protect the privacy of each person.) Many of those we talked with expressed the hope that their experiences might help other couples.

The 14 secrets we share in this book are the fundamentals of a good marriage that many people forget, ignore, or never put into practice. We also share with you doable methods of putting these fundamentals into practice that will bring happiness to every couple willing to use them daily. These secrets can help build or restore a strong foundation to your marriage no matter how long you've been with your spouse. Marriage is more than passionate romance. As you apply these fundamental principles, however, the deeply tender moments of romance will resurface again and again.

It is our hope that couples will work together in applying these principles. If only one uses them, the total effectiveness may be hampered significantly. One person, however, can start the process and make a difference.

For ease in reading we have written this book as though Gary were the only writer; however, the writing has been shared jointly by both of us. So now, please turn the pages and begin your journey in discovering the secrets that will help you achieve a happy marriage.

—Gary and Joy Lundberg

Married for Better, Not Worse

Return to the Beginning

Memories are the key not to the past, but to the future.—CORRIE TEN BOOM

ROMANTIC BEGINNINGS

Getting married is one of the most important steps in our lives. Whether our beginnings were blindly romantic or cautious and uncertain, all of us allowed hope to override any doubt when we said, "I do." We were able to do so because of our tender experiences with one another. Take a few minutes to think back and remember what your love was like in the beginning. This is an important step even if you are still a newlywed. It's amazing how quickly you can forget the very early stages of your romance during your courtship and even the first few weeks of your marriage. For those who have been married longer, the following three examples of other couples may stir your memories.

> **NEW LOVE IS VIBRANTLY PASSIONATE LOVE.**

➤ Devin remembers the anticipation he felt on the night he asked Laurie to marry him. His heart pounded; he checked the pocket of his jeans again and again. The ring was still there, just waiting for the moment. He took Laurie by the hand, leading her onto a rustic worn footbridge.

They had been here only once—the year before when they had accidentally run on to this quiet little park in search of a place to enjoy a picnic. This was where he had first told her he loved her. He knew this was the place to ask the most wonderful girl he had ever known the most important question of their lives.

Devin held Laurie in his arms, tenderly kissed her, then whispered, "I love you, Laurie." He took her hand, slipped the sparkling diamond on her finger, and said the words, "Will you marry me?" His heart nearly leaped out of his body when she cried, "Yes! Yes! I love you, too, with all my heart." And their lips met again in a passionate expression of their love for each other.

For the next few months they planned, talked, disagreed, then agreed, laughed, played, and were certain that their life together would be one of love and joy for always, no matter what happened.

➤ Elly's memory of the night Jay proposed to her remains vivid in her mind. She and Jay had been dating for three years. They were in love and they both knew it. They enjoyed concerts, ran together nearly every morning in Central Park, chattered endlessly about political issues they felt passionate about, and shared their job frustrations regularly. They were perfect for each other. So why wouldn't Jay pop the question? Every time Elly even hinted at marriage he would skillfully change the subject. One evening, as they sat sharing dessert in a cozy little restaurant, Elly tried again.

"This morning Maryanne came to work flashing a diamond ring on her left hand," she said. "She was two feet off the ground telling us all about how her boyfriend had finally asked her to marry him. Jay, honey, do you think we . . ."

He interrupted her, "Well, good for Maryanne. Hey, the Knicks are playing tomorrow night. Sam gave me a couple of tickets. Want to go?"

He had done it again and she was sick of it!

"Stop it!" she said. "Don't you get it, Jay? I love you and I want to be with you for the rest of my life, but I can't take this any longer. Either you and I are getting married or we're through!"

"I'm just not ready for marriage, Elly."

"Just what is it that you're afraid of?" she demanded.

"I don't know. My parents' marriage ended in divorce and I was devastated. I vowed that I would never let that happen to my kids. I'm not ready, Elly, and I don't know if I ever will be. I can't do it."

"Fine! Then we *are* through!" In tears she ran out the door as he sat watching her go.

That night Elly couldn't sleep; all she could do was cry. She loved Jay and couldn't stand to think of life without him. It was two o'clock in the morning when her phone rang.

"Elly, I love you more than anything in this world. I couldn't bear to lose you. Will you marry me?"

It wasn't in a quiet romantic setting with a ring in hand, but there he was, on the phone actually saying the words.

"Oh, yes!" she cried. "I love you so much."

The next day they went ring shopping and even set the date. And both of them knew it was right.

➤ Conner and Esther's beginning was less than ideal. They were sixteen when they started dating and their young love was intense. They planned to go to college and have successful careers. Their plan was to get married after graduating, but the summer before entering college something happened that changed it all.

They were sitting in the bleachers watching a baseball game when Esther mustered the courage to tell Conner. She knew he loved her, but was worried that the news she was about to give him could ruin it all. Looking at him with tears in her eyes she said, "I think I'm pregnant."

"You're what? Are you sure?" Conner asked in disbelief.

"The tests are positive. There's no question. We're going to have a baby."

"This really changes our plans, doesn't it?" Conner said.

She had been so worried about this moment. Would he push for an abortion? That just wouldn't be an option for her. Much to her great relief, he felt the same way. And no, they couldn't give their child up for adoption. He held her in his arms and they cried together. Then he said, "Esther, we can make it through this, but we're not bringing a baby into the world without married parents."

"Is that a proposal?"

"Yes, it is. A few years earlier than we planned, but a definite proposal."

"And my answer is yes. I love you with all my heart and we are going to make this work."

Even if your engagement experience wasn't like any of these, you can still relate as you remember the joy of that moment when you realized how deep your love was and how much you wanted to be together in spite of all the odds. New love is vibrantly passionate love. In the beginning, the love a couple shares feels like nothing could ever harm it. During that stage of your life you may have observed other married couples who were struggling and wondered, "Why can't they see how they're messing up their marriage? We won't let that happen to us. We'll be different." And you firmly believed it. You made strong commitments to each other and you intended to keep them. You *vowed* to keep them! Then life's tasks come in and overshadow those early intentions and your marriage journey becomes complicated. One day you realize that you, too, have begun having the kind of relationship problems that plague so many marriages. And you may be wondering, *How did this happen to us?*

WE NEED HELP

As Ted and Jill came into my office they carried a rather stern look and their faces had an ashen hue. They entered, rapidly moved to the couch, and sat rigidly, making sure they had some space between them. After going through the getting-acquainted phase, I asked them, each in turn, what brought them to my office. Each had his or her list of complaints and offenses, along with a laundry list of what the other person needed to do.

As I listened to their complaints, I wondered how these two people got together. So I asked them how they met. Then I asked Ted what motivated him to ask Jill out on their first date. He sneaked a quick glance at Jill and said, "I saw her, thought she was cute, and decided to ask her out." I then asked Jill the reason she said yes to his invitation and she, too, sneaked a quick look at Ted and said, "He was handsome and looked like fun."

WHEN COUPLES START TO REMEMBER THEIR BEGINNINGS THE WHOLE ATMOSPHERE CHANGES.

Then I asked Ted, "What caused you to ask her to marry you?" That question brought a longer glance and a little giggle from both of them. He began to relax a little and replied, "We had a lot of fun together and I fell in love with her and I thought she would be a great mother for our children." Jill's answer to "What caused you to accept his proposal?" was much the same. As she spoke she reached out and gently touched Ted's leg and he nervously shifted and slid a little closer to Jill. As they remembered their beginnings they relaxed and their natural color returned to their faces.

Ted and Jill's response is common. The answers to the

questions vary, of course. "A friend introduced us and I thought she would be fun." "I saw her walk down the street of our little town and I couldn't get her off my mind." Sometimes the wife was the first to ask for a date and the couple will laugh about that. Desirable attributes that attracted them to each other vary, and when couples start to remember their beginnings, they begin to relax and the whole atmosphere changes.

After Ted and Jill reviewed their beginnings, I asked them what they do for fun. The glance they gave to each other told the story even before they replied in unison, "Nothing!" Then Jill spoke up and said, "We used to have fun before we got married. We went dancing, out to eat, and would sit for hours just talking to each other. I don't know what happened. I guess we just ran out of time for each other."

Sometimes change happens so gradually that we are lulled into complacency and almost don't wake up until it's too late. What were the things that affected Ted and Jill's connectedness? Schooling, jobs, his wanting to stay involved in sports and be with his buddies, money worries, pregnancy and birth of their children, job changes, civic involvement, her shopping with friends, preschool, washing clothes, cleaning house, fixing meals, buying a new home and fixing it up, PTA, church involvement . . . and the list went on and seemed to grow almost daily. "It just seems we run out of time for us," mused Jill. "It's so easy to take each other for granted."

IN ORDER TO MAKE A CHANGE, YOU NEED TO FIRST FIND A PLACE TO BEGIN.

Change will not just come. We first must recognize that something is not working and then be willing to change that something. This reminds me of a saying attributed to that "great philosopher" Anonymous: "If you do what you have always done, you'll get what you've always got. Is that enough?" That's a good statement to think about regarding your marriage.

In order to make a change, you need to first find a place to begin. In an interview with *Newsweek,* Dr. John Gottman, author of *The Seven Principles for Making Marriage Work,* reported, "[One] quick way to test whether a couple still has a chance is to ask what initially attracted them to each other. If they can recall those magic first moments (and smile when they talk about them), all is not lost. We can still fan the embers."[2] I have used this strategy in my practice for years and here's how you can begin the process:

STEP 1. WALK DOWN MEMORY LANE Set the stage for your walk down memory lane. You can do something as simple as going for a walk in the park, taking a ride in the country, or having a nice quiet dinner at home or at a lovely restaurant. The point is to be anywhere where you can be alone stress free and without a phone (turn it off if you're at home). If you have children, arrange for them to be well taken care of so you won't have to worry about them. It won't work if they are upstairs in bed or in another room, with others in the house. Remember this is a time for just the two of you. You can enhance these conversations if you have the love songs that were popular when you were dating, softly playing in the background on a CD or tape player. If you have one particular song that was *your* song, play it. Milk those memories and let them flow.

This time together is for you to discuss things that will build and strengthen your marriage. Talk about good things—look at the positive side of your mate. Take this time to find out things you may have never known or taken the time to discover. The following are some suggestions and ideas of things to talk about. You could copy this list so you can more easily refer to it that night.

Questions to Help You Remember

1. Where did you first see each other? And how did you get introduced?
2. When you first met, what attracted you to your spouse?

3. What do you remember most about that first meeting?
4. What caused you to ask for the first date?
5. What feelings did you have when you first kissed?
6. What were the most endearing acts or words that made you realize that this relationship was intended to be a lasting one?
7. What physical features do you love the most about your spouse?
8. What characteristic brings you the greatest feeling of security or comfort from your spouse?
9. What characteristic has your spouse brought from his or her childhood home to your family for which you are grateful?
10. Name at least one area in which your knowledge or expertise has been increased by your association with your spouse.
11. Share with your spouse a time when you felt especially close to her or him.
12. What were your most fun and memorable dates during courtship?
13. What activities would you enjoy doing now for a fun date?
14. If you could have a day alone together how would you want to spend it?
15. What could you do to make your next anniversary celebration fun and memorable?

You can find a great deal of pleasure in revisiting the feelings you had in your courtship and early married life. Sharing your memories *of* each other *with* each other can be very romantic. If you allow yourself to be open and free with your memories, *without correcting or criticizing each other,* it can be a lot of fun. Chad and Shirleen, a couple who attended one of our marriage retreats, said they got so involved in this process that when they reached question number thirteen on the list they wrote down enough fun ideas to last for their next twenty dates.

Another couple, Maurie and Jessica, said they were surprised at what happened as they did this assignment. Jessica said, "We haven't had that much fun talking with each other for a very long time." By letting yourselves get involved in sharing and remembering, you can rekindle, as the song says, "that old feeling called love."

Some couples have had less than ideal beginnings. Maybe they weren't in love, but it just seemed right to get married. Or maybe they married because it seemed right to their parents or someone else. What then? If you fall into this category, don't despair. Yours can become an enjoyable, fulfilling love affair with each other as well. You can begin now to create loving moments that will make happy memories. Focus on the future—try using the answers to question numbers thirteen to fifteen on page 8 as a place to start. Let your imagination soar. Dream a little here—pretend you are independently wealthy and could go anywhere and do anything together you wanted to. What would it be? Fantasies that may never come true can be a lot of fun to dream about together. And, who knows, maybe someday they might. But if they never do, at least you've had the fun of dreaming about it. Then get realistic and plan something that is possible, something you'll both enjoy. It takes *doing it* to make it happen. We have seen it work. People who thought they were not in love, fell deeply in love by doing the fun things, the caring things that create romance.

> WE SHOW WE REALLY CARE BY PAYING ATTENTION TO OUR MATE'S COMMENTS, DESIRES, AND CHOICES.

STEP 2. GET BETTER ACQUAINTED We often assume that we know our mates very well, and that may or may not be true. Have you ever been at a social gathering when a spouse remarks, "I know my wife better than she knows herself."

Only to have the wife lean over and very quietly say, "He doesn't really know me. He just thinks he does."

Over time individuals change and so do their preferences. Or sometimes circumstances force us to make changes we don't want. For example, Fred loves to grocery shop, and when he does, he likes to buy little things for his wife Louise that she hesitates to buy for herself. She likes black olives, and because he dislikes them with a passion, she would rarely buy them. As a treat, Fred used to buy them periodically for Louise. But now she has to watch her cholesterol levels, which limits her olive eating. So when Fred wants to buy her a surprise he chooses something different. Louise never knows what he'll come home with—it may be her favorite fruits such as pomegranates, papayas, tangelos, or best of all, blueberries—but all elicit a big smile and hug for Fred.

Unless we talk about our likes and dislikes regularly with our mates, the changes may go unnoticed. If a box of chocolates has always been your favorite gift to your wife and she is now on a diet, she's not going to be thrilled with the chocolates. That's the time for her favorite flowers or something else that you know is appropriate for now.

As in the first step, the two of you need a place where you will have some uninterrupted time in order to accomplish this step of getting better acquainted. Keep in mind that this is *not* a test; it is a time of sharing and learning. Ask your mate for the information, and when you are asked, please do not reply, "Well, you should know that" or "You mean you don't know that after all this time we've been together?" Remember, this is time to enjoy talking, sharing, and possibly finding out something new or different about your mate. Make two copies of the list that follows so you can each fill in the blanks as you ask about each other's favorites. Don't just guess. And don't be a stick-in-the-mud. Talk! Laugh! Have some fun while you gather this information.

THIS IS NOT A TEST: IT IS A TIME OF SHARING AND LEARNING.

My Mate's Favorite Things

FOOD

RESTAURANT —————————————————————————

MAIN DISH ———————————— DESSERT ——————————

BEVERAGE ———————————— CANDY ——————————

MOVIES

TYPE —————————————————————————

MOST RECENT —————————————————————

ACTOR ———————————— ACTRESS ——————————

MUSIC

TYPE —————————————————————————

SONG —————————————————————————

SINGER/GROUP ——————————————————————

SPORTS

TYPE ———————————— TEAM ——————————

ATHLETES ——————————————————————————

RELAXATION

TV SHOW ——————————————————————————

BOOK —————————————————————————

HOBBIES ——————————————————————————

OTHER

CAR —————————————————————————

FLOWER —————————————————————————

COLOR —————————————————————————

Add anything else you want to the list. This list can be very valuable, so keep it and refer to it periodically. When you want to say "I love you" in your mate's language of love, use this information. Louise did this for Fred. He walked out of his study one afternoon and there sitting on the floor in the middle of the hall was one of his favorite candy bars with a little love note. The novelty of where she put it was half the fun; he nearly stepped on it. Earlier in their marriage he confessed he might have said, "How come you put it on the floor? I could have stepped on it." How loving would that have been? Get out of yourself and enjoy the fun. Remember, it's the little things that matter because they say "I'm thinking about you." That applies when you do something for your mate and when you graciously accept something that your mate does for you.

> **IT'S THE LITTLE THINGS THAT MATTER BECAUSE THEY SAY "I'M THINKING ABOUT YOU."**

STEP 3. GET BACK TO THE SIMPLE BASICS OF RESPECT

As couples come into my office, I watch how they treat each other. I see where they sit in relationship to each other, how they look at each other, and how they talk to each other. Often there is a lack of respect in their language and tone of voice. One or the other will become impatient and either finish the other's sentences, or just ignore what is being said and talk right over the top of the other. Here's an example of a dialogue I had with two of my clients, Tami and Will:

Gary: What brings you here?

Tami: We're having problems and we can't seem to fix them ourselves. We need help.

Gary: What kind of problems are you having?

Will: Nothing I do is ever enough.

Tami: What do you mean? That's all you do is *nothing*. I'm sick of having to do everything myself.

Will: I resent that. I work darn hard trying to keep a roof over our heads.

Tami: And that's all that matters to you. You don't ever help the kids with their homework. You don't ever help clean up the place. I do it all. And you don't ever appreciate *anything* I do. Yesterday I cooked one of your favorite meals and all you did was eat it, without a word, and then, like always, sat in your stupid chair and watched TV.

Will: So? I'm tired! What do you want me to say?

Tami: Nothing! You wouldn't know how to say it anyway!

Will: (Turning to Gary) See what I have to put up with?

Tami: What *you* have to put up with?!

That's when I stopped it. Now I had a view of their disrespectful attitudes toward each other. I couldn't help but ask myself, *Are these two people adults or little kids?* Sometimes I say to a couple, "I wish you could be in my position and listen to you two." They are startled at first, then look a little sheepish, and then make a remark of how awful it must sound.

These kinds of disrespectful interactions must be changed in order to build happiness and safety into a marriage. One place to start is in the very basic interpersonal treatment we learned as children. Most parents insist their children show respect by using common courtesy: saying "please" and "thank you." When I asked Tami and Will if they ever used these words with each other, Will said, "We used to all the time. I guess we just assumed that we didn't need to anymore. After all, we're adults and should know that's what we meant."

"Anyway," Tami remarked, "we make sure our kids use them." And yet one of their issues was the lack of respect they felt from each other. I asked them to think about how their conversation would have gone if, when Will said, "I work darn hard trying to keep a roof over our heads" Tami had responded with, "Thank you, honey. I appreciate how hard you work." Or if Will had ignored Tami's other comments and said, "Thanks for cooking that meal for me. It was delicious."

There is an interesting power in the use of those two simple words. In order to use "please" and "thank you," you have to get out of yourself because you become more aware of the other person and what he or she is doing. The recipient hears respect and recognition in your acknowledgment. Opportunities to use these words with your mate surround you. Instead of saying, "Hand me the newspaper," how about, "Please hand me the newspaper." And then, "Thank you." When two kids need you at once, instead of saying, "Take care of Suzie. I'll get Tommy." You could say, "Honey, please take care of Suzie while I get Tommy." And then follow up with "Thank you." After a couple of weeks of working at using "please" and "thank you" with each other, Tami and Will reported that there was a little more peace between them and they also saw a difference in their children.

THERE IS A POWER IN THE USE OF THESE TWO SIMPLE WORDS— PLEASE AND THANK YOU

There's another little courtesy phrase that gets forgotten. It's "You're welcome." When your husband opens the door for you, do you say, "Thank you"? Does he respond with "You're welcome"? These illustrations are the everyday occurrences that cry out for courtesy. They seem so obvious, yet many couples forget to use these simple words with the most significant person in their life—their chosen mate. Simple approaches, such as this, clear the path for being able to work on deeper and harder issues in marriage. After a few more sessions Will stated, "Without setting this simple respectful beginning, I'm not sure we would be as far along as we are."

One woman told me she went to work out of the home because that was the only place she was treated with courtesy and appreciation. Think of the contentment and love that could be restored to marriages if these caring courtesies were used.

IT WORKS

You can rekindle the early romantic feelings you had for each other if you refocus your thoughts about your mate and start to change by doing the three simple steps in this chapter:

1. Return to the beginning and remember those early feelings.
2. Take the time to get better acquainted with each other.
3. Show each other common courtesy and respect.

Please don't discount the importance of these three simple steps. They work wonders in a marriage when couples are willing to put forth the effort and do them, just as the following example illustrates:

> After twenty years of serving in military posts around the world, often without his family, a colonel in the marines retired in a Maryland suburb to work as a consultant. He was ready to spend more time with his wife and, in effect, make up for some lost time. His wife, however, had become involved in her own catering business and volunteer work. She didn't seem to have the time for him that he was counting on.
>
> The colonel decided to sweep his wife off her feet *just as he had so many years before.* In the evenings when he knew she'd come home exhausted from catering a big reception he would have a fire burning in the fireplace and greet her at the door with a refreshing drink. After checking her schedule with her assistant, he planned a weekend at a romantic inn on Maryland's Eastern Shore and sent her a formal invitation requesting the pleasure of her presence. These two now describe themselves as "a couple of honeymooners."[3]

Any couple can rekindle the loving relationship they had in the beginning by taking the steps that make it happen.

BEGIN TODAY

Set a date tonight when you will begin steps one and two, and *keep the date.* Have fun as you remember your beginnings and as you discover and review each other's favorites. Put step three into practice immediately by making a solemn promise to yourself that you will begin using "please," "thank you," and "you're welcome" when talking to your spouse. Be patient with your mate and yourself if the courtesies aren't used consistently at first. It takes a little time to break old habits and build new ones. Then get ready to enjoy the fun and the feelings of increased love that will inevitably come.

Keep Your Mate at the Top of Your List

*The path of true love is only wide
enough for two.* —HAL BOYLE

FALSE IMPRESSION

"Sometimes I feel like even the dog means more to my wife/husband than I do." Have you ever felt like that? Or has your mate ever expressed that feeling? There may be times when you give that impression to your mate and you don't mean to at all. Life can be like a freeway full of huge semi-trucks pulling two and three piggyback loads, bearing down at full speed and pushing your treasured little Corvette right off the road. That's what can happen to your spouse, your most valued treasure. Without even realizing it, you may be pushing him or her right off the road.

Or maybe you are in the category of being completely content just cruising along in that semi while your mate is off the road, stuck in the mud, and you don't even have a clue. Charese and Gordon are a typical example of this. Here's how she feels about their life together:

Gordon is very happy with life. He has his boat that he loves to work on and sail. When he's not doing that he's enjoying his other hobbies. He's been very successful in his business and has provided well for me. I shouldn't complain because I have so much, but what I don't have much of is *him*. I know he loves me, I think. And I love him. He's happy, but I'm not. I just wish he loved me enough to want to spend time with me. I don't think I'm very high on his list of priorities.

If you make a conscious effort to keep your mate at the top

IDENTIFY THE PRESSURES THAT MAY BE PUSHING YOUR MATE "OFF THE ROAD."

of your list of important people and events, then he or she will feel it, and your love will grow stronger and stronger. However long you have been married, now is the time to open your eyes to your own situation and identify the pressures that may be pushing your mate "off the road."

PARENTING PRESSURES

Children can bring a great deal of joy to a couple, and they can also put a tremendous amount of pressure on the marriage relationship. Let's look in on Cindy and Brent and see how they handled this challenge:

With oven mitts on both hands Cindy pulled the baked chicken part way out of the oven to check it. Not done yet, but at least it was beginning to smell good. She knew Brent would be hungry and nothing beats the aroma of delicious food after a hard day's work. The table was set and ready. One thing she had learned before quitting her job to be a full-time mom was that it is very smart to set the table early because even if dinner isn't on time, it looks like it's at least on the agenda.

"Mommy, read me a story. Pleeeeeease," came the plea from little Meggie as she pulled on Cindy's pant leg. *I need to take a minute and read to her,* she thought. *She's been feeling a little displaced lately.*

"Waaaaaaaah," came the cry from the nursery. Already it was time to nurse Timmy again. She and their two-month-old baby still hadn't hit on a convenient schedule. *Will we ever?* she wondered.

"I need to feed Timmy first. Okay?"

"No!" Meggie threw the book down and ran crying to her room. Timmy went into a full-blown hunger scream. Blowing a strand of hair out of her eyes, Cindy said to herself, *I'll get the baby and then take care of Meggie.*

As she hurried down the hall to get Timmy, ten-year-old Marc hollered from his room, "Mom, where's my hockey shirt? I need it right now and I can't find it anywhere. I'm going to be late for practice!"

Somewhere in the background Cindy heard, "Hi, honey. I'm home."

In this chaotic situation how does Cindy help Brent know he is number one on her list? How does Brent let Cindy know she is number one on his? First, consider the following scenario and how it would make each of them feel.

From the nursery Cindy yelled, "Thank heavens you're home, Brent! Go read a story to Meggie. She's driving me nuts!" She picked up the baby, went to Marc's room, and said, "I don't know where your shirt is. If you would take care of your clothes you'd know where they are."

"I've had a very hard day today," Brent said loudly as he made his way through a trail of toys into the kitchen. "I'm too tired to read to Meggie. What's for dinner?"

What's happening here? Do either of their comments help the other feel like number one? Brent probably feels pretty much like number four about this time. If this occurs often he will feel unimportant to Cindy, only valued as a helper, but not as a husband. Likewise, Cindy may decide he only cares about *his* needs. Hers don't matter, as if he's the only one who's had a hard day. And the only thing on his mind is what's for dinner.

Notice the difference as you read this scenario:

Somewhere in the background Cindy heard, "Hi, honey. I'm home." She quickly plugged in the binky, set Timmy in his infant seat with a few toys, ignored Marc's complaints and Meggie's whimpering, and made a beeline for the front door.

Throwing her arms around Brent's neck she gave him a big hug as she said, "Welcome home, you handsome devil!"

"Hey, I've only been gone for . . . let's see . . . about seven hours."

"Only seven hours! Well," she laughed, "I swear it felt like seven days."

"For me, too." And with that comment she planted a delicious kiss on his lips.

Meggie ran to the scene, "Hi, Daddy!" He scooped her up with a big hug. "Mommy won't read me a story."

"She won't? Good. That means I get to. Why don't you pick out a book while I change my clothes." Then smiling at Cindy he says, "Mmmmm. Something sure smells good."

"And it's coming right up, just as soon as I give some nourishment to Timmy."

"That kid has no idea how lucky he is, nestling into two of the most beautiful . . ."

"Watch it!" She smiled at the thought of Brent doing the nestling. And somehow, almost simultaneously, she remembered she may have washed a hockey shirt that morning. "Marc," she says, peeking into his room, "try the laundry room."

Now we're talking number one! On both counts. The chaos is still there, but Cindy is wise enough to put it on the back burner while she welcomes her husband home. He is the most important person in her life. She adored him and he adored her when they courted, and they have never lost the feeling of wanting to be together. With that feeling still intact, they are able to handle the family needs together.

> WHEN ONE MATE FEELS VALUED BY THE OTHER IT BECOMES NATURAL TO RETURN THE ATTENTION.

When one mate feels valued by the other it becomes natural to return the attention. Even though at times it takes effort and concentration, it pays off in a big way, and love will only grow stronger.

Some may read the last scenario of Brent and Cindy and think, *That's too ideal. It's just not real life.* If it's not real life in your house, then it could be. Paying attention to each other can change an otherwise miserable evening into a pleasant time of sharing family responsibilities.

This kind of loving attention can have the same positive result in any husband/wife situation, even when it's more complex than Brent and Cindy's schedule. When both partners work full-time and still have children to care for, the possibility of being knocked out of the number one spot increases. The greater the demands on time from outside sources, the greater the possibility of stress on the marriage relationship.

Kent and Sylvia are both employed full-time and have three children, ages nine, thirteen, and sixteen. In addition to the pressures of their jobs and children, they are actively involved in their church. Some days it seems like there just isn't enough time for all their commitments, let alone their marriage. To make sure their marriage doesn't fall into the background, they keep connected by working together fixing meals, cleaning up, and helping with the kids. It is their way of showing that they care about each other. Sylvia says, "One of the things that really helps us is the very simple act of touching each other. When Kent holds my hand or puts his arm around me it tells me I matter to him." They exchange these kinds of gestures when they are at the kitchen sink, at family gatherings, at church meetings, rushing to parent/teacher conferences and school concerts, or just sitting near each other trying to resolve family needs or watching the evening news. Tenderly touching your mate is a great way to say "I like being near you." And that translates into "you are important to me."

It is not only important for your spouse to feel this love, but it is also important for your children to see you doing the things that give this message. These gestures will make the marriage secure while also making the children feel secure. A *Family Circus* cartoon by Bill Keane illustrates this perfectly. It shows the mom and dad in the kitchen kissing each other with the little children watching from the other room and one of them saying, "I feel all warm and happy when I see Mommy and Daddy kissing!" The greatest gift you can give your children is parents who love each other.

CHILDREN MUST SEE THAT THEIR MOTHER AND FATHER LOVE EACH OTHER.

Carl Whitaker, a highly respected pioneer in the field of marriage and family therapy says: "In order for a family to work, the children must understand that the father loves the mother more than the children and that the mother loves the father more than the children." This does not diminish the importance of children, but it sets up the proper order in the home. Jack, who has been happily married for forty-five years, says, "I have often told this to my children: I love you more than anything in this world, except for your mother, and don't ever even try to compare the love I feel for you with the love I feel for her. They all seem to be very comfortable with that fact—especially their mother."

When this kind of strong marital love is established, the

children cannot play one parent against the other. Parents then have a greater capacity, not less, to show love to their children. When the marriage is not strong, then a lot of energy, emotion, and time is expended from both partners in worry and concern over the husband/wife relationship. These wasted emotions divert us from what could be given to others, especially our children. Children must see that their mother and father love each other.

The importance of this fact became very clear to Susan and Tom Williams. They had been arguing much too often in the earshot of their children. (And if you think your children can't hear you if the door is shut, you're fooling yourself.) Angry words and cursing had become their habit. After one such bout, they went to their bedroom to go to sleep and found a letter on the pillow from their ten-year-old son, Jason. In his childlike handwriting he wrote: "Please sign this and give it back to me. Jason." Attached was the following contract he had typed all on his own, misspelled words and all:

I, Tom Williams will never ever Divorce my Whiff, know matter what happens. Or may God have mercy on my soul.
Signature _____

I, Susan Williams will never ever Divorce my Husband. Know matter what happens. Or may God have mercy on my soul.
Signature _____

What a jolt! They realized that the way they were treating each other was affecting their children. They signed the contract and vowed to be more loving to each other.

Children must see their parents exhibiting caring and tenderness in their marriage relationship. This caring brings security to children *and* to the marriage. When children feel that their parents' marriage is solid they are less likely to act out and misbehave. And when children are not driving their parents nuts with bad behavior, more attention can be directed to the marriage relationship. Every relationship in the family is improved when spouses pay attention to each other.

EXTENDED FAMILY PRESSURES

What happens to the marriage relationship when extended family members' needs enter the picture? Without our even noticing, a needy parent can take precedence over a wife or husband.

SOMETIMES BOUNDARIES HAVE TO BE SET IN ORDER FOR A MARRIAGE TO REMAIN STRONG.

This happened to Doris and Steve. Steve's parents had been living in the same city as he and Doris; they had a pleasant relationship with their son and daughter-in-law while maintaining their independence. After Steve's father died, his mother became more dependent on him. He felt it was his duty to help care for his widowed mother, even though she was quite capable of caring for herself. As time went on, she began to call on Steve for help more and more often because she was lonely. She needed something from the store and it was too late for her to go for it herself, or her VCR needed adjusting, or she was crying and needed comforting, and on it went. At first Doris thought it was just a temporary need, but after several months she began to resent the excessive attention her husband was giving his mother.

When feelings of resentment set in, feelings of love can be pushed aside. Both Steve and Doris were feeling overwhelmed and guilty. When they finally sat down and talked about their feelings, they realized what was happening. As it turned out, Steve wasn't enjoying the unreasonable demands from his mother any more than Doris was, and yet he felt obligated. They both realized that if their marriage was going to survive and remain strong, they had to put each other first. They decided to set some boundaries with Steve's mother and yet still be there to love and help her. They made a plan where they, together or individually, would visit her on certain days. They went to her home and explained their plan to her. At first she felt hurt and was somewhat resistant, making comments like, "You don't understand how lonely it is. You don't care." They validated her feelings with, "We know it must be lonely for you without Dad. And we will be here to help you just as we have discussed." They called to check on her regularly, but, with a few exceptions, kept the visits to the outlined schedule. It was hard at first, but they were determined.

As it turned out, Steve's mother began to develop other friendships and interests, which made her life richer and more enjoyable. Best of all, Steve and Doris were able to spend more time together in pursuits that enriched their marriage relationship. It took planning and determination on their part, but the payoff was worth it for all of them. Steve's mother did not change immediately. It took time, patience, and consistency for her to accept their new boundaries. Sometimes boundaries have to be set in order for a marriage to remain strong. (See Secret #10: Set Your Boundaries.)

Others face far more difficult dilemmas with aging parents in need. These can be times of real sacrifice and can put a tremendous amount of pressure on a marriage. Still, with understanding and thoughtful consideration for each other, couples can survive these times of trauma. Such was the case for Henry and Phyllis. Here's their story, as told by Phyllis:

Henry's father lived alone nearly eight hundred miles away from us. His health was failing. After many trips to help care for his needs, it seemed the only good solution was to have him come and live with us so we could look after him. We knew it would be hard, but we didn't realize *how* hard it would be. We had a teenage daughter still living at home, as well as a married daughter, living nearby, with one child and another on the way. They needed my attention, too.

After several months, the pressures of caring for Dad began to wear on me, and when I would share my feelings with Henry, he became irritated and would often say, "Stop complaining. This is something we have to do and griping about it isn't going to help." Then he would walk away. I felt misunderstood and rejected by my own husband. I was doing my best, and he didn't seem to appreciate my care for his father, nor did he seem to understand what I was going through with all of the other family needs.

Actually, I was very willing to help care for his father, and I didn't think I was complaining. I just needed

> BURDENS ARE
> SO MUCH
> EASIER TO
> BEAR WHEN
> YOU ARE
> APPRECIATED
> AND FEEL
> LOVED BY
> YOUR MATE.

to talk about what I was going through with the one person who I thought really loved me. I began to doubt that love. All I really needed from my husband was a listening ear, a hug, and a "thank you."

Finally we had a heart-to-heart talk, and I was able to tell Henry my true feelings. And to my amazement, he listened and he hugged me. It had been too long since we had given each other any verbal or physical expressions of love. That night in bed we held each other, and he told me of his gratitude for me and his appreciation for what I was doing to help his father. It made all the difference.

Burdens are so much easier to bear when you are appreciated and feel loved by your mate. Sometimes it takes so little to put the balance back into the relationship. Listening to your spouse without being judgmental or critical can be one of the most effective ways you can help him or her feel like the number one person in your life. People can meet incredible demands when they feel secure in that position.

In some cases parents almost demand to be included in their grown children's lives and are intrusive from the first day of the marriage. Unless the natural child of the overbearing parents sets boundaries to protect the couple's privacy, the mate will feel that he or she doesn't fit anywhere. There are additional ways relationships with other family members can destroy the husband/wife relationship. For example, spouses who call their parents with exciting news before they tell their own spouse. Sadly, sometimes they don't even tell their spouse the good news. Or they will talk about issues of the day with parents, siblings, or friends and forget to talk about it with their mate. If this happens, a husband or wife can feel unimportant and left out.

Even more destructive than this are spouses who criticize their mates to other family members. You might as well order a coffin for your marriage because it's going to suffer a terminal illness if that kind of behavior doesn't stop.

God put it all in perspective when he said, "Therefore shall a man leave his father and his mother, and shall cleave unto his wife . . ." (Genesis 2:24). I'm certain He was referring to both spouses. There is no question that He intended us to put each other first.

CAREER DEMANDS

The demands put on us by our careers can take first place if we are not careful. During the early years of marriage when career preparations are being made, and even later when career changes are necessary or desired, extra pressure may be put on the marriage relationship. These challenges must be carefully considered and planned for by the couple or the marriage can be seriously damaged. Sherri and Jason's story is telling:

During his internship as a young doctor, Jason found that his intense schedule did not allow him much time at home. And when he was home he was exhausted and just wanted to sleep. After a time he began to feel he was losing touch with his wife, Sherri, and their three small children. He was overwhelmed with his career responsibilities and wondered how he could possibly keep his marriage strong. He was well aware of the high divorce rate among doctors and it scared him. He saw how easily it could happen.

Jason knew there wasn't anything he could do to change his schedule if he was to complete his training, but he *could* let Sherri know how much he loved her. Besides telling her, he started sending her flowers on special occasions with notes to let her know of his love and appreciation for her support. He started calling her from the hospital when he had a minute between duties. Sometimes the conversation was no more than a "Hi. I'm thinking of you. I love you." It gave her a chance to say she loved him, too, and it felt good to both of them. Often he would ask her to meet him in the hospital cafeteria for lunch, which she would do, though it was no small task to bundle up three small children and bring them along so they could see their "phantom" daddy. There were times when she would sit there and wait for him for as much as an hour, but she understood he didn't have much control over his schedule. She decided it was worth it to be with him.

It was a difficult time for both of them, but they were determined to make it work. Sherri said, "At times when I felt overwhelmed by the responsibility I had raising our children with very little help from him, I found great comfort in occasionally being able to pour my heart out to him. Jason is a good listener, and it helped so much to have him validate my frustration without trying to give me a lot of advice."

Their determination to make it work *has worked*. Jason is now a successful doctor and he and Sherri continue to work at making their marriage their number one priority. Jason said, "It takes effort, but there is no other way if we are to succeed, and succeeding with my family is very important to me and to Sherri. It's what our life is really all about."

James and Jodi are facing similar challenges as Jason and Sherri did. James is establishing a new mortgage company and his work takes so much time that it could easily take over *all* his time. "The irony of it is, I'm doing all this to make a good life for my wife and children, and if I don't keep it in balance I could lose them in the process," James reflects. He told his secretary that no matter what meeting he may be in, when his wife calls he wants to talk to her. "She's first on my list, and it's got to stay that way if we're going to enjoy our marriage and keep it strong." Knowing that, Jodi respects his time and keeps her calls short and free of whining.

You can also use these touching-base calls to add a little spice to the day. One businessman described a phone call he received from his wife that he will never forget: She said, "Hi, honey. Just wanted to let you know that I just stepped out of the shower and I'm standing here in your shirt and nothing else . . . feeling very close to you." Do you think he delayed his departure that day? His imagination soared and he could hardly wait to be home. He definitely felt important to her.

If the wife is also employed out of the home, perhaps that kind of call is just out of the question, although one or the other of you might take a day off and try it for the fun of it. And believe me, it would be fun. It wouldn't need to happen often. Like a full course turkey dinner, serve it too often and it's no longer a special treat. To take the analogy a step further, we enjoy a variety of good meals often, so be a little creative and have some fun—both of you.

Occasionally, some bizarre things can be done that really do spark a marriage and make your partner feel totally loved. For example, Lynne and her husband, Darwin, who are both employed and in their second marriage with primary custody of their combined four teenagers, thoroughly enjoyed a surprise she carefully planned for him. For several years he had dreamed of going on a cruise but it never seemed possible. Lynne started saving, and one day when a good deal came along, she made the daring decision and bought cruise tickets for his birthday gift. He was completely surprised and delighted. She said, "Darwin could hardly believe I would do that for him. We had a fabulous time! I'm so glad I did it."

> OCCASIONALLY, SOME BIZARRE THINGS CAN BE DONE THAT REALLY SPARK UP A MARRIAGE.

Leland planned a surprise that showed his wife, Della, how much she meant to him:

On the day I arrived home from serving in Vietnam, my wife and children met me at the airport. Shortly after we walked into the house I noticed a small package that had just arrived in the mail. I knew what it was. I asked the children to please excuse me while I took their mother for lunch so we could have a little time alone. I took the package along and when we were seated at a table, I gave it to her and said, "It's addressed to you. Open it." The return address was in Hawaii. Inside she found a ring custom-made for her by one of the highest-ranking officers of the Pacific Command. It was a diamond and sapphire in a white gold setting, done in the officer's creative design based on his evaluation of Della's personality. He had been our host during an R&R time we had enjoyed together in Hawaii a year earlier. His hobby was collecting precious and semiprecious stones and designing jewelry, and we had admired his collection. She was thrilled and has worn the ring ever since, knowing I had it created especially for her. It has been more than worth every dollar it cost me.

Those kinds of things are important and can happen once in a while, but what can you do on a regular basis to help each other be number one, particularly when both of you are working and have demanding careers?

Like the couples in the earlier examples, you can use the phone and use a little imagination with it. Some couples have little codes for their beepers. Janet and Ben know that when they see the numbers 1-2-3 on their beeper display it stands for those three little words "I love you." They may be rushing to an appointment and don't have time to talk or leave a long message, but the beeped code lets them know their spouse is thinking tender thoughts about them. A phone call to your husband or wife saying, "How about meeting me for lunch?" keeps him or her right up there on the top of your list. Arlo and Janice, in the following comic strip by Jimmy Johnson, give another idea to consider:

(*Arlo & Janice* reprinted by permission of United Feature Syndicate.)

Pull out your list of your mate's favorite things occasionally and zero in on one, even if it's just buying his favorite candy bar when you stop to fill up the gas tank. It shows him you're thinking about him. Love cannot resist these small gestures. It

SHARE A KISS THAT LASTS LONGER THAN THE PROVERBIAL PECK.

can be as simple as when Conrad stopped at a restaurant on his way home for a surprise lunch and bought a sixteen-ounce jar of his wife Rachel's favorite salsa and still-warm freshly made corn chips. They didn't have much to spend on extras and he said, "I got both items for only $4.17! Less than at the supermarket." It was a real treat. He said, "Even though our two little boys were there, too, their mouths were stuffed and their hands were busy, so we could actually talk!"

Remember to use the power of touch. Hug when you greet each other after a hard day's work. Share a kiss that lasts longer than the proverbial peck. Cal and Belinda enjoy their own version of this:

> Belinda loves it when I come up behind her when she's working in the kitchen and kiss her on the back of the neck. It doesn't take long until she's turned around, and we find ourselves in a full-body embrace.
>
> Then she's really happy when I add, "What can I do to help?" Of course, when I do the kissing I have to make sure I'm not taking her away from a pot that may boil over any minute.

What about when you are away on a business trip? What can you do to help your mate know that he or she is on your mind? People who travel a lot in their work face a big challenge in keeping the marriage strong. Meet the challenge. Sit down and make your own list of things you could do that would please your mate. Frederick travels often in his work and he and Nellie have developed a fun way to stay connected:

> I enjoy sending Nellie comic "I miss you" greeting cards when I'm gone for a while, and at times even

when it's only a few days. Sometimes I get home before the card does, but that doesn't matter. The surprise is still effective.

I can remember once having a card from her waiting for me at the hotel when I got there. I knew she had to have bought it and sent it before I ever left in order for it to be there. Wow, did I feel loved! There were times when I would find little love notes from her in my suit or pants pockets. I found one hot little message in my pajamas that made me want to hop the next plane home. Phone calls work for us, too. In fact, they are our greatest survival tool.

When you make time for each other on the phone and enjoy sharing the events of your day, your mate can't help but feel loved. One caution here: Keep overdoses of misery out of the calls. There will be times you have to discuss less than pleasant subjects, but don't let it be the norm or your mate will not look forward to your voice on the other end.

> OTHER ACTIVITIES CREEP IN LIKE A THIEF IN THE NIGHT AND STEAL YOUR TIME RIGHT OUT FROM UNDER YOUR SPOUSE.

Does your mate enjoy breakfast in bed? Every once in a while surprise your spouse with breakfast on a tray before he or she gets up. Have fun trying different things. There must be a concentrated effort on the part of both husband and wife to make this kind of giving work. If one partner isn't doing anything the other can at least start the process by doing *something*, without any strings attached. Your spouse just might catch on and join the fun.

EXTRACURRICULAR INTERESTS

All kinds of activities can creep in like a thief in the night and steal your time right out from under your spouse. Because you may be enjoying the other activities so much, you may not notice what is happening, but your mate will notice. One newly married wife found out rather quickly how debilitating this can be to the marriage relationship. She called our radio program and told us, "I thought getting married meant being together more. That's a laugh. I think I've seen less of my husband than I did while we were dating." When asked what he was doing she said, "He comes home from work, eats like a starving child, changes into his sweats, kisses me on the cheek, and runs out saying, 'See ya later.' Then off he goes to play basketball with his single buddies. Then he comes home and wants to make love. Believe me, I'm not in the mood!" She was feeling very low on his list of priorities. We told her it was time for a sit-down-and-clear-the-air kind of talk with her husband. He needed to know how she was feeling. They needed to make a plan that would give them time together and still allow him to play basketball once or twice a week, but not every day.

Sometimes a spouse has to set a boundary to preserve the marriage. This can be done by validating his feeling, such as, "I know you enjoy playing basketball and being with your friends. And (not *but*) I need time with you, too. You are the most important person in my life, and I need to feel like I'm the most important person in your life." Then, in a kind, gentle, respectful, and firm way, set a boundary by saying something like, "What's been happening is not acceptable. What can we do so we both feel valued?" He may not have realized what he was doing to her. Sometimes people just need a wake-up call. Don't let it go on and on and then give the wake-up call in the form of divorce papers—or worse. When you've been bumped out of the number one spot, let your spouse know how you are feeling and do it in a kind, caring, nonwhining way. And then reciprocate by helping meet his or her needs in a way that works for both of you.

Another thing that can take precedence over the marriage is the computer. We live in an era when the computer practically rules. It's helpful, intriguing, fascinating, educational, fun, and, if you're not careful, it can own you almost like a drug addiction. If you are spending more time in the evening with your computer than you are with your spouse, open your eyes and you just might see a big red flag that says "Danger! Marriage in trouble." Winnie and Charley faced this problem when Winnie got addicted to chat rooms and became involved with a man on the Internet. Now she feels he is her soul mate and is divorcing her husband. If she and her newfound love interest are both already captured by the chat room enticement, just how long will it be until one or the other finds a new soul mate? Probably just about the time the newness of their romance wears off.

Sports or computers may not be the culprit that knocked you off the list. It might be television, hobbies, shopping, exercising, a family member, or a friend. Anything or anyone that takes over someone's life and excludes his or her mate is the culprit. Nancy and Larry found this out when she became overly involved in her crafts projects. Most evenings would find her at work in the room she called her "shop," painting, sewing, crocheting, you name it—if it was "crafty," she did it. And she did it well. Lovely things she had created adorned their home. Friends and family loved her homemade gifts. She made so many, she would stockpile them and then have a craft sale. Larry didn't mind that she had this hobby; what he minded was that it seemed to take precedence over him. Sometimes he just wanted to sit on the couch and cuddle while they watched TV together, without her always having knitting needles in her hands.

For Christmas one year a friend gave them a warm cozy polar fleece blanket with their names, Nancy and Larry, embroidered in one corner, with a note that said, "This is for the two of you to snuggle under while you watch TV." It was her wake-up call. She said, "I keep it folded on the couch with our names showing to remind me that I must take the time to be there for Larry." And she's doing it. She said, "Our relationship is better and Larry feels like he's on the top of my list of priorities now. And we are enjoying the snuggling." They found their kids were enjoying seeing them snuggling, too. She said, "I learned that you can't snuggle and knit at the same time, but who cares." Of course, she still enjoys her crafts, but she has her hobby more in perspective now.

What about the obsessed reader? If you feel like your mate is married to his or her books instead of to you, that can be discouraging. Reading is an enjoyable hobby and even an important part of work. As in anything else, however, when it becomes excessive and excludes your mate for hours and hours repeatedly, that's putting it above your spouse and is a clear indication that changes need to be made. Excessive compulsive behaviors may exist or be developed. If it becomes extreme the person may need professional therapy to overcome it.

Sometimes couples allow community and church service to take precedence over their relationship with each other. While these things are important, remember that they are not the most important thing in your life—your spouse is. Janalee expressed her sadness over the fact that her husband was always helping friends and neighbors with their broken appliance, leaky roof, fouled-up sprinkling system, or whatever it would be. She said, "I'm glad he's kind to them, but any request I make of him is completely ignored. I *know* I'm last on his list. In fact, I'm not sure I'm even on it. When I remind him of what I need, he calls it nagging."

This "hero of the neighborhood" only seems to be after the praise of others. It feels good to be the good guy and have others admire you. Doing good is great, *after* you have seen to the needs of your spouse. Certainly, in times of critical need, your spouse will understand someone else needs you, but he or she won't resent it if you have made your mate feel important. In fact, your husband or wife will likely join you in meeting that other person's need. You must pay attention to your spouse.

BE CREATIVE

Put your creativity to work in your marriage and you'll be pleasantly surprised at how many ideas you can come up with that will keep your mate at the top of your priorities. Joshua, for example, describes how his wife, Heidi, greets him when he comes home from work:

> Hearing me drive into the driveway must be her cue, because when I open the door, Heidi comes around the corner into the entry hall and, grinning from ear to ear, says, "My day has just begun!" Then we kiss. What a welcome home! It makes me feel like a million bucks. I love it and so does she.

Couples need to consciously address their priorities *often*. If you do not already have a regular date night, this is a good time to establish one, preferably once a week. This night can include dinner, a movie, dinner *and* a movie, or going to a fancy restaurant and only ordering dessert. It can be a walk in the park, a round of golf, an evening roasting hot dogs and marshmallows in the canyon, going to a concert, or just going out for an ice-cream cone—or any number of things you might enjoy together. The object of this date night is to provide a time when you can be alone as a couple, occasionally including another couple, but not the children. There are times to be together with the family, but this is not it. It's also important to get away for a weekend or an overnighter now and then. You don't need to go far, just somewhere where you can be alone together. Make the time away as unpressured as possible, without scheduling a lot of things to do.

KEEP YOUR MATE NUMBER ONE ON YOUR LIST AND YOU WILL FIND YOU HAVE MORE TO GIVE IN THE OTHER IMPORTANT AREAS OF YOUR LIFE.

Being happily married takes thought and effort, and it's

well worth every ounce of that effort. When the marriage relationship is strong and each one of you is valued by the other an amazing thing happens—there is more energy, more freedom, more ability to share your love with children, family, friends, and neighbors. You are not bound down by the energy and emotion wasted on jealousy, injustices, or any other marital worries. Keep your mate number one on your list, and you will find you have more to give in the other important areas of your life.

BEGIN TODAY

Take a minute right now and evaluate where you have put your spouse in your life. Do something right now to let your mate know that he or she is at the top of your priority list. To be adored by your mate puts all of life into perspective. When you are number one in your spouse's eyes, you can make it through anything.

Be Each Other's Very Best Friend

The only way to have a friend is to be one.
—EMERSON

THE IMPORTANCE OF MARITAL FRIENDSHIP

Jeanette C. Lauer and Robert H. Lauer, the authors of the book *Til Death Do Us Part,* conducted a study of 351 couples who had been married fifteen years or more to determine what it is that makes a marriage not only enduring but happy. Of those responding, three hundred said both mates were happy in their marriage. They were asked to select from thirty-nine factors and list in order of importance what they thought it was that made their marriage lasting and enjoyable. Approximately 90 percent of both husbands and wives put the same thing at the top of their list: My spouse is my best friend.[4]

When observing happily married couples, you see the husband look at his wife and say "She's my best friend" and hear her say in return "And he's mine." These comments are accompanied by smiles and a tender reaching for his or her mate's hand. One of the saddest comments is, "We used to be best friends, but we just don't enjoy each other's company anymore. Any other lost friendship will never be as tragic as the loss of friendship with your mate. If you are a newlywed you may think this sounds impossible because of how close you and your spouse feel now. The only way it will be impossible is if you work at keeping your friendship alive and well. If the friendship in a marriage has been lost, it can be restored. It can also be developed if it was never there in the first place. Being married to your best friend is one of life's best gifts.

WHAT IS FRIENDSHIP?

Both husband and wife need to work on creating and expanding the qualities that make a friendship. Friendship in marriage is like a one-way street—two lanes, side by side, going in the same direction. It's not a two-way street with partners going to totally different destinations. There may be little side roads that you each take from time to time as you go through life, but they do not take you away from your main destination. It takes *both* of you putting forth the effort to keep going in the same direction to make your friendship grow.

GET RID OF ANY NOTION THAT YOU ARE GOING TO CHANGE YOUR MATE— YOU CAN'T.

To explore the different ways you can keep a strong best-friends relationship with your spouse, you first need to understand the meaning of a genuine friendship. A friend is (1) someone who accepts me as I am, (2) someone I can talk to, (3) someone I can have fun with, (4) someone who really cares about me, and (5) someone I can trust. Let's see how each of these applies in a marriage relationship.

A FRIEND IS SOMEONE WHO ACCEPTS ME AS I AM
Since friendship is based on acceptance, eliminate any notion that you are going to change your mate—you can't. True friends don't try. That doesn't mean your spouse *won't* change, it simply means *you* can't be the change maker. If you try, you will most likely be the road block that stops the change from happening. You may be wondering, *Why is that? If you love someone, isn't it part of your responsibility to help him or her be a*

better person? No! Your responsibility is to *be* the better person yourself. Of course, something interesting happens when you focus on making yourself a better person. It rubs off on others, particularly your spouse. But that must not be your motivation for self-improvement; it will simply be a pleasant by-product.

Think of what Henry Ford really meant when he said, "He is your best friend who brings out the best that is in you."[5] Remember that one of the most effective ways you bring out the best in a friend is to accept him for who he is, without criticism. Nothing builds a strong marital friendship like pure, unconditional acceptance from a spouse.

Ken and May understood this concept well. May was considerably overweight, and Ken was the opposite—lean and fit. Though May had been much slimmer when they married— five babies ago—he adored her, and they were, without question, happy. They were fun to be with. One evening at a party he looked over at May and said, "Isn't she cute?" Then Ken hugged her and added, "Well, if you think she's cute with clothes on, you ought to see her . . ." Embarrassed, though obviously pleased, May interrupted with, "Ken! Hush." You could see that he adores her and she him. They are the epitome of best friends and have been for more than fifty years now. They love each other just the way they are.

On the other hand, Curt hadn't quite come to grips with his wife's weight problem. He was always trying to get his wife, Sasha, to lose weight. She had been just the right size when they were married. With the birth of each of their three babies she, too, gained weight, which she found very difficult to lose. Curt noticed other women who had as many children, or more, and saw that they had lost their weight and were all slim and trim again. He didn't take into consideration that some women don't even have to worry about it because they have higher metabolism rates or other genetic "gifts." People are different for many reasons, and we have to allow for the difference.

Whenever Curt would impatiently say something to Sasha like, "When are you going to lose that baby fat?" she would feel hurt and jab him back with, "You don't get it, do you?! I wish I could!" Then he would add, "Well, if you would just exercise every day and watch what you eat, you could." That isn't love. True friends don't say that.

A LOVING RELATIONSHIP IS FAR MORE IMPORTANT THAN A SLIM BODY.

Curt had a buddy who gave him the clue that opened his eyes. His buddy said, "I don't tell my wife to lose weight. I'd never do that to her. What I did one day was look in the mirror at myself. That's when I decided I needed to start an exercise program of my own. When I started doing it for myself, my wife joined in with me. Now we're both a little slimmer, and we have fun doing it together." That's friendship, pure and simple. Curt got the message.

At one of our marriage seminars during a break-out session when Joy talks with the men while I talk with the women, a man in the audience said, "I told my wife I wanted her to lose weight so she'd feel healthier." Joy asked, "Is it working?" His answer was, "No." Right then another man shouted out, "A woman can see right through that one." The men laughed, including the one who made the first statement, though he added that he really did want her to be healthy. Learn to take care of your own goals, without criticizing her, and she may then feel liberated enough to join you. And if she doesn't, just accept her the way she is without nagging. A loving relationship is far more important than a slim body.

Usually, when people are critical of themselves they are critical of others, including their mates. Accepting your mate for who he or she is can best happen when you accept yourself for who *you* are.

Here's a little exercise that can help: When you step out of the shower look at yourself in a full-length mirror. Really do this—it's the beginning of being able to be comfortable with seeing and being with yourself as you are. The first time you do it just look yourself in the eye and say, "Hi," then get dressed. Do this again a few more times and don't look for imperfections and pick yourself apart. Soon you will be more comfortable looking at your whole body and will be able to accept yourself as you are. This exercise is to get you beyond being critical of your body and getting to the point when you can say, "I like me. I'm glad I've got a body and I'm glad that, for the most part, it works. I'm just fine the way I am."

> TRUE FRIENDS GIVE GENUINE COMPLIMENTS AND TRUE FRIENDS ACCEPT THEM AT FACE VALUE.

That doesn't mean you may not work on making a few changes if you need to; but that is not the main focus here. It means you can accept yourself and are happy to be you, just as you are. If you are continually critical of yourself it makes it harder for your mate to accept you the way you are. Your mate may never notice your defects or he may just be perfectly happy to ignore them, unless you draw them to his attention.

Another seminar attendee said, "I told my wife she had beautiful ankles. She answered, 'You must be blind. Just look a little higher and you'll see the real picture.'" He added, "Why can't a woman just take a compliment without berating herself?" Good question. True friends give genuine compliments and true friends accept them at face value. Take the compliment with a "Thank you, honey," and understand that he or she is loving you just the way you are. It's not too smart to give your mate negative points about you to ponder.

Here's another tip: Never ask your spouse if he or she thinks you're fat. That's just asking for trouble because there's no good answer for it. If the answer is "no," you think it's a lie. Yet if the reply is "yes," you're mad that your mate thinks you're fat. And if your spouse avoids the question altogether and says, "I love you just the way you are," then you think it's a cover-up for thinking you're fat. Just accept the fact that you are loved and don't put him or her on the spot. Accept yourself the way you are and if you are unsatisfied with something then make the changes that you believe would be in your best interest. That goes for both spouses.

Sometimes a mate can become impatient with his spouse if she doesn't understand what *he* so clearly understands, such as a computer function, a cooking technique, a new dance step, or a football play—anything. When you are teaching your spouse any new skill it's important to accept his or her level of expertise. Just because a person does not understand something as well as you do, does not mean the person is stupid. Consider how you would teach the same skill to someone at work; would you insult or berate a fellow worker or friend? Surely, you would not treat your wife or husband with any less respect if he or she doesn't "get it" right away. There will be other things that *you* will not easily "get," and you will appreciate a little patience and respect while your mate shares a skill with you. Remember that you want to keep your spouse as your best friend. Allowing him or her time to learn and comprehend as you share information builds your friendship.

Many areas in relationships require patience. For instance, are you the kind of person who is always on time and your spouse is always late? When you're meeting friends for dinner are you tapping your foot impatiently while he or she does just one more thing? This can be very irritating for both of you. This calls for some negotiating, but not in the heat of the moment. A simple discussion—without pointing fingers and saying the accusatory statement "you always make us late!"—can help your mate realize how important this is to you. Remember that you love each other and you want your mate to be happy. Find a compromise by asking: "How about giving me a ten-minute notice before we need to leave. That would help me be ready on time." Or why not create a loving signal such as a kiss on the back of the neck when it's nearly time to leave?

Patience in spiritual matters works as well. If you and your

husband are of different faiths or have diverg-
ing views about your own faith, you will have
to work at respecting each other despite your
differing views. One of our seminar attendees
told us this story:

CHANGES CAN HAPPEN WHEN PEOPLE ARE KIND, CARING, AND UNDERSTANDING WITH EACH OTHER.

> I attended the seminar you gave at our
> church about six months ago. You were
> concerned about how so many people are
> divorcing and you counseled wives who were married
> to a good man of a different faith to hold on to him. I
> would get mad at my husband for not putting forth any
> effort to learn about my beliefs. He would never go to
> church with me and seemed to resent me for going. I
> was sort of shaking my finger in his face over the mat-
> ter. He was making my life miserable, and I was regret-
> ting that I ever married him. I didn't realize, until that
> night, how I must have been making *his* life miserable.

We had suggested a dialogue to help wives and husbands
see the power of accepting their spouse the way he or she is
when it comes to religious differences, using the example of
a wife speaking to her husband. Here is the scenario:

The wife comes to the husband, who is a good man in so
many other ways, and says, "I'm going to church and I'd like
you to go with me."

He replies, "You know I'm not interested and I'm not going."

To which she hotly replies, "You never go! When are you
going to wake up and get a little religion? It's not fair. You
don't put forth any effort at all. Don't you care about me or
the kids?!"

Any husband is going to recoil at such statements.

Consider what the outcome might be if the conversation
went like this instead:

"Good morning, honey. I'm going to church and I'd really enjoy having you go with me."

He replies, "You know I'm not interested and I'm not going."

To which she kindly and with sincerity replies, "That's okay. I understand. Thanks for all you do for our family. I love you. I'll see you when I get back." She kisses him and says, "G'bye."

The woman who attended our church seminar went on to say:

> I was not being kind to my husband, and our life was miserable. I was only driving him further away. When I stopped what I had been doing and, instead, handled it the more loving way, everything changed. It really works. My husband began studying my religion and has now joined the church I belong to. And we both have never been happier.

Not everyone will have this outcome, but this kind of caring response will contribute to a loving environment in a home. All religions teach the power of love, and when you actually put it into practice with your mate, you are doing what you profess. Otherwise your mate may be thinking, *What good is that religion? I don't see it making a difference.* Changes can happen when people are kind, caring, and understanding with each other. It makes for a great friendship.

A FRIEND IS SOMEONE I CAN TALK TO The importance of listening to each other cannot be overemphasized. At a workshop a woman said, "That really matters. The other night when my husband and I were lying in bed I started pouring my heart out about how this woman at work had been rude to me and had really hurt my feelings. He just listened and didn't give me any advice or anything. He just listened and hugged me. It felt so good." That's what we all need—a listening ear from the most important person in our lives. Sometimes it is helpful if the person listening asks, "Honey, is this a listen-and-talk-about-it moment or a find-the-solution discussion?" This clarifies what is wanted or expected.

What if something wonderful happened to you and you can hardly wait to share it with your mate? Listen and share in the joy. It's such a treat to have your spouse allow you to relive a special part of his or her life. If a spouse won't listen, or seems uninterested, the other spouse often will find someone else to confide in. It's sad if your partner won't allow you to share the important events of his or her life. If you avoid listening because you think you have to make everything all better, remember, you don't need to do anything but listen. That's it. That's what any friend needs—especially your best friend.

Both husbands and wives need to be able to "pour out their hearts" to their mate, without being criticized or told what they should have done or need to do. Some men don't open up to their wives when they are worried about their job or some other thing that feels threatening to them. They believe they have to be the strong one and end up not being able to talk about some of their concerns, because it might worry or alarm their wives. Most women can handle whatever it is that may be troubling their man. In fact, they will feel respected and valued when that depth of confidence becomes a natural part of their relationship. If that's not the case, a wife needs to work at having more faith in her husband's ability to solve problems and enough courage to let him go through times of feeling down. In all that we do, we are a partnership. When there is something challenging happening that may threaten the security of a job, have enough faith in each other that you can meet the challenge together. When two people are working toward a

> FRIENDSHIP IS ALL ABOUT BEING ABLE TO TALK ABOUT YOUR DEEP CONCERNS WITH EACH OTHER.

common goal, the outcome is greater than when there are two people working separately. This is the synergy that Stephen Covey teaches in his book *The Seven Habits of Highly Effective People*. Often we are taught this principle at work, but don't apply it to our marriage. But it does work in a marriage relationship, too. Friendship is all about being able to talk about your deep concerns with each other.

Another reason husbands don't talk is because they don't want to be told what to do about what they are internally fretting over. All they really need, just like a wife, is a non-threatening listening ear. A retired marine officer underscored the importance of this principle with his own experience:

> Twice during my military career, my wife helped me successfully work through a devastating setback. Had I been so foolish as to have tried to go it alone, the results could have been far worse. Confiding in her, and receiving her instant understanding and strong support, was—and continues to be—of enormous value in my life as well as in our marriage.

Some couples avoid talking about anything beyond the surface stuff because it almost always ends up in an argument. To avoid such unpleasant moments they just simply avoid talking about their feelings and concerns. By so doing they miss one of the most beautiful and fulfilling parts of a loving marriage relationship. Learning and using a few simple communicating skills can make all the difference. Secret #8: Talk to Each Other, will show you how to help your mate feel that you are listening and are genuinely interested in what he or she is sharing with you, even though your needs and opinions may differ.

A FRIEND IS SOMEONE I CAN HAVE FUN WITH Best friends enjoy having fun together. I encourage you to find as many things as you can that you both enjoy. Don't be afraid to find new interests that you can share. Be adventuresome together. I remember a time when Joy and I went out with a group for a day on a deep-sea fishing vessel. She spent the day throwing up while I spent the day catching nothing. We've ruled that one out as an option for us.

Another time we went on a cruise with some close friends and had a marvelous time. This time she was prepared with seasick pills. If you've never taken a cruise, you may want to do it. Planning for one can be almost as fun as going on one. If you can't agree on which cruise to take, search until you find one you would both enjoy. If you still can't, you might try turning it over to fate by putting some options in a hat and drawing one out. How about taking up a new sport together, maybe biking, or walking together in new and interesting neighborhoods or parks, or hiking a mountain trail. Or try an activity your spouse already enjoys that you don't know how to do . . . yet.

That's how Lilly and Pete discovered how to have some fun together. Pete loved to play golf and was good at it. He was always looking for someone to play with and would go with different friends from work or church. He was having fun, and Lilly was spending many hours alone. According to Lilly, his fun was at the expense of their relationship. She had never played golf. One day Pete said, "Come with me. I'll teach you how." She hesitated, but went. He patiently worked with her, teaching her all the techniques and which clubs to use. It was awkward at first, but as she got the hang of it, she began to enjoy it. Now they play together often and have a great time. Lilly, with a wry smile, said, "I've become good competition now. Sometimes I even beat him, and believe me, he's not giving it away." Be willing to try something new; it could develop into something fun.

Having fun together must be a shared enjoyment. When you go camping or fishing, or do any type of vacationing, it must be fun for both of you. If one of you ends up doing all the packing, shopping, cooking, and cleaning up, then it's not fun for that person. Sharing these responsibilities makes it so your mate is more willing to go because he or she can then be part of the fun. Listen to Ranae and Logan's story:

> Logan and I pick out a new book to read together at the beginning of each year. We enjoyed reading aloud with the children and thought we might enjoy doing it with just the two of us. We read books on marriage, good wholesome fiction, and biographies of people we admire. We talk about the concepts, the characters, the story, how we feel about what is happening, why we feel that way, and what we hope will happen as we progress further into the book. This draws us closer to each other as we cry together, laugh together, and even get upset together as we find ourselves immersed in the story. It's turned into something we really enjoy.

Sometimes when spouses enjoy different kinds of activities, it may require some compromising, just for the sake of being together and pleasing your spouse. Connie and Kevin, who have had a devoted and happy marriage relationships for many years, are very good at this kind of compromising. Connie explains what they do:

> Kevin really loves basketball. He enjoys attending the local college games. I love this guy and want to be with him, so even though I'm not wild about basketball, I go because I know he enjoys it and he likes me there at his side. And I get a big kick out of how he gets so mad at the refs and how he cheers his team on with such vigor.
>
> Several years ago when he bought our season tickets for the basketball games, he also came home with tickets for two for the ballet! He knows I love the ballet and he goes with me regularly now because he wants to be with me; and he enjoys seeing how happy it makes me.

That's what best friends genuinely caring about each other is all about. In Secret #1: Return to the Beginning, you were encouraged to find out what your mate's favorite things are. Now is another good time to review your findings and identify any items that are the same on each other's list. It's fun when you make the most of a favorite thing you both enjoy. If there are none, no problem. Enjoy the differences, as Connie and Kevin did, or discover some new things you'll both enjoy.

Perry and Sarah are in their early thirties and found they needed to compromise in the music they listened to. He enjoys current pop music, and she enjoys the romantic oldies. In the process of trying to find a happy medium, they discovered some music that they both enjoy. They didn't quite realize what it was until one day when Sarah, pregnant with their second child, was lying on the couch experiencing morning sickness and listening to the radio. The deejay announced a contest—fifth caller would win tickets to the Garth Brooks concert. "I dialed the number and won!" she said. "I was so excited I almost forgot I was sick."

They went to the concert and they both loved it. She said, "We bought the album and enjoy listening to it and a few other country artists—together. At last we have some middle-ground music." When they're each alone they still listen to their own favorites, sharing a few choice ones with each other. "We're beginning to enjoy more and more music together," Perry said, "but we still like our own, too, and we respect that."

Not a bad idea to try something new once in a while. You just might like it. If you don't, then you can laugh together about the whole experience and try something else.

A FRIEND IS SOMEONE WHO CARES ABOUT ME To be genuinely cared about and to have someone desire to be with you is a need that everyone has. It is most important to have this need fulfilled by your mate. You need to feel that you are individually cared about. It's not a smothering caring—it's a feeling that you know in your heart and it becomes evident through little acts of kindness that are directed toward you. It's knowing that your mate cares about what you are going through—your successes, your failures, your hurts. It's believing that you are important to your mate as mentioned in the previous chapter. You're comfortable just being with each other, even when nothing is being said. It's a feeling of peace and contentment. It is one of the deepest elements of friendship.

An additional way of caring is to recognize that sometimes your mate just needs some time alone. It may be no more than taking a walk, reading a book, or listening to music. For a man it may be as simple as wandering through the local hardware or sports store. For a woman it may be browsing a boutique. It's any place where your spouse can have his or her own thoughts and know you won't feel threatened or left out. Kahlil Gibran describes this eloquently: "Let there be spaces in your togetherness."[6] It can be very rejuvenating for your mate and you, and it will end up being good for your marriage.

BEST FRIENDS ALSO NEED OTHER FRIENDS.

When you care about your mate you also realize that he or she needs other friends. Best friends also need other friends. Men need to understand that women need women friends. They may like to go shopping, or talking about recipes, romantic movies, their kids, their labor pains, their weight woes, or their new hairdo—things men just don't get into. Do yourself and your wife a favor by allowing her to enjoy her female friends, without complaining or criticizing. She'll love you for doing it. And vice versa, women need to similarly support their husbands' outside friendships. Sheldon is an example of this. He has enjoyed a long friendship with Richard because they share the same family values and are both determined to keep in good physical condition. They get together for one hour three times a week to play basketball or walk.

Sheldon says it gives them a chance to talk over ideas about work and family needs.

There is a nice by-product to this. One woman reported that she finds her husband more interesting because he has some good friends he enjoys. She said it's fun to hear about their adventures when he gets back from his "all male" fishing trip. Her husband in turn said he finds her more interesting, too, as a result of her friends. Because they have friends who are also devoted to their families, they feel comfortable about each other being with these friends. Friends with different talents and life experiences can introduce you to interesting new vistas, and it can be fun sharing them with your mate.

A couple of cautions need to be addressed here. One example comes from a woman who called in to Dr. Laura Schlessinger's radio show. She said she needed to get away with her girlfriends for a weekend. The problem here was that her girlfriends were single and they wanted to visit the bars and find interesting men to be with. She went along and found herself also visiting with an interesting man. Dr. Laura strongly cautioned her, as only she can do, and told her what a stupid thing that was. She is absolutely right. It's foolish and wrong for married persons to take such chances. Is it bad to occasionally spend a few days with your friends? Of course not, if the activities are appropriate for a married person.

When you are going to be with your other friends your mate needs to know what you're doing, where you're going, and when you'll return. This is just common courtesy. If get-aways with friends are covered up or hidden from your spouse it can be very damaging to your marriage, as was the case with Becca and her husband, Willard.

During the first couple of years of our marriage, Willard was in medical school and we were very poor. We hardly had enough money for necessities like food, heat, and rent, let alone enough to go on a personal pleasure trip. We had one child, only one car, no TV. I never had any money of my own, and we lived in a city without any relatives and very few friends. Under the guise of going "out" selling insurance or something (I forgot what) to make some money, Willard said he would be gone for a couple of days, which turned out to be a week. I found out later he had gone fishing for a week with another medical school student at a resort area hundreds of miles away, with no thought of our welfare, our supply of food, and so on. That's when I realized that Willard didn't really care about me. Being with his friends, regardless of our situation, was all that seemed to matter. This was a heartbreaking realization and has haunted me all of our many years of married life.

Each spouse must be cautious when it comes to spending time with other friends. It is vitally important that wives don't spend an inordinate amount of time with their girlfriends, and equally important that husbands don't go overboard in the amount of time they spend with their buddies. Fishing trips every weekend that don't include your wife—now, that's extreme. It can seriously damage your marriage. Does that mean your wife has to be included in every fishing trip? No, unless you both want it that way. As discussed in the previous chapter, your mate must feel like number one on your list. You can find out if you're spending too much time with other friends by simply asking your mate. If you plan something with friends when your best friend—your spouse—has plans that involve you, or if she or he may need you at that time, that can be hurtful. Work out solutions that you both feel comfortable with, doing the best you can to understand each other's needs.

A FRIEND IS SOMEONE I CAN TRUST Trust is an essential part of friendship. It does not come immediately. It takes time to build and then becomes the firm foundation that marriage is based on. When it is intact the marriage can endure the storms of life. The sad part is that small acts can weaken and finally break apart this foundation.

People can have casual friendships with members of the opposite sex, but they must stay very casual and with others present. Spouses need to stay away from any intimate setting with a co-worker or anyone of the opposite sex, such as dinner alone or other activities that have the appearance of a date, including becoming someone's confidant. There is danger in becoming a confidant, because when you share another's problems, you can start to have sympathetic feelings and a cry on the shoulder can become far more than you bargained for. Inappropriate passions are stirred when intimate problems are discussed, even in the most innocent friendships, and may lead to serious indiscretions that can ruin your marriage. Don't put yourself in vulnerable positions. Your mate needs to be able to trust that you will guard yourself and your marriage relationship in these matters. Some things never go out of style, and absolute fidelity in your marriage is one of them.

> SOME THINGS NEVER GO OUT OF STYLE, AND ABSOLUTE FIDELITY IN YOUR MARRIAGE IS ONE OF THEM.

Another situation to be cautious of is the danger of the two of you "hanging out" with the same couple all the time. This can cause too much familiarity with the other person's spouse. This familiarity with the other person's spouse in the name of friendship, may lead to separate meetings. Your spouse may "fall in love" with the wife or husband of your friend and have an affair. This has happened all too often and must be guarded against. It's a tragedy that may cause you to lose three important people in your life—your spouse and the two friends. Have a variety of friends whom you enjoy being with and you will prevent the possibility of this happening.

Another situation that can harm your marriage a great deal is when one spouse is jealous of the other. It sometimes wears a disguise called, "But it means I love her (or him)."

Wrong! Jealousy does not mean you love or really care about your spouse. It means you are frightened and don't trust your spouse. It also can be a demonstration of unhealthy over-possessiveness. For instance, if you're walking down the street together and your wife waves at a fellow co-worker who happens to be male, don't read anything into it. Or if your husband is in the break room having a soda with a female co-worker when you happen to drop by, don't read anything into that either.

Take the case of Sharon and Richard. Richard's first wife had had an affair that ended their marriage. He was continually accusing Sharon of what his first wife was guilty of doing. Whenever Sharon would talk with her first husband, discussing their children's problems or other issues, Richard would say, "Why are you talking to him? You just want to be with him. You just want to sleep with him." Not only did he object to her having conversations with her ex, he reacted that way when she talked with any man. He was so jealous and possessive that he was sure she was cheating on him. The truth of the matter was, she wasn't even thinking about it, and it was ruining their marriage.

Some people say "I'm jealous. I admit it. I want him/her all to myself. He's/she's mine." To be so extreme is pure selfishness and is a blatant lack of caring and trust.

There are other areas of trust needed in a marriage. It's a very good feeling to be able to tell your wife or husband something and know that it will go no further. Some things are just too personal and private to share outside the marriage relationship. Your mate needs to know that you will not talk about your private matters with friends, family members, or anyone else. To keep confidences is a must in a genuine friendship.

June and Arlen had an argument one morning, and June was still fuming when Arlen left for work. She was well acquainted with the people he worked with. Later that morning she remembered something she needed to ask Arlen, completely unrelated to their argument. She called him at work. One of the other workers answered the phone. She could hear a group of them talking in the background. Her husband got on the phone and rather arrogantly said, "So, are you still mad?" She was very embarrassed because she knew the others could hear and would know they had had a fight. And the way Arlen had responded made her feel he had told them about the argument. She felt this was a betrayal of their privacy. It was their issue and no one else needed to know anything about it.

Your spouse needs to have confidence that you will not say disparaging things about him or her to others. You have probably heard other people say pretty disgusting things about their mates behind their backs. How did you feel about the person saying it? How did you feel about the person he or she was saying it about? It puts both in a bad light. It can be a serious betrayal.

You also need to remember that your mother, or father, is also outside of the marriage relationship and should not be privy to the intimate details of your private marital life. Don't belittle your mate by complaining to your parents or others about certain character flaws he or she has. These are betrayals. Honor your spouse and keep private matters private. That includes the sexually intimate side of your marriage.

> **NO MATE HAS THE RIGHT TO PHYSICALLY, SEXUALLY, OR EMOTIONALLY ABUSE HIS OR HER SPOUSE.**

The exception to this rule is abuse of any kind. Spouses need to be safe around each other. No mate has the right to physically, sexually, or emotionally abuse his or her spouse. And no one needs to accept or put up with this kind of behavior. If you are not physically safe, then strong measures need to be taken. Calling the police may be all that is needed. If not, then you may need to go to a shelter for abused persons, then call the police. Never risk your own or your children's safety.

If you are experiencing sexual or emotional abuse you need to seek professional counseling. If you are a member of a church or synagogue you may want to seek guidance from your minister or rabbi. Not only is counseling needed for you as a couple, but the person doing the abusing may also need separate counseling to overcome a deep-seated problem. You may also need to have legal counsel. A point that cannot be overemphasized is that not only is the abused person being damaged, but the children are also being damaged and taught that abuse is acceptable behavior when they marry.

Money is another area in which trust can be threatened. In some marriages one or the other spouse misuses credit cards and stacks up debt. Couples must be able to trust each other with the family funds. When this principle is violated, trust is lost. When this problem becomes extreme, professional counseling may be needed. Trust in this area must be restored for the marriage to be strong. You've got to be able to trust your best friend with the family money and needs. Landon found this out the hard way:

> I travel a lot in my business and I needed my wife to take care of paying our bills while I was gone. Although she would pay some of the bills, others were left unpaid and any notices of their being due were destroyed by her. She used the money for other things and to this day I have no idea where the majority of it went. This continued for several months until I was home long enough to start receiving creditor phone calls. At first I fully believed her when she said they had been paid. The end result is that now I don't know when I can trust her.

If you have lost trust in your mate, it can be restored. First, the mate who broke the trust needs to be forthright and honest about the betrayal. A sincere apology needs to be given. If it is a matter of telling your personal business to others, then cease doing it. Or if it's regarding speaking ill of your mate to others, stop. The same is true of the misuse of money. The behavior must change. Whatever the act may be that caused the trust to be broken, make a pledge to your spouse that you will sincerely work on changing your behavior. Give your spouse time to get over the broken trust until he or she can trust you again. It may take more time than you think is necessary before your spouse believes you have changed, so be patient.

ADULTERY IS THE ULTIMATE BROKEN TRUST.

The person whose trust was broken must get to the point where he will ultimately set aside the incident or incidents and risk giving trust again. The one who has been hurt needs to forgive and then move on. The newly trusted spouse must then always deserve and honor that trust.

Adultery is the ultimate broken trust and one of the most devastating acts perpetrated against a spouse. Sexual intimacy is one of the most precious shared gifts a couple has. Once this trust is broken, it is extremely difficult to mend, but not impossible. If you still love each other, there is a way. If you can't stand him or her for doing it, but you want to save the marriage and both spouses are willing, it can be done. If there are children, do everything in your power to restore the marriage and make it stronger and happier than it has ever been. Though it may be very difficult it will be worth all it will take to make it happen. The first step is that all contact with the illicit partner must cease completely.

Some people may tell you that as time goes on you just have to forgive and forget your spouse's adultery. Forgive? Yes. Forget? Impossible. At least not for a very long time, and perhaps not at all. That still does not prevent you from restoring your marriage and enjoying happiness beyond what you thought possible. Sometimes the silent remembering keeps it from happening again. It is possible, however, that the memory will finally fade into the background as a new and loving relationship is built between the two of you. Chris and Shelly's story is one example of how this tragedy can be handled.

Chris and Shelly had been married for twenty-two years. They were active members of their church and attended services together every Sunday with their six children. One evening Chris could no longer carry his dark secret. He had had numerous affairs in the past ten years and finally admitted it to his wife. The affairs were only brief ones, with no desire on his part to continue the relationships. He loved his wife and children and didn't want to lose them. Shelly was devastated by the news. She was stunned, then filled with overwhelming anger, and then with the deepest sorrow she had ever known. That's when her tears started, and she couldn't make them stop for days on end.

He begged her to forgive him and promised absolute fidelity for the rest of his life. He pled with her not to leave him. She was repulsed by him and wouldn't let him touch her. *How could she ever let him touch her again?* she wondered. He pleaded for her forgiveness. She didn't know if it was possible to stay in the marriage even if she *could* forgive him. She was certain she would never be able to trust him again. And if that were the case, how could she possibly stay married to him? But what about the children? They loved him and needed him. She loved him. She had always loved him. And she needed him. He had been a good provider. How could she make it without him? How could he have done this to her? All of these things went through Shelly's mind as she mourned this tragedy in her life and worked to find a solution. She agonized and prayed for guidance about what to do and whether to stay in the marriage.

Chris did not press her for a decision and let her vent her anger on him whenever she needed to, always asking for her forgiveness and expressing his sincere love for her and his understanding of her disgust and disappointment in him. When she would shout, "I hate you, I hate you, I hate you for this!" He would respond, "I hate me for it, too. Please forgive me." He had learned not to ruin the healing Shelly's anger could bring by using any defense or justification. He just listened and tried with all his might to understand her feelings from her perspective. It was a deeply painful time for both of them, but Shelly decided to stay in the marriage.

It took many months before she would let him touch her in any intimate way. And when they finally made love, her imagination went crazy thinking about what he had done. They would talk deep into the night as she questioned and cried. He answered her questions, held her, and listened, pledging his love and fidelity again and again. He also made this same promise to God and asked Him to help him keep the promise. And he meant it. He never wanted anything like this to ever happen to him and his family again.

It took several years of patient understanding on both Shelly's and Chris's parts until finally the trust was restored. Their love for each other grew through the years, and now they share a wonderful life together, not only enjoying each other, but also enjoying their children and grandchildren, something they would have lost had they not been willing to work through the pain.

Dr. Carlfred Broderick gives wise counsel on how to deal with questions the betrayed mate has regarding what actually took place during the illicit sexual encounter.

[D]emands for clinical sexual details should be resolutely resisted. In response to an informed spouse's assertion of the right to know "everything," repentant mates all too often supply details so vivid and concrete that they can scarcely be set aside. Months and years later they flash into memory, triggered by a date, a place, a word, a circumstance—and they lose none of their power to hurt. It is natural, of course, to be morbidly curious about such things, and injured spouses may argue that nothing could be worse than their fantasies. They are mistaken. Fantasies fade; but sharply etched visions of certified reality live on and on.[7]

Forgiveness is the key to rebuilding the marital relationship after adultery. It is not always possible, however, as Ruth and Brandon's experience shows. Brandon simply could not forgive Ruth. She had been the unfaithful one. It had only occurred once, and she felt horrible about it; but Brandon would not let it go. He kept it alive in his mind as though it had happened yesterday and yet it had happened many years ago. He kept pressing for explicit details and verbally beat her with those details. His lack of desire to set it aside and move on destroyed their relationship. It's heartbreaking when that happens because it doesn't have to.

Dr. Broderick makes another important point about the benefits of working through this devastating betrayal:

> When infidelity is turned into a profitable experience by a couple it is because a combination of two things occurs: 1) despite marital hurts and resentments, there is a fundamental commitment to the marriage; and 2) through the terrific jolt which the infidelity and the discovery caused, the couple take a new hard look at their relationship and what they can do to revitalize it.[8]

Sometimes the only way to go through the process of healing your marriage is to have professional counseling. Many couples work through this heartache of infidelity and regain happiness and trust in their marriage. It can happen if both parties are willing to put in the necessary dedication, hard work, and time.

There is never an excuse for being unfaithful to your spouse, but there are reasons why it happens; both partners need to explore and understand what events led to the infidelity. Each must be willing to take his or her own responsibility and look openly at what needs to be changed. For instance, one partner may not be getting his or her needs met and may not be telling this to the other. The other mate may not be willing to listen. If there is a conscious effort on both his or her part to create a friendship and to use the different principles in this book, an affair can be avoided or forgiven.

NEVER BREAK THAT SACRED TRUST. IT CAUSES TOO MUCH AGONY AND SUFFERING.

To those of you who have remained faithful to your spouses: Please, never break your sacred marital trust! It causes too much agony and suffering for everyone concerned. The long-lasting difficulties divorced families have are not to be underestimated.

BEGIN TODAY

Developing a deep and loving friendship with your spouse is one of the most important secrets to a lasting, happy marriage. Review the five elements of true friendship and look to see what you are doing to incorporate them into your behavior. Take responsibility for your own actions without being critical of what your mate may or may not be doing. Then decide what you would like to do to put these five elements into practice. You will then be doing your part to open the door a little wider to a deeply fulfilling marriage. As you grow together in your marital friendship, though you still remain individuals, you will develop a "oneness" that transcends all other friendships.

Focus on the Positive

*Go to your bosom; knock there, and ask
your heart what it doth know.*
—WILLIAM SHAKESPEARE

THE CRITICAL EYE

The time of courtship is such a fun time. We have high expectations and we view each other with eyes of love and gentleness. We are very attentive to and aware of each other's
needs. Our manner of speaking is respectful and kind. Our
awareness is expressed in our gratitude for even small things.
It is as though our natural instincts inspire us to put our best
foot forward because we have found our desired mate.

This usually continues during the first year of marriage. It
seems, for most of us, we can hardly be pried apart. We want
to be holding on to or touching each other all the time. Sometime during that first year, however, our vision of our mate
seems to change and we become aware that some little things
could stand improvement. So our improvement suggestions
begin. It's funny that once we begin to look for little im-
provements the list grows. If our mate does not respond right
away then the suggestions become a little more adamant. We
view each other with a more critical eye and the cycle begins.

Our mate begins to dislike the critical eye and begins to

respond in a like manner. After all, isn't it all right to help your mate with the task of improving, particularly when she is so willing to "help" you? Our conversations seem to be dominated by criticism. The one being criticized starts to defend and justify what he or she does. The conversations become more and more spirited and erupt into full-blown arguments that go nowhere.

Roger and Vickie seem happy and quite congenial, yet as they shared their story Roger corrected Vickie and she became offended. Here's their dialogue:

Vickie: Stop that! You're always correcting me. I'm not dumb.

Roger: I know you aren't dumb; it's just that you forget some of the details and you need help.

Vickie: (She snapped back) Look, I wasn't the one who forgot our anniversary. You were.

Roger: (Shifting his position and moving away) Well, you're not so perfect. How come the house isn't cleaned up when I get home? I work hard all day long and the least you could do is have the house clean when I get home. After all, you're home all day long.

Vickie: You ought to try to take care of our kids day after day and meet all their demands. You get to go to work and have a nice quiet office to work in without all the howling kids and messy diapers. You wouldn't last two days here at home!

Roger: (Angrily) If you think it is so easy maybe you ought to get a real job and see how long you'd last in the real world. Your family has never been good at employment.

This type of conversation resembles a sword fight. It starts with an attack by one, then the other defends and must attack in return; then the first one must defend and return the attack. And so it escalates until one is mortally wounded and retreats to nurse the deep wounds and hurts. The end result is that the original subject is not resolved, the participants build a bigger emotional wall around themselves, and the critical eye sharpens.

When a person gets in the critical mode toward his or her mate all parts of the relationship are affected. The communication pattern becomes unfriendly, often sarcastic and cutting, and carries the tone that implies "stupid, dummy, or idiot, can't you do anything right?" The atmosphere in the home becomes guarded and strained. The desire to be together drops—as does the level of intimacy. The more critical we get the more wrapped up in ourselves we become. Each of us has a universal need to feel that *I am of worth, my feelings matter, and someone really cares about me.* Time and time again people ask, sometimes beg, for this affirmation.

> WHEN A PERSON GETS IN A CRITICAL MODE TOWARD HIS MATE ALL PARTS OF THE RELATIONSHIP ARE AFFECTED.

The responses to our survey included many comments about mates being self-absorbed and unaware of their spouse's needs, for example:

"She focuses on my faults."
"He's in a rut of fault finding."
"Selfishness, always thinking of himself instead of me and the family."
"I'm never good enough on my wife's scale."
"She's always keeping score—counting up how many nice things she does for me, compared to what I don't do for her."
"My husband only notices and comments on what's wrong. I clean and he points out the fingerprints."

One couple's response was, "There's no such thing as 'constructive criticism.' Being critical all the time is just plain

being negative. Happy couples look for and build on the positive." It's true that criticism in marriage is rarely constructive.
You need to notice the good in your companion and cease
focusing on the bad.

RUDE AWAKENING

Sometimes a wake-up call comes too late. Georgina started
divorce proceedings and the papers were signed, but the final
decree had not been issued when her wake-up call came:

> I had a horrible awakening this week—I realized that I
> still love my husband and now he doesn't love me. I was
> so sure it was right to divorce him. Now it's too late.
> He's already found someone else. I had been hurt by so
> many people this last year and I thought it was his fault.
> I built up a wall around me. Now he has a wall around
> him.
>
> I went to him and told him I was sorry and that I
> loved him. He was so cold and distant. He told me he
> didn't love me. Throughout the past year I was so
> wrapped up in myself that I didn't see what he was go-
> ing through. Now I've lost him.

In such a tragic case as this, not only are the husband and
wife devastated, but so are the children. The children sense
the stress and notice the changes, and often
their behavior deteriorates and puts greater
strain on the home and parental relations.
That was the case with Georgina. She had
children from a previous marriage and she was
very critical of how her current husband dealt
with her children and everything else he did.
The children's behavior became worse. When this happens,
negativism can become the pervading mood of all members
in the family. This generally happens over a period of time,

RECOGNITION OF EACH OTHER'S EFFORTS IS VITAL.

one step at a time. Unless something is done differently, it can progress to the point where the family splits up.

DESPERATE MEASURES

Recognition of each other's efforts is vital. Sometimes even the pleading for this recognition and the crying out for help doesn't work. That's what Marcia, the mother of six, found out. The more she did for the family the less everyone else did. Her husband criticized what she did and he and the children just demanded more and more of her. Finally, she decided to take a unique and desperate step:

> My husband traveled a lot and I took care of all the bills, kids, repairs, snow shoveling, animals, doctor and dentist visits, and so on. One time, when he came home, I was still doing it all with no help. A big snowstorm had hit and everyone, including the six kids, had something else to do besides help me. Well, around 6:30 P.M., when I still couldn't start fixing dinner and had no support from my husband or help from the kids, I called a family meeting.
>
> I sat them all down and I turned in my resignation. I quit! I informed my children that my name was Marcia and that Mom resigned and all things under that title were gone! Driver, maid, cook, doctor, and all. I told them that Marcia was a woman and Marcia needed her space to take care of things for her for a while. And if they needed anything Dad was still in position, so ask him. I was nice and I told them I loved them, just for the individual people they were, not just because they were my children.
>
> Then I turned to my husband, who was being quite smug by this time, and informed him that I quit being "wife" also. Boy, I wish I had had a camera—he looked shocked! I went on to say that I was a woman and had

a few needs that were not being met. I needed help and since he couldn't see fit to do it, I quit. I also told him I would talk to him later about personal needs.

About now all six kids were yelling and he joined in, "You can't quit. Who will do all the things you do?" I, still calm, told them that was something they would have to figure out among themselves, and I went to my room to escape to a warm tub and a good book.

Later, my husband came in and angrily broke a few photo frames, and I just looked at him. It took a while for him to calm down. He informed me that all the kids were in their rooms crying and he asked, "What should we do?" I very nicely told him that was something he and they needed to talk about. Twenty-four hours later they all came to me and asked me to return to my job with a few changes, because they really needed me.

The kids never forgot that day, and when life gets heavy they step in with no complaint. My husband never did remember and now we're divorced; he lives alone with all his rules, criticism, and lack of help!!!

TO TURN THINGS AROUND IN YOUR OWN MARRIAGE YOU MUST CHANGE WHAT YOU FOCUS ON CONCERNING YOUR MATE.

Maybe there is something simple that could be done without such a desperate measure and before this kind of terrible wake-up call is needed. It is amazing what recognition, appreciation, and help will do to motivate a mate. Imagine how different Marcia would have felt if her husband had recognized and appreciated what she was going through while he was gone so much with his job. What a difference if he had pitched in and helped her and insisted that the children do their part.

TURN THINGS AROUND

Abigail Van Buren shared a letter in her column "Dear Abby" from a woman whose marriage had been in need of repair. She and her husband were continually fighting and she had spent many nights crying herself to sleep. She wrote:

> One night I couldn't sleep because I was so upset with him. All I could think about were all the things that bugged me about him. I knew that if I didn't banish these negative thoughts from my mind, it would be a long time before I fell asleep. I decided to think instead of all the things that I loved about him. I wrote them down on a piece of paper, put it in an envelope, and placed it in his briefcase.
>
> The next morning, he called me from work to tell me how much he loved me. When he came home that evening, he put my "list" in a frame and hung it on the wall. We hardly ever fight anymore. I get love notes weekly and kisses daily.[9]

To start turning things around in your own marriage *you must change what you focus on* concerning your mate. If someone is told to *not* focus on something, somehow the forbidden thing becomes the center of focus. So this becomes an overt act on your part of focusing on something different. The following activity can help a couple change their focus.

Each spouse, take a piece of paper and write the following statement at the top:

Things My Mate Does That Help Me Feel Happy

Do this next part alone—no discussing any of it with your spouse at this point. Each of you take your paper and start to list the acts, both big and small, that your mate does that help you feel happy. Notice that it isn't what *makes* me feel happy; no one can *make* you feel happy. Happiness becomes a conscious choice and we each choose how we will feel about the things that go on around us. Still, certain things do *help* us feel happy and our mate can definitely make a significant contribution to our happiness.

The success of this part of the exercise hinges on your willingness to acknowledge the positive things your mate does and says. This is a time to get specific and avoid generalizations. Instead of saying something like "my mate is kind," write down exactly what he or she did or said that was kind. Each of us likes to be recognized in specifics. So let your mind wander over the past, both near and distant, and see what you can write down. There isn't anything that is too insignificant. Emphasize those things that were said and done to and for you. Also, recognize things he or she has done for family members and friends that generated a happy feeling within you. Remember how you like to have the little things you do honored and acknowledged. Now is the time for you to do the honoring.

Your list needs to be original, in your own words, stating your feelings. Give yourself a little time and think, not only with your mind but with your heart. You might be interested to see, as you begin to write, how your list grows as your memory is jogged by focusing on the little acts and expressions of kindness. This happens because you go inside and find the feelings of your heart that allow you to get outside of your self-absorption.

THE TOGETHER TIME

Now comes the fun. This is, again, a time for just the two of you, not a family time. If possible, farm the children out with grandparents or trade some baby-sitting with a neighbor. Or you could bring a sitter in while you go to a nice motel. Find a comfortable and intimate place to be—maybe sitting on your sofa or bed where you can face and touch each other. You might consider having some soft romantic music playing in the background (no TV!) to give some additional warmth and intimacy to this sharing time.

Let your mate know what has been meaningful to you. How you do the sharing part is up to you. Some couples have had one read the entire list and then the other read his or her entire list. Others take turns reading one item from each list as they go along. Remember, doing this involves a risk for each of you, and just as you want your list to be accepted, so will your mate. Be appreciative of the things that are shared. One caution: Do not remind your mate of other things you have done. Accept those things that your mate recognizes with no additions or critiques. If his or her list is longer than yours, that's okay. Just enjoy it and don't make comparisons. This is a beginning.

> **TO FEEL OF WORTH IN THE EYES OF THE MOST IMPORTANT PERSON IN YOUR LIFE GIVES MEANING AND ADDED ZEST TO EVERYTHING YOU DO.**

Many couples have reported that doing this exercise became a wonderful intimate time—one that they have not experienced for a long time. During one of our marriage retreats, three couples who attended were contemplating divorce. After the first session and that evening time of sharing, they arrived at the next morning's session with arms around each other and an obvious tenderness exhibited toward each other.

Ashley, who has been married for twenty years, describes a similar experience:

> I was once so caught up with feeling sad that my husband didn't join me in attending church that I wrote my brother, saying, "It's so hard to be married to a man who doesn't believe as I do." He wrote right back with

a long list of things my husband and I both believe in. It was a great letter. I still have it.

Whenever I tend to look at the 20 percent I don't have, instead of appreciating the 80 percent I do have, I think of that letter. Now I often say, "I'm married to the best man far and wide." And I believe that with all my heart.

To feel *of worth* in the eyes of the most important person in your life gives meaning and added zest to everything you do. It takes so little time and effort and pays such great dividends.

KEEP IT ALIVE

To help keep this feeling alive, give the paper you have written to your mate so it can be referred to again and again. Now that you have started the recognition, make it a habit. Each day look for the things that have helped you feel happy and tell your mate—even if you said something like it yesterday. Suzanne describes how she and Mark have made this a habit:

Every day we consistently tell each other what we appreciate about the other. We talk about the little things we did for each other that helped us feel happy. For instance, Mark said to me, "I appreciate your picking me up from work today." I added, "And I appreciated the way you made me laugh when I lost the file on my computer." Recognizing the caring day-to-day actions and comments keeps us focused on the positives.

WE OFTEN BECOME WHAT OTHERS BELIEVE WE ARE.

This is a process every couple needs to continue throughout their life together. Make it fun and then it will spread to your children. As they hear you acknowledge each other's good points, and they are also acknowledged, who knows, they might start doing the same for each other. And one day, they will know how to do it in their marriage.

BEGIN TODAY

Think of something positive about your mate right now and tell him or her today. Also, set the date for making your list of "Things My Mate Does That Help Me Feel Happy."

We all need a mate who loves and respects us, in spite of our weaknesses—someone who recognizes our strengths. Faults that used to be in the forefront of our minds become insignificant and our marriage will be much stronger and happier. We often become what others believe we are. Think of the possibilities as you apply this concept to your marriage.

Appreciate the Differences

*. . . male and female
created he them.*—GENESIS 1:27

HOORAY FOR THE DIFFERENCE!

By grand design, male and female are supposed to be different. Otherwise God would have made Addie and Eve or
Adam and Steve. But then none of us would be here had that
been the case! The fact that the sexes are different is not new
news. We can visually see the differences. And yet we seem to
waste so much energy in trying to change the grand design.
Somewhere someone decided that there was a need to prove
which one is better, woman or man. Or sometimes there
seems to be a push to make them more alike. This quest
seems to be taken more seriously by some people than their
trying to understand and enjoy the differences between males
and females. Dr. Denis Waitley, author of *The Psychology of
Winning,* said at one of his lectures: "Some women adopt the
worst attributes of men in an effort to be more like them,
such as swearing, swilling, and swaggering. Please, women
if you want to take on some of our characteristics, choose
the noble ones. However, remember that what you have
to bring to the world as a woman—your unique femi-

nine characteristics—is desperately needed and every bit as valuable."

WE COME LOADED

Consider the histories of the following couple and what kind of baggage they each would bring into their marital relationship. Here's their history, and as you read it, consider what chance of success you would give this marriage.

THE WOMAN

- ➤ Raised in a small farming town in the West
- ➤ Forth of nine children (seven boys)
- ➤ Older of two daughters
- ➤ Went to high school of 395 students
- ➤ Very popular
- ➤ Cheerleader and Letter-man Ball queen
- ➤ Very strong father in the home
- ➤ Strict religious upbringing

THE MAN

- ➤ Raised in a big metro-politan city in the East
- ➤ Youngest of three boys
- ➤ No sisters
- ➤ Went to high school of 1,500 students
- ➤ Not too popular
- ➤ In student choir and marching band
- ➤ Very strong mother in the home
- ➤ Same religion, not as strict

How successful do you believe this couple would be at marriage? What percentage chance would you give them for having a lasting marriage: 100, 75, 50, 40, 30, 20, or below? When this exercise was given at a seminar for singles the majority voted 20 percent or below. When asked what their reasons were for thinking this couple couldn't make it these were at the top of the list: She was like an oldest child and was probably used to getting her way; she was probably very cherished and spoiled; small town versus big city; she was popular and the center of attraction while he was in the background; he was the youngest and spoiled, and two spoiled people can't make it; she was used to a strong father and he was used to a strong mother; he didn't have any sisters and probably didn't understand females; and the last nearly unanimous statement was "they are too different."

After the discussion was finished, I introduced the couple who had been happily married for nearly forty years. That's when my wife came out and we took a bow. This group of mostly divorced people had experienced differences and baggage from their past and they were surprised that we had worked through such a history and had made it. By acknowledging differences and working with and through them, couples can have a very successful marriage.

BAGGAGE OF YOUR OWN

Differences show up in many ways. We each bring with us the baggage of the past, some of which is good and some of which needs to be discarded. No matter what our family was like when we grew up, we each believe that most families are like our own family of origin. When we experience differences with our mate we automatically react the way that seems natural to us because that's the way we grew up. We have a knee-jerk reaction—it happens without our thinking. For instance, if you were spoiled by having your family cater to your wants most of the time, you will expect your mate to do the same. If your mate doesn't, you may resort to the behavior that manipulated your parents when you were a child. Now, if your mate was not catered to, the stage is set for a battle for control.

This same type of difference may show up in more subtle ways. If you were reared to be a people pleaser, you will do almost anything to get approval. At first, this may seem great, but in the long run it can be very damaging. The pleaser eventually gets tired of not getting his or her needs met and then begins to react angrily at even small things. The mate doesn't understand what happened to their peaceful life and this wonderful person who was so agreeable.

Dr. Carlfred Broderick, the noted therapist and author, tells a great story. When he was newly married he got sick with a cold and wandered around their apartment coughing and moaning, waiting for his wife to tell him to go to bed, just like his mother had done. Finally his wife said, "If you are that sick go to bed." As he lay in bed he kept coughing and waiting for his wife to bring him some orange juice, just like his mother had done. In desperation, he finally asked his wife if they had any orange juice, she answered to the affirmative, and he weakly asked her to bring him some. A little later, the same scene happened again. Later, as he waited to be automatically taken care of (like mama used to do), in desperation he coughed loudly and asked for juice. His wife brought him the juice and in exasperation said, "Do you have some fetish with orange juice? If you want juice ask for it or get up and get it for yourself." He said he had assumed that all families functioned like the one he grew up in and this was the first clue to let him know that it was not true.[10]

One of the first spirited discussions (the politically correct way to say "argument") Joy and I had after getting back from our honeymoon concerned who was going to pay the bills. We had not discussed much about money during our courting days except for the need to have jobs so we could have money to live on. When the bills came in she started writing out the checks to pay them. I said, "What are you doing?" She said, "I'm paying the bills." I said, "That's not your job. It's mine," and her reply was that the wife pays the bills. You see, she grew up on a farm where her mother paid the bills. I grew up in a home where my dad was an accountant and he paid the bills. We were both dedicated to doing it the way our parents had done it and were both quite stubborn. I was more stubborn so I got the privilege of paying the bills. My system was not as organized as my dad's and I called it the *round to it* system—you know, I pay when I get around to it. This drove Joy crazy.

> IT'S A WISE MOVE WHEN A COUPLE CAPITALIZES ON ITS INDIVIDUAL STRENGTHS.

Two years later when I went into pilot training she had the time and I didn't, so she took over paying the bills. Since then she has been more than a bill payer; she has managed our money and she is far better at it than I ever was. My philosophy was, if there was money to be spent, why not spend it. She seemed to always find a few extra dollars to tuck away in a savings account. We've been much better off because of her ability.

It's a wise move when a couple capitalizes on its individual strengths. Recognizing these differences without feeling threatened or discriminated against is important and beneficial.

CULTURAL DIFFERENCES

Differences arise from many sources: your cultural backgrounds, what part of the country you were reared in, the country of your origin, the economic status of your family, the strength of your religious background, the traditions carried on by your family, your birth order, how your family communicated and showed love, and the list could go on. Each of these contributes to who you are and what makes you different from each other. Different backgrounds and family experience can mesh depending on the desire and motivation of the couple. Keith, for example, grew up with abusive and angry parents. He vowed that he would not be like that with his wife, Meg, and family.

Keith said: "It is hard for me to understand and identify with her family. They are fun-loving, kind, and

happy. Meg has been very patient with me and is helping me learn how to be different than my family was.
She has seen my family and knows of my vow and she
helps me with great love. It is that love that has gotten
us through some pretty hard times."

Meg said: "I have watched how hard Keith has
worked to control his temper and how much he desires
to have our family [be] different than the way he grew
up. He really is such a kind man and has developed into
a loving father."

We can learn from each other and have the best of both
our worlds. Some families have marvelous traditions and customs that build memories. Foods, celebration

**CELEBRATE
YOUR
DIFFERENCES
AND EXPAND
YOUR WORLD
TO LEARN
NEW THINGS.**

customs, and cultural costumes all combine to
make life more enjoyable. The statement
"we're so different" is used too often as an excuse. Instead, celebrate your differences and
expand your world to learn new things. Who
knows, you might like it!

Joseph and Nicole have blended two cul-
tures over the years they have been married.
Joseph and his parents immigrated from the Ukraine during
World War II. Nicole's family is thoroughly West Coast
American, having moved from California to Utah when she
was young. As exciting as it was for them to have such different backgrounds, they also learned that not all parts of cultural differences are easy to blend. When Joseph's family got
together it was natural for them to speak Russian and Nicole
was unable to participate. This was hard for her, even though
she tried to learn some of the language. At times she felt very
alone. But Nicole has learned that "every home is a different
culture. Focus on what's working and what you have in common." She found out that food was very important to Joseph's
culture. It was the way they extended themselves to others.

You convey deep respect through the food you serve and the way you prepare it. She developed a love for Russian food and learned to prepare it, and in turn "this has expanded my personal world." Easter is one of the big holidays in Russia and she decided thirty years ago that they would celebrate it in their own family the way Joseph's family had celebrated it. This would be a way to honor and teach their children her husband's heritage. So each Easter, Nicole and other women in his family prepare traditional foods and they honor the customs that surround that holiday's celebration. "This is a deeply spiritual time," she explains, "and over the years has expanded to include more of his family and at times some of our neighbors."

Embracing those things unique to your spouse's culture broadens your experience and brings greater depth to your relationship. Just imagine the respect that is built when spouses celebrate each other's interests.

GENDER DIFFERENCES

Our genders have built-in differences; recognizing and understanding them can help us enjoy each other more. There are many publications that treat this subject extensively, including *Male and Female Realities* by Joe Tanenbaum; *Men Are from Mars, Women Are from Venus* by John Gray; and the seminar tapes *Hidden Keys to Loving Relationships* given by Gary Smalley. Each of these approaches the male/female differences from a unique perspective and is interesting to study. The differences between men and women that follow suggest they are the predominant characteristics in most males or females, but keep in mind they are not necessarily true of all males or females. All of us are individuals and may have a different mixture of characteristics. There is no particular order of importance in the presentation of these differences.

TALKING

Phyllis, like many women, has this complaint about her husband: "He doesn't talk to me very much. I talk and explain and all I get in return is either a grunt or a groan, or just silence. When I push him to say something . . . anything . . . then out of the blue he just blows up." Phyllis brings up a number of classic male/female differences. The first being that men do not talk as much as women do. As a matter of fact, this starts very early. Newborn baby girls have more lip movement than baby boys and that seems to increase as the girls grow older. Girls usually learn to talk earlier and talk more throughout their lives.

In one study, children at a preschool were observed and the noises coming from their mouths were analyzed. All of the sounds the girls made were recognizable words and it was noted that the girls spent a great amount of their time talking to other children, and when alone, they talked to themselves. The little boys used recognizable, understandable words about two-thirds of the time. The rest of the time their noises were sound effects like the roar of an engine or siren, the sounds of a crash, or one-syllable sounds like "yah" or "maaaaan" or "huh." This tendency starts early on and goes into adulthood. Most wives realize that this has been going on for a long time with their husbands. Men need to understand that they can become more talkative. Both need to understand that it will take a conscious effort for him to change even a little bit.

MEN NEED TO UNDERSTAND THAT THEY CAN BE MORE TALKATIVE.

PHYSICAL BRAIN DIFFERENCE

Another difference occurs during the development of the fetus within the womb. Sometime between the fourth and sixth month's growth, a chemical fluid is released and washes over boys' brains and causes the right side of the male brain to become slightly smaller, and it destroys some of the fibers of the connecting tissue between the right and left sides of the brain (corpus callosum).[11] This influx of fluid and the reaction it generates causes boys to be left-brain oriented. The logical, analytical, and factual functions are contained in the left side of the brain, which also houses the aggressive and physical tendencies. Girls do not go through this chemical bath and brain change. They are predominantly right-brain oriented. The characteristics of this hemisphere are emotional, nurturing, creative, artistic, and communicative skills. They can draw on both sides of their brains more easily and generally process information faster. A woman receives almost twice as much input from her main senses. Thus she is more sensitive to and aware of her surroundings and the relationships around her.

Understanding the sensitive nature of women helped Tony DiCicco to coach the World Cup Championship-winning U.S. women's soccer team. Having once coached the men's national junior team he found that women responded subperbly to challenges, but terribly to chastisement. "Men can absorb tough criticism because they don't really believe it anyway," he said. "Women believe it and take it to heart."[12]

Women can more clearly communicate what they are experiencing and feeling. Just as it is important for men to understand this difference in women, it is equally important for women to understand that a man needs more time to process the information being shared. In other words, he needs time to mull things over in his mind. So when Phyllis stated her husband was either grunting or silent, that was a sign he was mulling things over. When he is pushed to reply before he has had a chance to think things through in his mind he may explode. This explanation does not justify the explosive reaction; it just explains what happens. If a man needs more time to think about a subject then he needs to say so with a simple comment like, "I need a minute to think about it." If women understood this need then they would not keep pushing a man for an answer and would give him time to think at his own pace.

This anecdote illustrates what science has proven:

A gentleman entered a busy florist shop that displayed a large sign that read "SAY IT WITH FLOWERS."

"Wrap up one rose," he told the florist.

"Only one?" the florist asked.

"Just one," the customer replied. "I'm a man of few words."[13]

Studies have shown that the average man speaks about twelve thousand words a day and the average woman speaks about twenty-five thousand words a day. And all too often when a man comes home from work he has used up the vast majority of his daily allotment while his wife has just gotten warmed up. Add to this the fact that, as Joe Tanenbaum states, a woman "receive[s] almost half again as much input from her senses as a man, store[s] more information, and can retrieve it more quickly and with more accuracy than he, which automatically gives her more to talk about."[14] The result is that when their husbands are not talkative, women often feel neglected, ignored, or lonely even when their husbands have no intention of shutting them out. Samantha, married nearly twenty-five years to Rulon, describes these feelings:

I yearn to talk with him. He just doesn't seem to have anything to say. I would give anything to have a conversation with him that goes beyond his usual five words. If he would only tell me about his work, his hopes for our children, his interests, it would make such a difference. I am so lonely for a conversation with him.

SOMETIMES THE REASON MEN DON'T TALK IS BECAUSE WOMEN DON'T STOP TALKING.

Husbands, you need to talk to your wife. She needs it. Wives, let your husband know you want to listen to him, that you want his opinion, then accept it without criticism. Sometimes the reason men don't talk is because women don't stop talking and give them a chance. If this is the problem, consider asking your husband some questions and just be quiet and listen to his response. For more help with communication see Secret #8: Talk to Each Other.

MEN COMPARTMENTALIZE

Men have the ability to compartmentalize. When they are ready to deal with an issue they can take it out of their "pocket" at a later date and go on where they left off. Usually it does not sit in their conscious minds and weigh on them. This also means that when a discussion is coming to a completion, and he has a grasp on all of its dimensions, then a man can put it away or set it aside.

For example, if a husband and wife have been arguing and the argument is becoming resolved, the man will set the subject aside, and when it seems to him that there is no further need for discussion, he might say to his wife, "well, honey, let's make love." She will likely respond with, "in your dreams!" The reason for this reaction is that a woman needs the time to work through the emotions generated by the discussion. We each need our processing time—men to process information and women to process emotions.

REASONS FOR COMMUNICATION

There is a basic difference in the main reason men and women communicate. Men mainly communicate to find a solution to a problem. They will try to solve the problem internally and when they can't find a solution they'll ask for help. Women also solve problems; however, their main purpose in communicating is to share. They share feelings, thoughts, experiences, and needs.

Often when a woman is trying to solve a problem, she will think out loud. This is the same process a man goes through only she is doing her reasoning verbally. Because a woman is able to take in more information faster and can store it more globally, she receives more input from her senses, processes faster, and can focus on many things at the same time. When women think out loud they often bring up other subjects. Men think in a linear fashion and focus on one thing at a time, and they have a hard time relating to the female way of problem solving. This is a foreign process to a man and he may accuse her of being scatterbrained.

An additional problem arises when a woman is in her sharing process. Because the main reason a man communicates is to solve a problem, he thinks that the reason his wife is telling him something is because she wants a solution. So he begins to tense up and go into his problem-solving mode to come up with the answer to her problem. When he begins to tell her what to do, she gets frustrated because all she needed was to be listened to and understood. He also reacts with frustration because all he was trying to do was to help. If a woman is in her sharing mode, it is helpful for her to tell her husband that that is what she is doing. On the husband's part, it would also be helpful if he would listen, and if he wonders if she needs help or a solution, ask something like, "Is there something you would like me to do?" or "Can I help you in any way?"

MEN HAVE A BUILT-IN ABILITY TO JUDGE DISTANCE, SPEED, AND SPATIAL RELATIONSHIPS.

JUDGING DISTANCE

Men have a built-in ability to judge distance, speed, and spatial relationships. Some scientists posit that this skill dates back to our hunting days when our ability to feed our families depended on the accuracy of throwing a spear or shooting an arrow. Regardless of its origin, this can cause a problem in driving on the freeway or a canyon highway. For example, Lucia gets very nervous when she and her husband, Bart, are coming down a mountain road, particularly if she is on the cliff side. She is sure they are going over the edge at almost every curve. Of course, Bart thinks that's silly because he can judge the distance and knows they are safe. Here's Lucia's account of this difference in men and women:

> I have a real concern here. I know of some men who will use this to scare their wives and I think that's cruel. You married her because you love her, so, for goodness sakes, show it. Bart understands my fear in these situations, although, in all honesty, I have to say he didn't always. However, he never used it to scare me. He was just annoyed by my nervousness. Now his response is different. Knowing that I can't judge the distance with as much accuracy and that I am imagining us careening over the edge to our deaths, he slows down and moves over a bit. At that moment my heart is filled with new love for him, because of the care he has shown to me.
>
> Also, because I now understand that he has an eye for judging distance that I don't have, I have become more confident in his driving and feel less vulnerable. It works both ways. Respecting this difference in each other matters.

PHYSICAL MAKEUP

The physical makeup of our bodies is very different. On average, women have lighter bones, smaller hands and weaker thumbs, more flexible joints; are 23 percent muscle and 25 percent fat; burn fewer calories; wrinkle easier; bruise easier; and have nerve endings that are closer to the surface of the skin. Men tend to have heavier bones, thicker skulls, tighter joints; have 50 percent

MEN'S AND WOMEN'S BODIES PROCESS FOOD IN A DIFFERENT WAY.

stronger arms; are 10 percent taller; are 40 percent muscle and 15 percent fat; and are less buoyant in water.[15]

Muscular strength is very different in men and women. For instance, a man's hands are larger, his grip is much stronger, and the strength in his thumb can be about twenty times greater than a woman's. I know the reason for the thumb strength—so we can open all those bottles and jars used in the kitchen. Joy says it's for using and abusing the TV remote and, of course, I have to disagree. I believe we have to keep up our thumb strength through use of the remote as our exercise machine.

Men's and women's bodies process food in different ways. Metabolism is affected by our hormones, brain organization, and muscle mass. Proteins and fats are processed at different rates and in different ways. Females store body fat in greater amounts and have a harder time burning it. This is partly due to the type and amount of muscle tissue in each body. Women's muscles are smooth, and men's are more defined or striated. Striated muscles burn more calories and burn fat at a higher rate.

It is also interesting to note that "male hormones encourage the accumulation of fat mainly around the waist and the female hormones encourage the fat to accumulate in the hips and thighs."[16] The fat cells in the abdominal region are larger and fewer in number than the fat cells in the hips and thighs. With the combination of muscle construction, metabolism, and the size and location of the fat cells, men can loose weight easier and faster than women.

Men need to understand this difference. Women are very frustrated as they try to lose weight. For example, Stacy describes a typical situation: "It seems no matter what I do the weight doesn't come off. My husband and I went on a diet together and the weight is just dropping off him and he even snitches ice cream. It's not fair." Some men become very critical, even harsh and demeaning to their wives over this difference. This struggle is real for many women. Listen to this doctor's story:

> A friend of mine, who is thin and has a heavy wife, took his wife on a trip for five days. They did everything together—exercise, slept, golfed, and ate precisely the same food in the same amount. He lost three pounds and she gained six pounds.

Did he have a medical explanation for this difference? No, except that men and women have different metabolisms. So, husbands, harsh words and demeaning comments are not motivating to your wife. Stacy said she was more motivated when her husband backed off and just loved her. One day he discovered a book she had bought on weight loss. He said to her, "You don't need to do this for me. I love you just as you are." She replied, "That's what makes it possible for me to try."

Men and women also differ in some of their food cravings. Studies show that many women crave yeast products and given a choice, will often take bread over dessert. However, they do rate sweets high on their list of loves, especially—can you guess it? Chocolate! Men seem to crave meat, particularly red meat. There may be some connection with this need and the way men differ physically from women.

IT'S NOT COLD!

Rose said, "My husband and I were watching television the other night and he said to me, 'You must be comfortable.' That's our in-joke about the room temperature. What he really means is 'I'm too hot.' When he's just right, I'm too cold. Our personal thermostats rarely seem to match. Either he starts shedding clothing or I wrap up in a blanket."

You may wonder why it is that women generally seem to be cold—after all, according to their body types, it would seem that they have more insulation in the form of fat. There are multiple factors that influence our temperature differences. Two of the main factors have to do with our ability to stop the loss of heat and the ability to generate heat. The male body has a higher metabolism rate and higher muscle proportion, and the fat is distributed more evenly through the torso area, better insulating against heat loss.[17] All of these factors combine to make men better at generating heat and retaining it. It is true that the female body has better insulation, but this benefit is lost by a lower metabolism rate and poorer blood circulation. Thus, women feel colder more often and their bodies experience greater temperature changes. So when your wife complains about being cold it is not all in her head—it's real. Of course, there is an exception to this when a woman is going through menopause. Until her hormones are balanced she will have moments when her body feels as though it's on fire.

MALE NEED FOR INDEPENDENCE

While growing up, a boy has to pull away from his mother to prove he is a man. In contrast, a girl doesn't have to pull away from either parent to prove she is a woman. She can maintain close ties with both throughout her life. The proof of manhood, however, is a male's ability to be independent and strong, stand on his own, solve problems, be looked up to, and be depended on. He cannot be tied to his mother's apron strings and at the same time show the world that he has become a man. After all, how could a woman lean on his strength if he is holding on to another woman's apron?

A BOY HAS TO PULL AWAY FROM HIS MOTHER TO PROVE HE IS A MAN.

This need to pull away continues into his adult life. Both Joe Tanenbaum and John Gray write about this need for men to pull away; each has a slightly different perspective, however. Tanenbaum says that a man has a need to recharge his energy because being in a relationship takes energy, and he needs a certain amount of energy to sustain his life. Each man unconsciously allocates energy for the task at hand and then must recharge in order to continue. This process requires him to be on his own while he recoups the energy he expended. Gray believes it is a need to maintain his independence and autonomy. He states that a man loses part of himself when he connects to his partner and he must pull away to reestablish that independent feeling for himself. Men, he says, are like rubber bands and they will spring back with renewed energy ready to pick up where they left off.

When a man wants to withdraw so he can mull things over and come up with a solution, it can be threatening to a woman. Since a woman needs to talk things out and only withdraws if there is a problem or if she's angry, she thinks something is wrong. So she starts pressing her husband with questions like, "What's the matter?" or "Is something wrong?" or "What did I do this time?" This confuses her husband because there isn't anything wrong; he just needs some time to think. She doesn't believe him and so the stage is set for a discussion that will go nowhere.

Here again, if we can realize this difference we can do some things to help each other. If the wife will understand that her husband needs some time to process and mull things over, she will allow for this and not be threatened. And if the husband will recognize his need and what her natural reaction is, then he could say, "Nothing's wrong, honey. I need some time to think this over."

Even in normal conversation, men often respond more slowly. I notice this in my practice. When I ask a question to both the husband and wife, she usually responds more quickly. When I have a male client alone, I see him taking a longer time to respond than my female clients. This is normal behavior for both of them. It goes back to the fact that women have 40 percent more interconnections between right and left brain.

WHAT ABOUT THE MOVIES?

When you want to go out for a movie do you always agree on what movie you want to see? If you do, you are a rare find. Of course, there are times when you will agree on some hit movie whose TV commercials have captured the fancy of nearly every viewer. Usually, though, women are more inclined to want to see romantic, heart-touching films, and men seem to favor high adventure. Again, this goes back to the right- and left-brain predominance. That doesn't mean a man can't enjoy a good three-Kleenex flick now and then. Or that a woman won't become engrossed and enjoy suspense and adventure.

VIEWING VIOLENCE OVER AND OVER CAN HAVE A NEGATIVE EFFECT ON THE WAY PEOPLE TREAT EACH OTHER.

No matter what your tastes, be cautious about the movies you choose to see. Viewing violence over and over can have a negative effect on the way people treat each other, including spouses. The tender marital relationship needs to be guarded and nourished, not sabotaged.

BEGIN TODAY

Learning to understand our differences as married couples can significantly enhance our relationships. Look at these differences with new eyes and discover their benefits and learn from each other; by doing this you can find greater happiness together. Your world will expand, your burdens will lighten because you no longer need to be troubled over not being more alike, and your enjoyment of being with each other will increase. Hooray for the difference!

Have a Sense of Humor!

*A merry heart doeth good like a
medicine . . .* —PROVERBS 17:22

MAKE A CONSCIOUS DECISION

A wise man once said, "In all of living have . . . fun and
laughter. Life is to be enjoyed, not just endured."[18] Having a
sense of humor can be a saving grace for marriage. Like all
things that are worthwhile, it takes a little effort, but it has a
big payoff.

Make a conscious decision to laugh a lot. Actually talk
about it as a couple and decide to find the humor in your life
as much as you possibly can. Enjoy the comical moments for
all they're worth. See the humor in the little tragedies that
come along. They *are* going to happen, so just accept that fact
and find the funny bone among the aches and pains of life.
Marie Osmond gave a suggestion worth considering when
she said, "If you're going to be able to look back on something and laugh about it, you might as well laugh about it
now."[19] Laughter is great therapy and it's free!

Candyce figured that out when her third baby was born.
After going through nine months of misery and what seemed
like endless hours of labor each time her babies were born,
Candyce thought the least her husband, Wayne, could do

FINDING HUMOR IN SITUATIONS THAT COULD GO EITHER WAY IS A GREAT WAY TO LIVE JOYFULLY WITH YOUR MATE.

would be to bring her some flowers. All she got from him was a "Good job, kid." Somehow it wasn't quite what her hungering heart needed. However, when this new baby arrived, so did a beautiful bouquet of a dozen red roses. She was thrilled! At last Wayne was starting to be a little romantic. She threw her arms around him and thanked him profusely. He nonchalantly said, "No problem. I'm glad you like 'em."

Later that day, after he had left the hospital, she found an envelope that had fallen to the floor. She thought, *Oh, good. He wrote me a note to go with the flowers. He's such a sweetheart.* She pulled out the note and read,

Dear Wayne,
Here's some money. Go buy Candyce some flowers this time.

Love, Mom

Don't get mad, she thought, *laugh.* After all, it was very funny. She *had* to laugh. And they have both laughed about it many times since. She has received many bouquets of flowers from him since then, without prodding from anyone.

There is a choice little verse in the Bible that says, "Live joyfully with the wife whom thou lovest . . ." (Ecclesiastes 9:9). Finding the humor in situations that could go either way is a great way to live joyfully with your mate. Naomi and Gil discovered this secret early on in their marriage and it has served them well. After one of their less desirable days when they had a rather heated discussion, she found the perfect card to give him. On the outside it said, "You're the answer to my prayers . . ." Then inside: "not quite what I prayed for, but nevertheless, the answer." It broke the ice and they laughed. And they have continued the practice of giving humorous greeting cards to each other ever since.

LAUGH MORE THAN YOU CRY

Joy and I made a decision one day and actually said the words, "Let's laugh more than we cry." We had many reasons to cry in our early married life and have had many others since. We wanted very much to have children and we wanted them right off the bat. She came from a big family that she enjoyed and wanted us to have a big family of our own. I wanted it, too. Having the idea and making it come true were two different things—it just wasn't happening for us. At the time I was a fighter pilot, having the time of my life, while she was bottoms up in doctors' offices trying to find out why she couldn't get pregnant. Not fun.

At one point, the doctor told her to try the temperature method. She was instructed to take her temperature at a designated time every morning and when it was at a certain level it meant she was ovulating. That was to be the moment of action. She told the doctor that I would likely be up in the air flying at that time of the day. He said, "Hey, just call the control tower and tell them your husband has to come home right now and make love." When she told me what he said she started to laugh. We both ended up laughing and imagining all kinds of scenarios. We got completely carried away as we envisioned the expression of the flight controllers and other pilots on the same radio channel, who might even try to volunteer for the duty. Laughing about it was a great stress reliever.

Next we were told about all kinds of positions that would likely lead to pregnancy. And what was once high eroticism became high hilarity. You've got to laugh or some things in life are just too difficult. Of course, we—mostly she—did our share of crying once a month when the bad news would manifest itself. When we had been married nearly five years, Joy had a tubal pregnancy that ruptured and serious complications were discovered during the surgery. The doctors gave us the sad news that she would never be able to give birth to children. It was a low point in our life. But blessings came and we were able to adopt our children . . . all five of them.

It's good that we learned how to laugh during those early years because it came in handy later when we discovered that out third child, our little daughter, Carol, was mentally impaired. That's when we decided again that we needed to laugh more than we cried. We consciously looked for things to laugh about. One day when I came home, Joy could hardly wait to tell me what had happened with Carol, who was about six years old at the time. She had been hitting her brother, and Joy was reprimanding her for it. Carol looked at her upset mother with her big brown eyes and said, "But Mommy, I can't help it. I'm brain bandaged." We don't know where she heard that expression, but we thought it was absolutely hilarious and laughed! Then we decided how very clever it was of her to think of it and decided she was smarter than most people thought. Laughing helped lift our burden. Let it help lift yours.

LITTLE INSIDE JOKES

Something wonderful happens when couples have their own little "inside humor" moments. These moments are based on funny past experiences that you both relate to in a fun way. These are the experiences that, whenever you're in a group and you see anything akin to it, cause you to look at each other and give a little knowing smile, a nudge, or a wink, and you both know that you're remembering that old event. Sharing and enjoying such a moment again and again becomes almost more fun than the actual event. Start to laugh about life's happenings over and over again. Let the fun memory have a full life and enjoy these moments to the hilt.

Mindy and Chuck had one of those experiences when they were in a Mexican restaurant with their two sons. As they looked over the menu their nine-year-old son, Billy, looked up at his mother and said, "Mom, what's a fadgitah?"

He was trying to pronounce "fajita" and she thought he said, "What's a vagina?" She looked at her husband, who thought he heard the same thing, and replied to Billy, "Please, not here, son. We'll talk about it at home." He said, "No, Mom. I want to talk about it right here. What is it? I might want it." Before they could be too horror stricken, and much to their great relief, he pointed to it on the menu. Now Mindy and Chuck have this little inside joke that makes them giggle every time they look at a menu in a Mexican restaurant.

ONE OF THE PRICELESS THINGS ABOUT LASTING MARRIAGE IS THAT YOU HAVE A DELIGHTFUL HISTORY TOGETHER THAT CAN'T BE ENJOYED WITH ANYONE ELSE.

One of the priceless things about lasting marriage is that you have a delightful history together that can't be enjoyed with anyone else, even another spouse if you divorce and marry again. It's a precious piece of your life that becomes irreplaceable.

Janice and Doug continue to enjoy a choice piece of their history together. It happened in a music class when they were in college. Janice had noticed Doug and thought he was very good looking and wished he would ask her out. The most she had gotten out of him was a casual, "Hello." She was sure he hadn't really noticed her, and she was not the type to pursue him. The day of their performance exams Janice was nervously waiting for her turn to play a piece on the clarinet. Just before her turn to get up and perform, Doug, who was sitting behind her, leaned forward and whispered in her ear, "Those lips were made for something better than playing the clarinet." She can't remember how well she did on her performance, but she'll never forget what he said. That was the beginning of their dating and courtship. Whenever they tell it, mostly at the prodding of someone who has already heard it, they can't help but laugh.

Humor is all around us. We just need to notice it and make the most of it. It's surprising how often the well-intended moments of life gone awry can be the catalyst to a humorous moment made memorable, if we let it. Austin (now a doctor) and his wife Ashley's experience is a perfect example:

> Austin was in his first year of medical school when he decided he needed to have a job to bring in some extra money. School was very demanding, but he was sure he could do it and found a night watchman job for an industrial plant. He was young and felt somewhat invincible—"I don't need much sleep." He began the job the evening of the day we brought our first baby home from the hospital. My mother was there helping me and off he went to work. He thought he could study some and maybe even doze off occasionally while he sat guard. The reality of his folly came into focus when he realized that the job did not just include "watching," but doing cleanup as well.
>
> As the night wore on, one disaster after another occurred as he worked. First he locked himself out of the building he was supposed to clean (having dropped the keys in the mud and couldn't find them), had to break in through a window, and had to empty huge drums of oil with a forklift and backed into a wall, causing damage. On it went through the night—one catastrophe after another.
>
> When he finally came home he shared his night of horrors with me and my mother, who had been up nearly half the night with the baby. As he went on we could not help but laugh and he, too, began to see the ridiculousness of it all and joined in the laughter, making the stories even grander. By the end of his tale we were all exhausted not only from our lack of sleep but from our convulsions of laughter. Then he sobered a bit and said, "I have to pay the company for all the damage I've done." That was it—we decided he didn't need to work, because the point of it all was to earn money, not pay it. He also realized there was no way he

could study or sleep at this job, and he quit. Fortunately, the boss had a soft heart and told him he wouldn't pay him for the night's work and Austin wouldn't have to pay him and he'd call it even.

They have told this story many times and never fail to laugh and enjoy the fun they shared that night.

HUMOR CAN STOP AN ARGUMENT

Melissa and Jake hit on a valuable tool that has stopped the arguments they always seemed to have whenever they were driving in their car. They were in business together and often drove to give speeches at different locations. At their meetings it was a miserable feeling to have to pretend to be in good humor, when, in fact, they were very upset with each other. Here's Melissa's report of their discovery:

On one of our trips we took our Blazer, not the usual sedan we drove. Jake was driving and as we began the trip I said, "Don't you think we need to get some gas? The tank is only three-eighths full." Jake said, "No it's not. It's five-eighths full. We have plenty of gas to get there." I said, "You're wrong. I can see that it is exactly three-eighths full. I'm counting each tick on the gauge and it *is* three-eighths!" He hotly replied, "I'm counting and it's five-eighths. You're wrong! We have plenty of gas." I couldn't believe he could be so foolish and said, "Okay, run out of gas if it will make you feel better!"

With that comment, Jake pulled the Blazer over, abruptly got out, and insisted that I sit in the driver's seat to see that he was right. With arrogant assurance, I did. Just as I said, "I'm right," Jake, somewhat

KEEP YOUR EYES OPEN FOR LITTLE OPPORTUNITIES WHEN YOU CAN CREATE AND ENJOY A GOOD LAUGH WITH YOUR MATE.

embarrassed, said, "I know what happened. The gas gauge in my car reads in the opposite direction." We both laughed at the stupidity of our argument, which had reached the high blood pressure stage.

Not long after that trip, I said to Jake as we drove along on another trip, "I think we only have about twenty-five more miles to go." He said, "No, we've got at least fifty miles left." I jumped in with, "Well, I saw a sign back there that said . . ." And the argument began. Then he looked at me and said, "three-eighths full!" And we both started laughing, realizing that we were falling into the same type of stupid argument. Just saying "three-eighths full" whenever an argument begins makes us laugh and it stops the fight instantly.

Shelby found another way to end an argument with humor. She seemed to have a gift for saying just what needed to be said and in a most unusual way. During one argument she said, "We've got to stop arguing in front of each other." Who could keep a straight face after that? Laughter can usually break the ice of an argument whenever it begins to form, particularly if a couple can find a key phrase, like Melissa and Jake did, from their own history, and use it.

Lydia and Tyler had an experience that shows how humor can stop an argument, though their's was a delayed reaction. Lydia said:

Tyler and I had a heated argument and I was so mad at him I said, "I've had it with you! I'm going out!" and with that I slammed the door and left. I got in my car and decided to go to a movie and get him off my mind.

When I came out of the movie I realized that I had left the car lights on and the battery was dead. I had to call Tyler to come and get me. How humiliating. When I climbed in the car beside him I knew he was silently laughing in the dark. I said, "Are you laughing?" At that point he could no longer hold it back . . . and neither could I. We laughed all the way home.

DON'T MISS THE LITTLE OPPORTUNITIES

Keep your eyes open for the little opportunities when you can create and enjoy a good laugh with your mate. Everyday occurrences provide a rich source of humor, once we push ourselves out of a deadpan existence.

Darrell was good at looking for ways to put some humor into his and Melanie's life. One day he spotted her shopping list posted on the refrigerator. He added his own item. Here's the list:

> *Potatoes*
>
> *Eggs*
>
> *Cereal*
>
> *Chicken*
>
> *Hamburger*
>
> *Fruit*
>
> *Veggies*
>
> *A naked snuggle*

Later when Melanie went shopping she saw it and laughed right out loud. And Darrell got one—that night.

Opportunities for humor abound. And they can be a lot of fun. Eleanor and Cameron discovered how bringing a little humor into their lives could do just that. One day they decided to play a joke on their kids by hiding in a closet. It was a tight fit. As they heard their children trying to find them, they laughed silently—the kind of laugh that makes you jiggle all over as you try to hold it in. Eleanor said, "To feel Cam's arms around me as we hid in that tiny closet, playing a trick on our kids, was so much fun."

To be able to laugh about life's unpleasant twists of fate can put a lot of fun into your marriage. Jared and Stella discovered this when they were about to celebrate their wedding anniversary. The day before, Stella was hit with a horrible back pain unlike anything she'd had before. It was unbearable. Jared rushed her to the emergency room where tests showed she had a kidney stone. After a miserable night with no luck in passing the stone, the doctor sent her home, with catheter still in place, to wait it out on pain medication. At home the pain had eased somewhat, and she got up from her bed, where her husband was lying beside her as they watched a TV show, and went out to the kitchen. She returned holding her catheter bag in one hand and a bottle of sparkling Martinelli in the other. She looked at Jared and said, "Happy anniversary!" They laughed as she gently collapsed on the bed beside him.

When things don't go quite like you thought they would, you might try seeing the humor in the situation and then just collapse on your bed and laugh. It works wonders.

FUN WITH MONEY

Collins told of a fun little experience he had with his wife, Bridgette.

I decided to have some fun with my rather meager paycheck. I cashed it into small bills—fives and ones. When I came home I walked over to Bridgette, who was sitting on the floor playing with our little son, and threw the money into the air above her head. It filled the room and felt like tons of money was raining on us. She laughed and laughed, gathering up the money like crazy, saying, "We're rich! We're rich!" It was very fun.

Marsha and Shane had an experience with money that left them both laughing. It was Valentine's Day. They realized separately that they hadn't bought each other a valentine card yet. Marsha said:

I told Shane that I needed to go get a few groceries and he said he had an errand to run, too. We both left in separate cars.

As I stood browsing through the card rack, trying to find the perfect card, musing and chuckling over different ones, I heard a rather hearty familiar chuckle. I looked up and saw Shane on the other side of one of the card racks. He, too, was browsing the rack and enjoying one card after another in search of the just-right one for me. Our eyes locked and we started to laugh.

I said, "Are you buying me a valentine?"

"Yes," he said, rather sheepishly. "Are you buying one for me?"

"Yes," I answered and then asked, "Have you found one yet?"

"Yes," he said. "Have you?" I had.

With his card in hand, he walked over to me and said, "How much is yours?"

Four dollars and fifty cents. How much is yours?"

"Three dollars and twenty-five cents." The humor of the situation was escalating and we started to giggle.

He said, "Why don't you show me the one you picked and I'll show you the one I picked and we'll read them and then put them back on the rack. It'll save us seven dollars and seventy-five cents."

That's exactly what we did and then hugged each other and went home laughing all the way. Every Valentine's Day we laugh again about that chance encounter and our thrifty decision.

Some couples know how to have fun with money without spending a cent. Here's Della and Durant's story:

I asked Durant what he wanted for his birthday. He said, "One million dollars." So I wrote him out a million-dollar check and gave it to him for his birthday—from *his* checkbook, no less. His response was, "Oh, thank you so much! It's just what I wanted."

That was years ago and he remembers it more than any other present I have given him. And it's always good for another laugh.

WHEN HUMOR HURTS, IT'S NOT FUNNY

Sometimes couples get caught in the sarcasm trap. If you are trying to be funny and clever at the expense of your mate, it will backfire. Even if your mate laughs at the time, he or she is doing it only to save face. This kind of humor carries a deep hurt. Here is the story of one husband and wife who were a prime example of this: In social gatherings he would make clever sarcastic remarks about her that were funny and people would laugh, as would she. She never said anything about her feelings concerning this matter. On the outside they appeared to be a happily married couple while she good-naturedly took the brunt of his jokes.

WHEN YOU ARE TRYING TO BE FUNNY AND CLEVER AT THE EXPENSE OF YOUR MATE, IT WILL BACKFIRE.

One day, she was seen with her two children driving away with her car packed to the brim. She had had it, saying, "I will not be insulted and humiliated by his sarcastic humor ever again." She divorced him and never returned. No one knew she had been suffering all those years, pretending to go along with it, until the pain was just too hard to bear anymore.

In your use of humor you must be certain that your spouse is never hurt by it. It's okay to have a little fun by making *yourself* the brunt of a joke, but never your spouse. If your husband wants to say at a party, after stuffing himself, that he is the veritable Pillsbury doughboy, fine. Just don't *you* ever say it, even if the thought occurs to you. It will crush him, even if he were to laugh. Remember, you love him and would do nothing to hurt him. Love doesn't cause hurt.

Gerald was conscious of that one day when he and his wife, Hillary, were on a vacation in Mexico with other couples from their office. Hillary describes how they all had to make their way to a sandbar in the beautiful blue Pacific waters:

> To get there, we had to fight the waves in a sort of trough between the shore and the sandbar. It became more than I could handle. Gerald and I started out hand in hand and a wave bowled me over. Unable to catch my balance, I was rolled back onto the shore. Being very large, I felt like a beached whale, but got up on my feet with Gerald's help and began again. This procedure was repeated three more times until I was so absolutely helpless with laughter at the picture I knew I was creating for all those watching, that I couldn't get back on my feet, even with his help.
>
>   Poor Gerald just stood there chuckling. He didn't want to outright laugh—even though I was—for fear of hurting my feelings, but there was no way to suppress a chuckle. That was okay because I felt that he loved me

enough to see the humor in my dilemma, but wanted to take care of my feelings by not laughing at me.

We've all been there when the fine line between laughing at our mate and merely chuckling respectfully is hard to define, or hard to resist. Gerald earned a medal of honor for this one. And his wife felt loved for it. If you keep in mind that your first priority is to show genuine love to your companion, then the choice is not so hard.

Anna was not so fortunate. Grant went a little too far with a statement that was funny once, but became hurtful when continually repeated. She was a very good cook, but burned part of their dinner one night. He said, "Oh, we're having burnt offerings, I see." She could have replied, "Yes, a meal for the Gods. Aren't you lucky." However, that never occurred to her because she was used to hearing so many "funny-to-him" barbs that really hurt her feelings. He was relentless with this one, and nearly every night after that he said, "So, are we having burnt offerings again?" She felt like making him the object of the next offering. If you are being hurt by such an ongoing joke, tell your spouse. He may not be aware of the hurt he is causing you.

Remember this final caution: You need to be careful about making light of something that is very serious to your mate. He or she may feel that you don't understand. If you are sensitive to his or her feelings you will know when humor is appropriate and when making a joke later, or not at all, would be better. Some people become extreme in their humor and don't know how to be serious when seriousness is needed. It's a little like overeating—a constant barrage becomes uncomfortable. There must be balance in all things, including the use of humor.

GOOD HUMOR IS HEALING

The appropriate use of humor plays a vital role in our lives. It has been said that "a good laugh is sunshine in a home."[20] Every home needs it, and it starts with parents being able to laugh with each other and with their children—not *at,* but *with.* It takes away the heaviness of the storms. In some cases, it may even keep some storms from coming at all.

PATIENTS IN HOSPITALS WHO LAUGH HEAL FASTER AND FEEL LESS PAIN.

There is growing medical evidence that laughing has a healing effect on the body. No doubt you have visited someone who had surgery, and when you asked how he felt, he would jokingly say, "It only hurts when I laugh." Strangely enough, scientific studies are now showing that that kind of hurt can heal. The evidence has proven that, in a majority of cases, patients in hospitals who laugh heal faster and feel less pain. Steven M. Sultanoff, Ph.D., who has done extensive research on therapeutic humor, says, "Humor can help build physical and emotional resilience as it stimulates the production of physical and psychological antibodies. [Therefore] humor strengthens both our physical and psychological immune systems."[21]

Perhaps this is why the comic greeting card business has boomed. When you're feeling down it's always fun to receive a card that makes you laugh. The giver laughs when he buys it, when he shows it to someone else, and when he gives it. The receiver laughs when she opens it, and again each time she reads it or shares it with someone. The laugh goes on, blessing whoever it touches. Laughter is a great gift to give.

Other studies have shown that laughter does much more than we think. It increases the heart rate like a good exercise would, stimulating blood circulation and breathing, and improving muscle tone. William F. Fry, Jr., M.D., found that "he could double his heart rate while convulsed by Laurel and Hardy and calculated that 100 laughs equals 10 minutes on a rowing machine."[22] His studies, and others, have also found that laughter "stimulates mental functions, such as alertness and memory, perhaps by raising levels of adrenaline and other chemicals that prepare the body for action."[23]

One study recorded ". . . a wave of electricity sweeping through the entire brain half a second after the punch line of a joke."[24] That could be very stimulating. If your spouse is a student, you might consider telling her a really funny joke just before she takes a test. Do your best to help her get a hearty laugh going. Who knows—maybe it will kick in some brain power she never knew she had. You might try it with your kids and raise their GPA. It might work. Go ahead, laugh.

BEGIN TODAY

The suggestions in this chapter may sound like a lot of fun, but they won't do any good at all for your marriage unless you put them into practice. Even if it means going out and buying a good joke book, or a funny "thinking of you" card—do something right now that could put some humor into your marriage.

Reader's Digest is also loaded with humorous anecdotes. Here is a prime selection:

My wife claims that we're so busy, we hardly take time to actually look into each other's eyes, and so we now do that before bed. One night my wife suddenly said, "We forgot to look at each other."

Sleepily, I asked, "Don't you think I know what you look like by now?"

"Okay," she said. "What do I look like?"

"You're gorgeous, beautiful and sexy," I replied.

"You looked," she said.[25]

The comic section of the newspaper is full of fun. For example, you may be familiar with *The Lockhorns*. They are the ultimate miserably married couple.

The Lockhorns reprinted by permission
of William Hoest Enterprises.[26]

Okay, it's your turn. Look in your newspaper comics, click
on "Jokes" on the Internet, find a cartoon in a magazine, ask
a friend for a good joke, or use one of these and share it with
your spouse. Whatever you do, do something. Be creative and
lighten up your life, your home, and have a good old-fashioned
hearty laugh together . . . today!

Enjoy Sexual Intimacy—Both of You

Love is the irresistible desire to be desired irresistibly. —LOUIS GINSBURG

HOW IT USED TO BE

Can you remember the intensity of the lovemaking in the early days of your marriage? You couldn't keep your hands off each other. After work, in your little apartment, you would eagerly greet each other. A simple hug and "I love you" would end up with his hands slipping under your blouse, touching in places that gave you goose bumps all over. Your hands would make their way under his shirt, where you would run your fingers through the hair on his chest. In no time you would be on the bed, undressing each other, touching and kissing passionately, and loving every minute of it. You couldn't resist each other. It was the deepest, most beautifully satisfying kind of love you could possibly express for each other.

SEXUAL INTIMACY . . . BECOMES A PHYSICAL RENEWAL OF YOUR LOVE FOR EACH OTHER—A RECOMMITMENT OF YOUR DEVOTION.

In Secret #1 you went back to the beginning and talked about the fun things you did then. To revive a floundering sex life, do the same thing—remember together how it was. Where were you when you first made love on your honeymoon? Was it like the movies portray it—soft music playing as she walks out of the dressing room in her flowing sheer gown, and he, in his silk pajamas, romantically enfolds her in his arms as they fall onto the bed and make mad passionate love? Or was it awkward and unfulfilling? Talk about your early sexual experience with each other. If you struggled while you learned, then laugh about that compared to what you know now. Talk about the ecstasy and passion you have felt as you have learned about each other's sexual pleasures. Vivid memories can be very stimulating.

WHY IS SEX IMPORTANT?

Sexual intimacy is a vital part of the marriage relationship because it keeps you connected in a way that nothing else can. When enjoyed by both partners, it becomes a physical renewal of your love for each other—a recommitment of your devotion and your determination to honor your marriage vows. It is a release of stress for both when both find pleasure in it. It bonds a couple, reviving your ability to face the world and all its pressures, together.

At one of our marriage seminars a young woman made that point clear when she said, "If we go very long without having sex, he gets grouchy, and I get easily offended." She went on to explain that "it's amazing how much better things go in every other part of our marriage if we take the time for some sexual intimacy." Others nodded in agreement.

Emily, married thirty-five years, agreed with this premise and told us what she had discovered.

When I ask my husband to do little favors around the house, like fix a leaky faucet or mow the lawn, he usually balks. Not that he outright refuses. No, he just complains or doesn't get around to it. It's not a high priority at all. If I remind him, he acts irritated. One day I realized that when we have had sex, he's willing to do whatever I ask, and usually without reminders. At the time I thought, *This is a great discovery. I can get whatever I want if we just have sex*. Then I realized that it worked both ways. I found that I wanted to do things for him, too. We are both happier and treat each other with greater tenderness and caring when we take the time to make love.

All married couples need to realize how vitally important their sexual relationship is to the success of their marriage. But beware: Never withhold sex as a punishment or use it to manipulate as a means to get what you want rather than as a fulfillment of love. Chuck and Evelyn's marriage suffered for years over this. They are the extreme example of what not to do. She wanted an extra room built onto the house, and Chuck knew how, but was busy at his accounting job. Finally, she said, "You're getting no sex until the room is done." It was her pattern for getting things. Chuck was a quiet guy, who responded to her orders. And they were both miserable.

EXCUSES

There are all kinds of excuses for not having a regular sex life as part of marriage, and one of them that some couples use is that they just don't have time to fit it in. When compared with the rest of your day or week, your sexual encounters are but a small moment. Think about it. You have at least sixteen waking hours a day; that's 960 minutes. Making love can take from 10 to 15 minutes, if you're short on time. Or when you want to make the fun last awhile, it may take up to an hour, or even longer. At the hour rate, that's only 60 minutes out of 960. At the shortest it's only 10 minutes, and that leaves 950 minutes! And that's if you do it every day, which is rarely the case, except for most newlyweds. Not having enough time just isn't a valid excuse. The powerful and lasting effect that those few minutes have on the rest of the day, the week, the month is incredible.

One problem I find in my therapy practice is that, because sexual intimacy isn't fulfilling to one spouse or the other, couples end up not *wanting* to make time for it. Or they put everything else first and are just too tired. Couples need to start giving this part of their marriage high priority.

In some cases, couples suffer from the early bird/owl syndrome. Their personal sleep clocks don't match. Mindy and Leo had this problem. Mindy goes into a near-drugged state of sleepiness after 10:00 P.M. Leo, on the other hand, is still in the full function mode as though he just received a shot of adrenaline, and he makes it to bed around midnight, slipping quietly into bed beside his sweet little zombie. At 6:00 A.M. Mindy's eyes pop open and she's ready for the day while Leo is still peacefully snoring away. Sound familiar? How do you make love when you're not awake in the same bed? You plan. Or you punt. Leo said if he happens to wake up in the mood and Mindy is in her study, he will sometimes invite her back to bed, and she responds. He used to lie there and resent that she had gotten up so early, without considering that, on most occasions, she would be happy to return to bed for a while.

At other times, Mindy will invite Leo to bed before she zonks out in the evening. Having time together in bed before she goes to sleep doesn't mean Leo has to stay and go to sleep, too. On many occasions he tiptoes out of the room after the fun is over and returns later when he's sleepy. It's working for them. Discuss your needs with each other on this issue and decide what will work for you. Put some passion into the act and you *will* more likely find the time for it. People don't resist doing what's fun.

MALE PRIDE GETS IN THE WAY

Sometimes one partner or the other isn't willing to make love, regardless of when it may happen. There are a few cases

when the husband is not willing, but most often, it seems to be the wife. At least, that's how
it often appears to men, and many women
agree, adding, "He wants it all the time. I
don't." The *American Journal of Obstetrics and
Gynecology* reported that "perhaps 75 percent
of all women derive little or no pleasure from
the sexual act . . ."[27] That evaluation was done
several years ago. In our seminar breakout session when I ask for a raise of hands (with all

**IF YOU WANT A
HAPPY SEX LIFE
WITH YOUR WIFE,
THEN YOU WILL
BE WILLING
TO LEARN THE
THINGS THAT
WILL MAKE IT
HAPPEN.**

eyes closed) of those who experience no sexual pleasure, I
find the percentage much lower, but still a significant number
indicating they find little or no pleasure. No wonder women
are not as willing as their husbands. Part of the reason they
aren't is due to the lack of men's understanding of what
women need. And, often, his unwillingness to learn. Pride
can get in the way with men. Some feel less than manly if
they have to ask for help regarding how to make their wife
happy in the bedroom.

When you have a problem with your computer, or if you
just bought a new one, you waste no time in finding out how
it works or what is wrong. You get out the instruction man-
ual and you start reading, or you talk with someone who
knows a lot about computers and find out what to do. When
you buy a new car you read up on all of its fancy bells and
whistles. And if you want it to stay new, you take care of its
needs—lube jobs, wheel alignments, and so on. If you want
to progress in your career, you find out what you have to do
and then you do it, whatever amount of effort it takes. If you
want a happy sex life with your wife, then you must be willing to learn the things that will make it happen. Ask her what
will bring her pleasure during the act of lovemaking, and begin doing it. And wives need to answer. If you don't know, be
willing to experiment with your husband and find out. This
works both ways—women, you need to ask your husband
what he enjoys. This is how you learn about each other.

There is something additional that men need to know: A woman's pleasure points change. Be willing to learn and be flexible. Again, the only way a husband will know is if his wife gives him some indication of what feels good to her.

WOMEN ARE DIFFERENT

Remember that you adore each other because you're different and yet you are confused because you're different. Keep in mind that what usually turns a man on is not the same thing as what turns a woman on. Men are sexually stimulated by what they see and women are sexually stimulated by what they feel. Don't confuse what gets you hot to go with what gets your mate in the mood.

WHAT SHE FEELS IN HER HEART MUST FIRST BE UNDERSTOOD BEFORE SHE CAN ACCEPT WHAT SHE CAN FEEL FROM YOUR TOUCH.

Valerie told us about her wedding night experience.

My husband and I were in our forties when we married. He wanted to make sure he set the stage for making love on our first night, and so did I. I put on the lovely, alluring nightie that I had carefully chosen for this night and then waited and waited for him to come out of the bathroom. I began to wonder what in the world was taking him so long. I think he must have been trying to work up the courage to do what he had planned.

Finally, he danced out, doing sexy gyrations like some kind of male belly dancer. And he was wearing a leopard skin bikini-type Speedo! I burst into laughter. I couldn't help it. I thought he was playing a joke, but when he saw me laughing, he stopped and said, "I thought this would turn you on." He was dead serious. Because an antic like that done by me would appeal to him, he thought his doing it would appeal to me. The truth of the matter was that it had the *opposite* effect on me.

Fortunately, he was willing to learn and we began our marriage with his asking me the question, "Then what does turn you on?" He really wanted to know, thank goodness, and we've had a great relationship ever since.

A WOMAN'S EMOTIONAL NEEDS

So what turns a woman on? Some husbands find that to be a real challenge. It's almost as if a woman is born with a protective privacy shield—that which covers her emotionally and physically and keeps her from letting you in. A man needs to know how to open the shield. One husband said, "parting the Red Sea would be easier." At times it may seem nearly *that* impossible, and yet it's not at all. It all comes down to knowing what to do. First you must understand that what your wife feels in her heart—the emotional—and on her body—the physical—has everything to do with your being able to effectively open her shield and turn her on sexually.

The importance of what she feels in her heart must first be understood before she can accept any part of what she can feel from your touch. As discussed earlier, generally speaking, women are predominantly right-brained and, therefore, more emotional. This is a God-given attribute necessary for family maintenance and success. Perhaps there may be times when you feel overwhelmed by her emotional responses and how long she seems to hold on to them. That is normal. Remember, men are different than women in this regard. It will be to your advantage in your sexual relationship, however, to understand the importance of her emotions and acknowledge them, even value them.

Understanding what she's feeling, or at least trying to understand, will, in effect, be the first step in removing her shield. This can easily be done by using the principle of validation. Keep in mind that as she expresses her feelings to you, about anything, she simply needs you to genuinely listen and understand without trying to fix her. Some men make it far too complex by trying to explain their wives' problems away or by trying to solve them. Just listen with the pure intent of caring about her and what she's feeling. She'll take care of the problem herself. She just needs to be heard by a husband who cares. Here's an example of how this could be done when sexual intimacy is on the agenda.

Sybil and Tyler are lying in bed and he wants to make love to her. He has just slipped his arm under her shoulders and is ready to move in closer when this conversation begins:

Sybil: Tyler, I feel so bad about what my boss said to me today.

Tyler: [thinking, *Oh, please don't go there right now,* but instead says]: What did he say?

Sybil: I was ten minutes late and he yelled at me. I'm almost always on time. He's so critical of the slightest mistake. Why can't he just notice some of the good things I do? Sometimes I just want to quit.

Tyler: I don't blame you, honey.

Sybil: Yesterday he was griping about some other insignificant thing. He's such a jerk!

Tyler: He must be. Obviously he doesn't realize how lucky he is to have you working there. [And he means it.]

Sybil: You're right. He doesn't know how lucky he is. [Then, romantically] Do you?

And with that comment, she puts her arms around him and is ready to enjoy a romantic time together. She feels listened to and cared about. If Tyler had said, "Please don't talk about that now. I want to make love," Sybil would not have felt cared about for anything other than fulfilling his sexual needs and would not have been as willing to participate. Or if he had said, "Oh, don't worry about your boss. You get too upset over nothing," she would have known he didn't care about how she felt. Instead, by his listening to her, her feelings changed from being upset about her boss to being understood by her husband, and it took very little time. This is an important emotional step in helping your wife get "in the mood."

WHAT HAPPENS DURING THE DAY HAS DIRECT BEARING ON WHAT MIGHT HAPPEN AT NIGHT.

Another important way to address her emotional side is to be willing to apologize for a sharp word or unkind statement you might have made, and the sooner you do it the better. If it festers, it grows tentacles as she remembers other unkind statements from the past. What happens between the two of you during the day has a direct bearing on what she is willing, even wanting, to do with you at night. If an apology is in order, give it and mean it—soon! When you sincerely apologize, you become *more* of a man in her eyes, not less. Genuine apologies work.

A WIFE CAN HELP

Because a woman sometimes has a difficult time setting aside the events of the day, she becomes her own worst enemy in preventing her intimacy process from even beginning. She can be lying in bed being tenderly touched by her husband while her mind is cluttered to the hilt like some kind of massive bulletin board of to-do lists. While her husband is completely engrossed in the excitement of the moment, with nary a thought of anything else, she may be thinking any one of the following:

"I should have mailed that bill. They're going to tack on a late fee if I don't get that out in the morning."
"I forgot to call Julie to tell her about the meeting tomorrow."

"I've got to figure out a way to help Tommy with his math. He's really struggling. Maybe I should call his teacher tomorrow."

"Did the cat get fed?"

"Why can't Susan and her husband just get along. Maybe I should take the kids for the weekend so they can have some time alone."

And on go the myriad things that fill a woman's mind. All of those extra interconnecting links that women have seem to be hot-wired to full capacity at the wrong time. Fortunately, there is something a woman can do about it. We all have the power to control our thoughts, and in order to control them we must consciously put forth the effort. To put this ability to use to aid in sexual fulfillment try the following three things:

1. Before you go to bed sit quietly for a few moments and write down any concerns that come to your mind. Make a to-do list, if you're feeling burdened with all that must be done. Do the same with a particular worry you may have, such as Tommy's struggle with math or your daughter's troubled marriage. Acknowledge your worry by writing it down on paper. Just a simple statement: "I'm worried about Susan's marriage. Tomorrow I will think about it, but not tonight." Once it's on paper it will no longer clutter your mind. Then put it in a box, maybe even a fancy little box you buy or make just for this purpose, and make sure it has a lid. This process is somewhat like what men do when they mentally compartmentalize and set things aside, out of their conscious thinking space. Women usually need a more hands-on physical action to do this. Write these items on paper, put them in the box, put the lid on, set it aside, and then go to bed.

2. Once you're in bed, relax. Visualize yourself in the most romantic place the two of you have ever been, or to which you wish you could go. Allow ideas of sexual ecstasy to fill your mind. Focus on your husband's touch and let yourself fully enjoy it. Enjoy touching him. Surrender to the moment and let everything else stay in that little box.

3. If you need help doing this, then pray to be able to set things aside so you can fully enjoy your husband sexually. God created this whole process and meant for you to enjoy it as much as your husband. I'm convinced He will help you find that enjoyment if you ask Him for help.

LOVE YOUR MATE AS SHE IS

Another thing a husband must understand is that his wife needs to believe that he loves her just the way she is, the number two element in a marital friendship. If you make derogatory comments about her weight, the size of her breasts, her legs, her hair, or any other part of her that you consider less than perfect, that privacy shield is going to become more impenetrable than you ever thought possible. Or if she does have sex with you, it will only be routine—no emotion, no real feeling, no chance of her having any real ecstasy in the process. But more than likely, she won't be open to even the routine version. You shoot yourself in the foot when you criticize her body.

Not only will she respond negatively to you, but you will not be able to find the full enjoyment with her that you would have had had you focused instead on her positive physical attributes. Put yourself in her bedroom

> A WISE HUSBAND WILL FOCUS ON THE AREAS OF HIS WIFE'S BODY THAT ARE ATTRACTIVE TO HIM.

WOMEN ARE ROMANTICS. THEY LOVE ALL THE NUANCES OF SETTING THE STAGE FOR LOVE.

slippers, as it were, and think how you would like it if she were criticizing parts of your body. This is a good place to be reminded of the Golden Rule: Do unto others as you would have them do unto you—especially your mate. Ricky learned this the hard way one night.

All three kids were finally in bed asleep, including their three-month-old baby, and he and Cynthia were in bed snuggling. There hadn't been much of it since the baby's birth. They were both looking forward to this time together. As Ricky's hands gently touched Cynthia's body, starting at her neck and moving downward, he stopped at her tummy. It felt like bread dough and he just couldn't resist jiggling it with his open hand. She was crushed and said, "That's it. We're done!" And she rolled over to the other side of the bed. She already felt terrible about the stretched stomach muscles that were sagging on her body. Ricky laughed and said, "C'mon. I was just teasing."

It wasn't at all funny to her. Even though he didn't mean anything by it, it carried a negative message to Cynthia, and she couldn't bring the mood back.

At one of our marriage seminars while I was talking to the women in the breakout session, I told them about a man's need to see his wife's nude body, and one woman in the back called out, "Tell them we don't need to see theirs." Most of the women laughed in agreement. I then asked them, "What if your husband said that about your body? How would you feel?" The room went to an immediate dead silence. I went on to explain that a man is no different than you are. He wants to believe he is physically desirable and sexually attractive to his wife. Many women only focus on their need to feel physically desirable and don't give a thought to their husband's need. A compliment from you about his body would certainly please him.

Men like their bodies to be appreciated, too. They enjoy a compliment about their looks as much as women do. A man may not shed a tear over the lack of such attention, but he will feel hurt by insults about his physique. He doesn't want you to make fun of his fallen chest any more than you want him to make fun of your stretch marks. Notice the things you like about him and tell him. Ignore the rest. None of us is perfect.

SET THE STAGE

It's not as complex as it might seem. Women are romantics. They love all the nuances of setting the stage for love. That's why they like the lights down low, an aroma candle burning, the TV off, and some soft music playing. If you're smart you'll go along. Lex understood the advantage of setting the stage. One evening he started a bubble bath for his wife, Dina, then told her he would put their two kids to bed while she took a leisurely bath. He read a story to the kids, then tucked them in, allowing her plenty of time. When her bath was over, she was calm and ready for romance, and both were well rewarded. Dina said, "I loved it. He was so sweet to care about me that much."

Another way to set the stage for love is to put your bedroom on a priority list. In some homes it's the last room to get any attention. Furnish it as nicely as you can reasonably afford. Choose furniture for it together with both of you agreeing on the style. That doesn't mean you need to buy a new bedroom set. The point here is, you need to create pleasant surroundings. One couple remarked that their bedroom was so cluttered that they could hardly get to the bed. All the dressers and night stands were piled high with "stuff." It's obvious why they avoided an early retreat to their bedroom.

Keep this special "love place" inviting. Keep the linens clean, put on a nice bedspread, dust the dresser, keep it clear of junk—at least most of the time—hang up your clothes, put things away. Make the bed every day—together, when you can. It just feels good to make love in a lovely setting. Let your bedroom be that lovely setting. Judi and Carlos got the picture:

> We like our bedroom to have its own appeal so we carpeted and decorated it in a different color than the overall theme of the rest of the house. We have always considered it our private place. Our children grew up with a clear understanding that it was *our* room, not theirs. If the door was shut they had to knock and be invited in.

WOMEN ARE EASILY DISTRACTED

Women have extremely sensitive built-in antennae. They can tell if a child is moving in his bed three rooms away, and they're sure he is on his way into your bedroom at any moment. Women need assured privacy. The door has to be locked. Don't give her a bad time about it, just lock the door.

GENTLENESS REINS SUPREME IN THE LOVEMAKING PROCESS.

Sometimes the phone can be a bandit in the night that steals away your moments of passion. Most men can completely ignore a ringing phone during lovemaking. It's the male ability to compartmentalize. Most women struggle with that. They have a nagging worry that the ringing phone is a dire emergency. It's their nurturing side in full gear. Have you ever picked up the phone during a hot embrace? If you can't say good-bye to the party on the phone you will certainly be saying good-bye to whatever else you had in mind. The phone is a definite mood dampener. To resolve this, you may want to unplug the phone and protect your privacy and her emotional need.

THE POWER OF TOUCH

Now that you have a glimpse of what she needs to feel in her heart, it's time to explore what she likes to feel on her body. Nothing is quite as magical as a soft, tender touch. When Joy told that to the men at a marriage seminar, a big tough-looking fellow stood up and held out his rough calloused hands, palms up, and said, "But look at these hands. What do I do?" Before she could say anything, another man in the group shouted, "Hey, Joe. Lotion!" The perfect answer. Some men don't realize the importance of using a good hand lotion every day, though obviously, some men do. It will help keep your hands soft, men. Perhaps not baby-bottom soft, but soft enough to make a caressing touch much more pleasurable for your wife.

Does this scene from a television show sound familiar? A husband and wife lie near each other in bed, discussing some event of the day. As the wife talked, the husband listened and began to tenderly stroke her cheek. With a soft gentle touch, his hand moved down her neck, onto her shoulder to her upper arm where he slowly and lightly moved it down her arm. She moved a little closer and the scene

> MEN'S BODIES CRY OUT FOR SEX PARTICULARLY AFTER THEY HAVE EXPERIENCED IT.

changed, leaving the couple to whatever might follow. In a real-life scene you will be smart if you continue the soft touching to her back, then down to her lower back and bottom. After a few minutes of that soothing and tantalizing touch, she will turn over and you can begin on the front side, ever so gently, followed by tender kisses on her body. She will tingle with readiness. And bingo! that metaphoric shield is history.

Since the nerve endings are very close to the surface of a woman's skin, gentleness reins supreme in the lovemaking process. Remember the song, "I Love a Man with a Slow Hand." There's a lesson to be learned in those lyrics. Be gentle and slow. She will then be ready for you to touch her genital area, softly and rhythmically. Most women need this slow, gentle touching to enjoy sexual fulfillment and make her ready for the orgasmic sensations from intercourse.

There are some great books out there (some titles are given at the end of this chapter) that will explain anatomy and teach you more explicitly what to do to discover techniques that enhance your lovemaking. If you need more information, try one of them. Our purpose is to help you understand certain specific needs that will open the door to the ecstasy and loving feelings that can be achieved.

WHY MEN WANT TO MAKE LOVE SO OFTEN

The reason men usually want to make love more than their wives is simple—they're made that way. Earlier in this chapter we discussed how important it is for men to love their wives just the way they are. Now it's the wife's turn. Love him the way he is, and needing to have sex more often than you is part of the way he is. He didn't plan it that way. A Divine Creator did, and for vitally important reasons, among which is: How else would the human race be propagated? Perhaps women are different in this regard because there needs to be a balance. Whatever purpose behind it, the fact remains that men need to make love for some very physical reasons.

Men are born with testosterone coursing through their bodies. And it sometimes seems to women that it's working overtime. Men's bodies cry out for sex, particularly after they have experienced it. When they are denied, a tension builds up and they actually feel discomfort, even pain for some, in the groin area. When sexual relations are not possible, nature provided a release in the form of wet dreams. Some men get caught in the trap of substituting masturbation for nature's wet dreams or sexual intercourse. In his book *Kosher Sex* Shmuley Boteach makes this important point:

> [M]asturbation is not a solitary practice, or a private
> matter with which public pronouncements on moral-

ity are concerned. It lessens the necessity for physical closeness that one human being feels for another. It is beyond the realm of the private and personal and is squarely an issue with which others are involved. Every act of masturbation serves as a powerful sexual release that in turn lessens our vital need for sex with someone else. In the context of marriage, this is disastrous.[28]

Boteach told of the experience of a man who traveled frequently in his business and claimed that masturbation was an important release for him while he was away. Yet this man felt less need for sexual passion with his wife upon his return, which lessened the joy in their marriage. There is no question that this practice takes away from the beautiful fulfillment of sexual intimacy between husband and wife. This applies to both men and women. You must rely on each other for your sexual release and enjoyment.

Another reason a man needs to have sexual relations with his wife is that there is an expectation built into him that says it validates his manhood. Also, he wants and needs to feel that he can bring sexual satisfaction to his mate. Helping him in this process can be a very loving act on the part of his wife.

WHAT MEN LIKE

A man usually likes to see his wife without any clothes on—naked, top to bottom. If this is something your husband enjoys, then give him this gift. You love him and want him to be happy, remember? Some women don't want to be seen in the nude because they are embarrassed. Their modesty prevents them from letting go and letting him enjoy looking at her. If this is the case, make a concentrated effort to get over this and let him enjoy seeing your body.

A MAN WANTS TO BELIEVE HE IS PHYSICALLY DESIRABLE AND SEXUALLY ATTRACTIVE TO HIS WIFE.

Faye and Bill were in my office discussing

some of their sexual needs. Bill said, "Faye wants the room dark and the covers up to her chin." As I talked to Faye about a man's need to see his wife naked, and as Bill agreed by nodding his head, she said, "How could he possibly want to see my body? After three kids and all the stretch marks—what's there to look at?" I asked Bill how he felt about Fay's body and he said, "She's beautiful." I asked, "Do you like to see her naked?" He answered, "Oh, yes, anytime I can!" I then asked him, "What about the stretch marks?" He replied, "She's so sexy I don't even see them!"

This same type of conversation has been repeated many times. Oh, there are a few inept husbands who make comments about their wives' physical defects; the great majority, however, love their wives' bodies just the way they are. It's so important for both of you to ignore the defects and just enjoy each other, focusing on what you do like about each other's bodies.

A man enjoys having his wife wear something sexy. This is very tantalizing for a man. And it can do wonders to put a woman in the mood, too. He loves you to look feminine and pretty. If you don't feel comfortable in a filmy nighty or less, keep in mind that it won't be on for long. After the fun is over you can crawl back into your favorite sleepwear.

A man likes to touch his wife's body—every part of it. He appreciates it when she relaxes and enjoys his touching. Remember, men, gently. He also likes her to touch him, especially in the genital area. It's very important that you both talk about what kind of touching feels good. You can guide each other in these pleasures. There are little signals you can give when what is being done feels good—an "ahhhh," or a little moan of delight, or just a quiet, "That feels so good." Let each other know so your needs can be met. Direct each other's hands at times.

WHAT WOMEN LIKE

Women like to be told they are beautiful. A wise husband will focus on the areas of his wife's body that are attractive to him. If she has beautiful blue eyes, tell her. If you have always been enchanted with her long, slender legs, tell her. If you like her hair, tell her. If she's got a cute dimple that has always charmed you, tell her. Notice the things you *do* like and make sure she knows about them by telling her.

Some men—far too many—think these good thoughts, but never say them to their wives. There was an excellent example of this sad truth in the comic strip, *For Better or Worse,* by Lynn Johnston. The couple, Michael and Deanna, dressed in casual attire, were walking along the beach as the sun was setting. As they walked hand in hand, sometimes an arm around each other, the strip showed Michael's silent thoughts. He was thinking:

> What an extraordinary evening! The sunset is brilliant, the sand is warm—nothing could be more perfect! And I'm walking with the most beautiful girl in the world! I'm so in love with Deanna, I'm intoxicated! Just holding her hand is . . . magic!
>
> [The sun went down and it was getting dark. They sat on a small bank, snuggling together. His thoughts continued:]
>
> It's as if this night was made for us . . . and I'll never forget it as long as I live!
>
> [Deanna looked up at him, dreamily. And he said to her:]
>
> I'm hungry. Do you wanna go grab a burger?
>
> [She replied:]
>
> Oh, Michael! You're so unromantic!!
>
> [He looked stunned.]

Is he unromantic? Of course not, he's intensely romantic, but she has no way of knowing. Husbands need to say the words.

Your wife needs to hear the tender thoughts you have about her. She needs to hear your compliments and romantic musings. There are a few other statements that women love to hear that you may not think are a romantic turn on, but they are. She loves it when you say: "You're a wonderful mother to our children, honey." Every woman with children wants with all her heart to be a good mother, and it isn't an easy job. To hear a compliment regarding her mothering is romantic music to her ears. Another ongoing difficult day-in-day-out job that most woman face is cooking. If your wife is the cook in your home she will love hearing, "That was really a delicious dinner you cooked tonight." These compliments must be sincere and honest, so make them on the day you admired your wife's parenting skills or particularly enjoyed the dinner she made. Also, whenever you're feeling especially blessed to have her for your wife, you might say, "I'm so lucky to be married to you." Whatever you say, you must be sure it's your true feeling.

Most important of all, she needs to hear you say the words, "I love you." Some men really struggle with this, partly because they never heard their father compliment their mother or say he loved her. If that was the case during your childhood, then make the generational change and say the words! Give your children the opportunity to hear you tell their mom you love her. Show them how to be a loving husband. And most of all, give your wife the sweet pleasure of hearing it and knowing how you feel about her. Don't assume she knows it. Tell her! Tell her during the day. Tell her at night. Absolutely tell her while you're making love.

A woman likes to share her feelings, her hopes, her dreams with her husband. This can be a very important part of sexual intimacy for her. Remember, sexual intimacy does not always mean sexual intercourse. She likes to be held. Sometimes she just wants a back rub.

There is nothing wrong with trading favors with your mate. Lauren said:

My husband and I have discovered how to bring pleasure to each other. He enjoys intercourse and I enjoy a
soothing foot massage. I feel very loved by him when
he takes the time to give me one of those wonderful
massages, using my favorite lotion. It feels so good and
so relaxing. He knows what I like. And I know what he
likes, and we're both satisfied.

Joslyn knew what she liked:

One of the things I really enjoy is my husband stroking
my arms and back—kind of like tickling softly. It feels
so good to me. The whole world can be falling apart,
but when he does that as we're lying in bed or sitting
watching TV, I relax and feel like all's well in my world
after all.

Meeting each other's needs and honoring each other's "likes"
is paramount in a fulfilling marriage relationship. This in no
way condones "holding out" sexually until you get what you
want. On the contrary, it should be an equal giving and receiving partnership.

If you, as a wife, don't know what you like, then it's time
to think about it and discover what kind of intimate acts you
would enjoy receiving from your husband. If *you* don't know,
there is no way *he* can know. And once you know, tell him. A
loving husband will be happy to respond.

NEVER MAKE COMPARISONS

If you have been married before, never discuss what your former mate did that you liked, or disliked. Leave him or her
completely out of the picture. Don't say, "I really liked it
when Sara kissed me right here." The picture your current
wife will suddenly have in her mind will kill all desire. You

can only hope she doesn't kill you, although she would almost be justified. You could simply say, "I like to be kissed right here." Leave everyone else out of it as well. One of my clients said to her husband, "My father was always affectionate to my mother, my sister tells me how loving her husband is to her, my friend Bev told me about how much fun her husband is in bed. Why can't you be like them?!" Bringing all those people in makes for a very crowded bedroom, and who can make love in a crowd? Certainly no one can and enjoy it, particularly a crowd you're being compared to.

Another comparison to avoid is asking your spouse, who was married before to Sara, "Do you like making love to me more than you did with Sara?" Sara was probably the farthest thing from his mind at that moment. Why in the world would you bring her into your bedroom?

TALK ABOUT YOUR SEXUAL RELATIONSHIP

It's amazing how few couples actually talk about their sexual needs with each other. It seems they are too embarrassed to discuss such a private subject. And yet it's a subject they participate in together all the time, often in an unfulfilling way. Monique and Jeff were a prime example. They had been married thirty years before they had a down-to-earth heart-to-heart discussion about sex. They had gone out to dinner, just the two of them, in a quiet restaurant and sat in a secluded booth . . . and talked. Monique expressed her needs to Jeff and he to her, without any criticism—just a desire to know how the other felt and what they each needed. Their sexual relationship improved considerably after that. It opened the door for the freedom to talk about it at other times.

THE ONLY WAY TO KNOW WHAT YOUR SPOUSE IS NEEDING IS TO TALK.

You need to talk about this vitally important part of your marriage relationship with your spouse. The only way to know what your mate needs, is to talk. During the talking time, however, it's very important to refrain from any criticism. You're after information and understanding. Make sure you have your discussion at a time and in a place out of the heat of the moment where there is no pressure to perform. Anywhere where the two of you can be alone, and away from the telephone and people you know, will work.

Here are a few questions you can ask to get your conversation started:

➤ How can we make more time for making love?

➤ Regardless of how often other couples say they have sex, how often do *we* want and need it?

➤ What would make it more fun for you?

➤ How about quickies? When?

➤ Could we take longer sometimes? When and how?

➤ Does having sex cause any concerns (such as getting pregnant, discomfort during intercourse, impotence, and so on)?

➤ What sexual activities are appropriate for us?

A couple of things that you might want to discuss are the following bits of information Joe Tanenbaum includes in his book *Male and Female Realities:*

➤ Once a man finds some "secret" places on the woman's body, he will go after those places with vigor. I suggest that 99 percent of all men would be very happy to have *one place* on his body receive all the woman's attention, and she doesn't have to get fancy! Not only does a woman have more erogenous zones than a man, but they also may change from night to night, or even from moment to moment. This is very confusing to men. (If it worked yesterday, it should work today, right?) If "the place" is not working this time, the man thinks there is something on the woman's mind, or he might think she lied the previous time, when she said she liked what he was doing.

➤ The man knows he is "done" when he climaxes. Not only are most women capable of multiple climaxes, but women can also be content with simply the romance, the holding, the intimate giving and receiving of pleasure. A woman doesn't necessarily need to climax every time she makes love in order to experience satisfaction with lovemaking. This concept is difficult for a man to understand, since he wouldn't be satisfied if he didn't climax.[29]

Discuss these topics and be completely open with each other. It will make the next time you make love more exciting and pleasurable than it's been for a long time.

Allie and Patrick would still be married if they had taken this counsel. She said:

For nearly ten years I've put up with Patrick's selfishness. All he ever thinks about are his needs, never mine. We get into bed and he wants sex. He doesn't know the meaning of foreplay. It's wham, bam, and not ever a "thank you, m'am." He doesn't give one thought to my needs. I'm through!

ALL SEX EXPERIENCES SHOULD BE THOSE THAT BOTH HUSBAND AND WIFE WANT.

Allie meant it. She divorced him. Allie quickly found someone else and had a sizzling short-term affair that ended in a great deal of sorrow and shame for her. Patrick was devastated by it all. Tragedies like this need never happen. Don't let it happen to you, no matter how long you've been married or what your age may be. Make time to talk about and share this part of your marital relationship.

WHAT SEXUAL ACTIVITIES
ARE APPROPRIATE?

Dr. Herbert J. Miles, in his book *Sexual Happiness in Marriage,* gives this caution:

> All sex experiences should be those which both husband and wife want. Neither, at any time, should force the other to do anything that he does not want to do. Love does not force.[30]

A Christian pamphlet on marriage offers this valuable counsel:

> Keep yourselves above any domineering or unworthy behavior in the tender, intimate relationship between husband and wife. . . . Tenderness and respect—never selfishness—must be the guiding principles in the intimate relationship between husband and wife. Each partner must be considerate and sensitive to the other's needs and desires.[31]

The pleasure a husband and wife give to each other in these deeply intimate and personal expressions of love is theirs to decide upon, jointly and in harmony with each other and their personal convictions.

Some men, and perhaps some women, think that by watching pornographic movies their sex life will be stimulated and enhanced. When they watch these movies, alone or together, this can only diminish the tender relationship that generates true caring and love. Too many marriages have fallen apart because of pornography. In his book *Standing for Something,* Gordon B. Hinckley writes that "[pornography] . . . destroys and distorts the truth about love and intimacy. . . . We cannot risk the damage it does to the most precious of relationships—marriage."[32]

WHEN ILLNESS PUTS A DAMPER ON SEX

When illness strikes it can affect the sexual activity of a couple. This is a time of sacrifice, of caring, and of understanding. When intercourse is not an option, many couples find creative ways to enjoy their sexual relationship without having intercourse. Sometimes just holding each other, or stroking each other keeps the close relationship alive. Caring couples do whatever is needed to help their mate enjoy feelings of love throughout the duration of the illness.

If you suffer from chronic or acute illness, you may want to investigate how to enjoy your sexual relationship in ways that do not endanger your health. Doctors and therapists can be very helpful. For example, the Jewish center for Immunology in Denver, Colorado, teaches patients with acute cases of asthma how to have sex without health risks. If you think you are at risk, ask your doctor. If he doesn't know, he can put you in touch with someone who does. It's well worth pursuing.

The same is true when you are expecting a child. Neither partner will feel like having sex if a wife is sick and throwing up. That's just not very inviting . . . for either. There is, however, a great need during this time to feel love from and for each other. Consider all the ways that you can still keep emotionally and physically close. Whatever the health issue may be, do not abandon each other sexually during these crucial times.

NURSING MOTHERS

Women who nurse their babies often lose their desire for sex. This can be hard on the husband. Just when her breasts are at their most voluptuous and he can hardly take his eyes off them, she feels like saying, "Look, but don't touch!" Now, that hardly seems fair. Nevertheless, it's real and there are a couple of reasons for it: Many women experience breast pain, especially during the first few weeks of nursing; to complicate matters, "the hormone prolactin, which supports the production of breast milk, is a notorious lust buster."[33] This is not true in all cases, but many. Some women have reported an increase in sexual desire during the months of nursing. This is one of those times when you must consider the needs of each other and do the best you can to meet those needs in the most sensitive way—both of you.

THE EFFECTS OF SEXUAL TRAUMA

When a woman or a man has experienced childhood abuse, incest, molestation, abuse in a previous marriage, or rape it can seriously affect the couple's sexual relationship. In order to survive, the victim builds emotionally protective walls around him/herself. They fear intimacy because they believe they are vulnerable and could be hurt again. They have the desire for intimacy, but the protective walls prevent it from happening. They keep trying to find the intimacy and fail and then feel defeated and incapable of achieving it. If your mate has had this happen you need to be sensitive and understanding. What appears to be your spouse's lack of sexual interest has nothing to do with you. It is very important for you to seek professional counseling. Find a good therapist so he or she can eventually set aside the pain of the past and its devastating effect and be able to enjoy sexual intimacy. Be patient with each other during this time of healing.

> BY THE TIME YOU HAVE IT ALL FIGURED OUT, YOUR ANATOMY SEEMS TO SABOTAGE YOU.

THE EFFECTS OF AGING

Usually, age takes a toll on your ability to function sexually. It's not fair. By the time you've got it all figured out, your anatomy seems to sabotage you. Still, you can have a regular, if not overly active, sex life together. The actress Bette Davis once said during her later years "growing old is not so bad. You can't do everything you always wanted to do, but it's okay because you don't want to anymore." That's only a little true about sex. You may not want to do it as often as you used to want to do it, but it is still a necessary and important part of your marriage relationship, no matter your age. You simply need to talk about what you can do to stay physically close.

One of the problems that men may face as they age is impotence. In many cases, it is a temporary condition but, nonetheless, very disturbing for a man. Women don't have to perform to make sex happen. Men do. Without an erection, there is no intercourse. Most women do not understand that when a man first experiences this problem it is devastating to him. He truly wants to satisfy his wife and now he can't. So he worries about it and this creates anxiety. The more he worries the worse it gets. That can be a terrible burden for a man, unless he and his wife have developed a loving, open relationship where they can talk about what is happening and be creative in finding solutions.

Sometimes when a man experiences impotence he turns away from his wife. Sharla experienced this with her husband, Kirk. She said, "I thought he had lost interest in me, and I was heartbroken." Kirk was too embarrassed to tell her the real problem. Please put embarrassment aside and confide in each other. Sharla said, "He didn't need to do any kind of performing. All I needed was his arms around me and his loving concern. And that's what I wanted to give him back." Once again, a little creativity can go a long way in this department, and the right kind of creativity may get the juices going again. If not, don't be offended. Try other avenues, or just enjoy the closeness of each other, remembering that love responds to the needs of each other.

You may need to go to a family doctor or a good urologist, and yet "less than 10 percent of the estimated 30 million men in the United States with some form of erectile dysfunction . . . ever seek medical help."[34] It's unfortunate that so few with this problem consult their doctor. There may be some physiological problems that can be easily corrected or it may be caused by something as simple as stress—remove some stress and it might do the trick. Or your doctor may prescribe medication.

In a *Newsweek* article, Geoffrey Cowley reported that "Some 4 million American men take [Viagra] regularly . . . studies suggest it has a success rate of 70 percent."[35] New drugs are coming on the market as drug companies race to expand the options for erectile dysfunction treatment. As with any medication, caution must be used because these drugs can have harmful side effects in some men. Your doctor will be able to advise you regarding medication.

When some women go through menopause they can experience a roller coaster of emotions. Their hormones sometimes go "crazy," and that can be a deterrent to enjoyable sex. This is another logical time to seek medical help. A leading sex researcher, Gina Ogden, Ph.D., says, "Menopause is inevitable, but the sexual lack of interest associated with the postmenopausal years is not inevitable. Women have the physical capacity to sustain a rich sex life into old age."[36] Monitored hormone therapy can help, as well as lubrication. Vaginal dryness is not uncommon and there are many intimate moisturizers on the market to assist with this need. Do all you can to help make your sexual life normal and fulfilling.

Dr. Marian E. Dunn, director of the Center for Human Sexuality at the State University of New York in Brooklyn, sees a strong link between health, fitness, and sexuality in older couples. Barbara, sixty-five, reported the following:

> I went on a low-fat diet and joined an exercise class to shape up for my son's wedding. Suddenly I had more energy. I was interested in sex again. Losing twenty

pounds turned out to be better than an aphrodisiac for me.[37]

A FEW EXTRA TIPS

Keep yourself smelling clean and fresh. Personal hygiene matters. Women have a keener sense of smell, especially during ovulation. Women are not the only ones who want a clean-smelling partner. So do men. Both need to use deodorant. Some men have expressed being repulsed by unpleasant odors from their wife's private areas. Body powders and perfumes are nice, but never use them to cover up uncleanness. Use them to enhance your clean, natural fragrance, if you like. There are fresh personal fragrances on the market that may enhance sex and sexual attraction. Both husband and wife who use colognes should keep in mind that subtle is best. Too much can be a turnoff. And so can bad breath. Do what it takes—brush your teeth regularly and use a mouthwash, if needed. See a dentist if you have a chronic problem.

Allow each other private times in the bathroom. It will enhance your feelings of romance. Of course, there are times to share the bathroom, too. Don't be afraid to invite your mate to share a shower once in a while. Enjoy soaping each other down and just having a little spontaneous fun.

Fatigue can diminish the desire for sexual intimacy for men and women. If this is the case with you, take a nap so you will feel in the mood later. Stress also puts a person's libido in limbo. Minimizing stress, at least on some days, will help renew your sexual desire.

BOOKS TO READ

To find out more detailed information on anatomy and sexual functions, both husband and wife could read a great little book called, *The Act of Marriage,* by Tim and Beverly LaHaye, written to help "Christian couples maximize their joy in sexual union." Another well-presented book on marital sex is Schmuley Boteach's *Kosher Sex*. People of all religious persuasions, or no religious persuasion, will find valuable information in these books. Of course, there are many others that could also be helpful. As in all things, it is important for husbands and wives to decide what is right for them.

BEGIN TODAY

Making love will be a fulfilling, wonderful part of marriage if couples remember that the most important part of the phrase is *love*. Love means tenderness, caring, sacrifice, holding on, forgiving, sharing, and responding to each other's needs. When all of these elements go into making love, then it can't help but enrich your marriage and bring joy and contentment to both husband and wife. What can you do to show your spouse how much you love him or her tonight?

Talk to Each Other

Listen or thy tongue will keep thee deaf.
—AMERICAN INDIAN PROVERB

A PLACE OF SAFETY

One of the great joys of married life is being able to come home at the end of a day and pour your heart out to your mate without feeling misunderstood or criticized. Marriage is enormously enhanced when each member of the couple can talk to, listen to, and understand each other. It's the relief valve in a pressurized world. The ability to talk and share helps make your home a safe place for you and your spouse. This safety then spreads to your children and creates an atmosphere that others will feel when they come to visit.

Not all homes have this feeling of safety. Some of the respondents to our survey pointed out problems that exist in communicating with their spouses. Here are some of their comments:

➤ Things that have made our marriage rough are the times that we don't communicate or validate well. My husband and I don't always see things the same way and it's frustrating when we walk away from a conversation or argument not feeling, at the very least, listened to.

➤ I have found that we both get very involved with busy schedules and don't take time for each other or take time to communicate. We get irritable and we both begin to think our partner is mad at us, even though he's really not. . . . I learned that our marriage went better when I kept him informed.

➤ One of the things that prevents our marriage from being a truly happy one is that my husband refuses to discuss important issues that are keeping us from being close.

➤ One problem I see is not having the skills or ability to communicate with my spouse or him with me. Many times I've been frustrated with our lifestyle and could carry on long conversations in my mind about my concerns. However, when it came to discussing the things I wanted to change, I didn't know how to communicate without blowing up or crying. I was afraid of having my feelings discounted and ignored.

➤ Those times in our marriage when I am miserable are the times that I feel that he doesn't care about my opinion or thoughts.

➤ Poor communications: When I make plans or would like to make a plan, I tell my husband; he says nothing and I take that for a "yes." Then when the time comes to do whatever, he grumbles or refuses because he never said he would.

➤ My husband wears hearing aids and whenever the batteries go dead I can speak but he can't hear. We're out of touch even when we're within reach—solved by carrying extra batteries.

➤ Misery comes when lines are drawn simply because I don't take the time to see things from two different perspectives—hers and mine.

➤ [The problem is] not being able to communicate with someone you feel cares. You need to be married to your best friend. Being able to communicate and understand is vital to a best-friend relationship. Pretty lonely without it.

IT OUGHT TO BE EASY

Talking ought to be easy. All you have to do is open up your mouth and start using the words you have been using since you began speaking. If that is true, then what makes it so difficult? Sometimes in my practice, I witness husbands and wives who seem to be speaking in a foreign tongue because of the reaction each spouse has to the other. One spouse says something that when interpreted by the other seems to mean something entirely different. When each spouse comes from a different country, such misunderstandings are understandable, but when they are both from the same country, how can they use the same words and understand such different things?

When you stop and think about it, we each come from a different miniculture with similar but different dialects. Certain words have particular meaning for one person that may differ in meaning to another person. For example, the word "fishing." For my father-in-law, the meaning is as close to heaven as you can get on earth. For me, fishing is close to banishment to the far dark side of the galaxy. When I think of fishing I remember tripping in a river and having my waist-high waders fill with water, trying with all my might to stand and being completely incapable of doing it. My father-in-law, on the other hand, saw himself reeling in his limit of beautiful rainbow trout nearly every time he went fishing. I not only came up empty-handed; I nearly didn't come up at all. Same word, different meaning, because of the experience associated with the word. There are many words that could be used as examples, such as *love, work, affection, mealtime,* or *home.* The list could go on and on. Everyone has his or her

FOR COMMUNICATION TO TAKE PLACE WE MUST BE ABLE TO UNDERSTAND FROM THE OTHER PERSON'S POINT OF VIEW.

own experiences relating to each word, which give it its own special meaning.

So you see, talking has some difficulties to start with. We aren't just talking about talking, however; we are talking about communicating with each other. When we communicate we are able to understand the ideas, concepts, and feelings of another person. These ideas, concepts, and feelings are represented by the words we speak, and in order for communication to take place, we must be able to understand them from the other person's point of view—what the words mean to that person.

For a marriage to succeed we must develop our own mutual culture and joint dialect that we each speak and understand. Some words take on special meanings because they are based on experiences we have shared with each other. One word may bring to mind a whole scenario as it flashes before your consciousness and all of the emotions are reexperienced in an instant. Harmon's experience illustrates this:

The words "broccoli soup" bring laughter to some of our family. A friend gave us some broccoli from her garden. Jolene washed it very well, cut it up, and made a delicious soup. As we and our two youngest boys were sitting at the dinner table eating the soup, our seventeen-year-old son, Buzz, was scrutinizing his. "What are these things floating in the soup?" he asked. Jolene quickly replied, "That's just some of the seasoning." He asked, "Are you sure?" She said, "Yes, now eat your soup, the seasoning is what makes it have good flavor," and she took a nice big spoonful to prove it.

As Buzz looked closer he said, "Mom, my seasoning has legs." Jolene exclaimed, "Impossible!" She ran to get the magnifying glass. Sure enough there were little dead bugs floating in the soup. When she examined the balance of the uncooked broccoli with the magnifying glass she found that there were tiny bugs on it that would not wash off. Homegrown broccoli sometimes gets these little bugs that don't seem to come with the store-bought kind. Needless to say, Jolene has been very diligent in inspecting broccoli ever since, and anytime "broccoli soup" is served we immediately ask if the seasoning is doing the backstroke.

Every family has experiences that are unique. They are what make up the culture and traditions of that family. Not all of the experiences are funny. Some are sacred, painful, or embarrassing. The ability to recognize them and share them is important. Otherwise, we develop no closeness or true intimacy. The more you listen and ask questions when your spouse is talking, the more you will understand the meaning of his or her words and the closer your relationship will become.

CHANGE OF FOCUS

Changing the focus of a conversation is a problem that makes communicating difficult. This means that the person who initiated the conversation has it taken over by another person. It often happens at the beginning of a conversation. Here's an example of how this can happen:

> Wife: "I have really had a bad day today and everything seemed to go wrong."
>
> Husband: "Honey, you don't know what a bad day is. Let me tell you what happened to me!" and then he launches into a nonstop recount of his day.

Has this ever happened to you? Or have you seen it happen to someone else? Or, heaven forbid, have you ever done this to your spouse? When this happened to you, do you remember

THE FOCUS
NEEDS TO
STAY WITH
THE PERSON
WHO STARTED
THE
CONVERSATION.

how you felt? This may be one of those times when you felt more than one of the emotions of mad, glad, sad, and afraid. The first may be mad—mad that you were interrupted and not cared about, and that he is playing one-upmanship, claiming he had a worse day. The next emotion may be sad—sad that what happened to you didn't seem to matter.

If you are able to get your mate to listen to you, the change of focus may happen in yet a different way. The shift happens when your mate tries to fix your problem or make you all better. You hear things like, "Well, what you should have (done, said, or felt) is . . ." or "You don't need to worry, I'll take care of this by . . ."

In both of these instances, the focus has been shifted from you, the one who started the conversation, to the listener and the roles have now reversed. When this happens, it is like having a bucket of ice water thrown on you. In my therapy practice, I have seen this happen and watched the eyes and facial expressions change from engaged to a withdrawn sadness. Sometimes there is an exhaling and a soft murmur of "Oh, what's the use." The focus needs to stay with the person who started the conversation. You can achieve this by understanding and using the principle of validation.

THE UNIVERSAL NEED

Validation starts with understanding the universal need that each person has to feel that *I am of worth, my feelings matter, and someone really cares about me.* If you were to ask most people they would say that they do understand the needs of their mates and they are trying to meet those needs. The problem is they are going about it in a manner that discounts their mate.

We often think that caring is demonstrated by fixing the other person's problems. Think for a moment about the last time you started to pour out one of your problems to your mate or another person and he broke in telling you what to do. How did you feel? Valued? Understood? Cared about? Or did you feel just the opposite? Ask yourself, "What did I need at that time?" Most people would say they needed to be listened to and understood.

Wanda and Bill are a classic example of this:

Wanda started to tell Bill about her day and the struggles she had had with her children. He listened attentively and then said, "I am really sorry you had such a bad day." [Excellent validation!] He continued, "You need to be more strict with the children and not let them walk all over you. They need to know you mean what you say. They need to have immediate consequences."

With a combination of tears and fire in her eyes, Wanda replied, "You really don't care. They are not your kids, they are mine and you don't know what they have been through. All you want to do is come down hard on the kids and me."

He quickly retorted, "I do care. Why do you think I'm trying to help you deal with the kids? I watch them run all over you and I get angry. I know what they need and I am helping you."

Wanda said, "You're not there and you don't have to deal with them all day every day." With that, her shoulders slumped and she began to cry tears of frustration and hurt. Bill looked away and sighed deeply.

> VALIDATION MEANS WALKING WITH ANOTHER PERSON EMOTIONALLY WITHOUT CHANGING HIS OR HER DIRECTION.

What did Wanda need at that moment? "I need him to listen and understand—and not criticize me. I need him to be on my team, not fight me. My ex does that enough." Bill quickly spoke up and said, "I do listen and I do understand and I want to be on your team but you won't let me." Wanda was trying to tell Bill he didn't need to fix her or her problems—that was her job. She just needed to be heard and understood. His validating statement at the beginning of their conversation was immediately invalidated by his advice.

PRINCIPLES OF VALIDATION

It is important to know and visualize the definition of validation. It is "the ability to walk with another person emotionally without trying to change his or her direction."[38] The visual part is to picture yourself walking beside that person. As soon as you try to guide someone, it is as though you are either walking behind, pushing, shoving, steering, or you are walking in front of them, pulling or yanking that person in your direction. Nobody likes to have that done to them. It is comforting and freeing when your mate walks beside you emotionally, allowing you to explore and wander where you want to go.

WE GET DESIRE MIXED UP WITH POWER.

The concept of validation is both simple and complex. The principles it is based on are simple; however, the unlearning of old habits is complex. We grow up being taught that we need to help each other and we have observed how others have given help, thinking that taking over and fixing whatever the problem may be is the best way. We know we truly cannot take another's responsibility, yet when we try to fix, we are doing just that. We do it with the best of intentions. Strange, isn't it, that when we are doing the taking over we easily forget how we felt when someone did it to us. So one of the important principles of validation is to *leave the responsibility where it belongs.* This is possible when you understand this basic underlying premise:

I do not have the power to make anything all better for anyone else. I can offer my help, but I cannot make it all better.

Often when people read this statement they say that it's not true. The main reason for this is that we have an inbred desire to help others and we get this "desire" mixed up with "power." We begin to think that because we have the desire, we also have the power to change and fix other people's problems. The only thing we can do is to offer our help, and even then we can't help unless the other person accepts our offer. When you believe this underlying premise you are then free of the burden of needing to solve your mate's problems, allowing you to give your full attention to what is being said. If you believe it is up to you to solve the problem, you will listen to only part of what is being said, then go into the problem-solving mode and not listen completely.

There have been many times in my office when I have turned to a husband and asked what he thought about what his wife had said. Sometimes he replies, "I didn't hear what she said because I was thinking what I was going to say." This example is a good one because the husband clearly admitted his mind had wandered. More often a husband gets a startled, panicked look on his face and replies, "I don't know." When pushed a little harder, he will say he missed part of what was said. This happens with the wives, also.

Have you ever been talking to your mate and the reply he gave seemed like he had been listening to another conversation—not yours? Or have you been listening to your mate and thought that something was missing from what you thought you heard? Check yourself out and see if you go into the problem-solving mode by getting ready with a solution. If you do that you have missed part of what was said. Practice concentrating on the entire conversation and then pausing at the end before giving a reply.

The idea of validation is to be able to view something through the eyes and feelings of the other person. Realize that each person has his own set of feelings and experiences; when you seek to understand them from his or her viewpoint you are showing great respect. You do not change or discount your own beliefs, feelings, or experiences. You get out of yourself for a while and into the "other" orientation—the most important other: your spouse.

RULES OF VALIDATION

There are four rules of validation: *listen, listen, listen,* and *understand.* The first "listen" means give your full attention to your mate, eye contact and all. Because your mate is so important, put down the paper, turn off the TV, turn away from the computer, put down the book—in other words, give your undivided attention. If you are the one asking for the attention, ask your mate if now is a good time to talk or ask when would be a better time. This, too, is respectful.

The second "listen" is to listen to the emotions being expressed. Each of us has emotions and it is important to be able to acknowledge what they are. Remember, these are personal and do not need to be corrected by anybody. How do you feel when someone says, "You shouldn't feel that way."

The third "listen" means to listen to the needs being expressed. Keep in mind that you can listen to those needs with full interest because you don't have to fix them or solve them. That's not your job. A man, after learning this principle commented:

> This is such an important point. I used to think I listened. I thought listening was just being quiet while the other person talked. I would be quiet, then I would tell the person all that was wrong and all that needed to be done—based on what I heard. I didn't know that I never really listened because I didn't understand that listening is about putting yourself in the other person's shoes. It's about walking with the other person emotionally. What a change when I started listening and validating.

Then comes the fourth rule: All you need to do is understand the best you can from your mate's point of view. You do not need to agree, although you may—just do the best you can to see your spouse's perspective.

Suppose you are having a hard time understanding—then ask questions to find out information or let your spouse know you don't understand, but you want to. You might say, "Help me understand. What happened? What are you feeling?" Too often, we ask questions to guide our mate to our perspective. Stephen Covey said:

> Seek[ing] first to understand involves a very deep shift in paradigm [your view]. We typically seek first to be understood. Most people do not listen with the intent to understand; they listen with the intent to reply. They're either speaking or preparing to speak. They're filtering everything through their own paradigm, reading their autobiography into other people's lives. . . . We're filled with our own rightness, our own autobiography. We want to be understood.[39]

You don't need to be right or to guide your mate. Your mate doesn't need your input at that point. You need to understand your mate's feelings, needs, and desires from his or her perspective. Milt describes a good example of this:

> I became aware that my wife was crying as she hung up the telephone. She said, "That was mom and she just returned from the doctor, where she found out she has breast cancer." With that she really started to sob. I thought I had to say something to help her feel better so I said, "Honey, it will be all right. They have probably discovered it early, so cheer up."
>
> She quickly looked up at me with fire in her eyes and said, "You don't understand! That's my mother and

she might die. She's not all right. In fact, maybe I could get it and also die." I stood there feeling horrible. All I wanted to do was make her feel better. I found out that all I needed to have done was listen and understand. I could have said, "That's really upsetting news. I am so sorry this is happening to your mother." If I had asked some validating questions and looked at it from her viewpoint, I would have been the hero instead of the guy with egg all over his face. It would have been so simple and loving. I think I get it now.

QUESTIONS—THE RIGHT KIND

It is important to ask the right kinds of questions. First, get rid of the question "why?" Why questions immediately put your mate on the defensive, having to justify his or her actions or what was said. Nobody wants to have to defend himself, particularly in his own home or to the person who is supposed to love him.

Another type of question to avoid entirely is the one that contains the answer. For example: "You really don't believe what you're saying, do you?" "You're feeling mad, aren't you?" "You agree with me, don't you?" "That's how we feel, isn't it?" You don't want your spouse to feel that it doesn't matter what he or she thinks, that you don't want to know because your mind is made up, and that all you want is for your spouse to agree with you.

The right kind of questions are those used to find out information and to clearly understand what happened. Instead of why, use what, where, when, how, is, do, can, are, or did. For instance, if your wife bumped into a car in front of her, instead of saying, "Why did you do that?" ask some of the following questions: What happened? Where did it happen? When did it happen? How did it happen? Did anyone get hurt? Are you all right? Do you need any help? Can I help?

What do you think needs to be done? How do you think it can be done? How did you feel about it? Each of these questions encourages your mate to report her own view and information. These questions say, "I am interested and I care about what's happening to you." But remember not to bombard your spouse with questions; ask one or two at a time, not all of them!

OPERATIVE WORDS

The art of questioning employs the skill of listening without translating what you heard. You must hear the exact word or words your mate used because they are the clues to what he or she is really feeling. We all use words that carry our emotions such as *hurt, sad, hard, frustrated, mad.* They are the *operative words* that need to be repeated in your questions. If you translate your mate's words into your own words, then your mate will not believe you are really listening. Individuals use words that have a particular meaning in their lives. By using those words—their words—you will not only be perceived as listening carefully, you will also be perceived as understanding what they are saying.

This however, is *not* reflective listening nor parroting what your mate says. Having to repeat all that was said to make sure your mate knows you understood is laborious, demeaning, and unnecessary. For example, your spouse may say, "I am feeling very sad." With reflective listening you might say, "I understand you are feeling very sad." Instead, using the operative word allows you to follow his lead without diverting his attention with your repetition of what he just said. The operative words your spouse uses lead to the place she or he needs to go. Now when your spouse says, "I am feeling very sad," the operative word is "sad." So your question could be, "Sad about what?" The answer may be, "Grandma is having such a hard time." Here the operative words are "hard time."

To that you could ask, "Oh, I'm sorry to hear that. What is she having a hard time over?"

When formulating questions around the operative words, remember to use *how, what, when, where, is, do,* and *can,* instead of *why.* If you focus on operative words, you focus on listening. Your mate can know that he is being listened to because he hears his lead being followed. His path is not being challenged or diverted, and the processing of what is needed flows on.

All of us have developed our own perception window through which we view life. This window is made up of our life's experiences and teachings. It is like the lens of a pair of glasses made to the needs of our own eyes. It is rare to have a pair of glasses work exactly the same for any two people. Therefore, it is important to concentrate on attempting to look through the other person's perception window by understanding her words and how they are used. If you don't understand a particular word, or how it is being used specifically, gently ask with a question such as "you say (give the word or words). I think I know what you mean, but I'm not sure." Then follow with a question: "Can you help me understand exactly what you mean?" Remember that everyone has her own language based on her experiences. By using this method you can learn to speak your spouse's language with greater understanding.

During a session with Ann and Judd, he said, "I would like to know where you are going when you leave." When I asked Ann what she heard she turned to Judd and replied, "You don't trust me and you want to control me." He explained to me, "All I wanted to know was where she was going in case I needed to get in touch with her for some emergency." This simple example effectively points out not only the need for careful questioning but careful listening to—and understanding of—the response.

The next time your mate starts to tell you what happened to him or her, listen very closely and follow the operative words. Keep in mind that you don't have to make it all better and you do not have to come up with a plan. Just listen, try to understand, and show that you care.[40]

CONFLICT RESOLUTION

Conflict resolution is not an easy thing to accomplish. Most couples come into my office struggling with a variety of conflicts and are very frustrated because their attempts to find resolution seem to end up in full-blown arguments. All too often, they start out with the desire to go from point *A* (where they are) to point *B* (the desired destination). As their conversation continues it resembles a road map. They start along the highway, and at the first street they turn off the highway onto a side road; at the next possible road they turn again, and so on until they are so lost, frustrated, and angry that they abandon the trip. Each turn represents the start of another subject and they end up with a whole bunch of unresolved items and far away from their original intended subject.

DEFENSIVENESS AND JUSTIFICATION STOP ALL INTERPERSONAL COMMUNICATION.

There are two things that cause many of these side trips: defensiveness and justification. As soon as either of you enters one of these modes, the original journey is lost. Defensiveness and justification stop all interpersonal communication and become the fuel for arguments. In fact, this part of the journey resembles a sword fight. It seems we each have a desire to be right and even if we are wrong we don't want to admit it. So we defend our position and justify what we said or did by pointing out our mate's faults and mistakes. This draws the other into the game because nobody wants to take the blame. One feels attacked and must defend oneself and in the process brings in one's justification, which resembles an attack and draws the same type of response. If you have a basic belief in yourself and your good intentions, you will not need to defend or justify what you did. Instead, you might try to find out what it was you did that didn't match what you were intending or wanting to do. Of course, if you meant to be nasty and rude, then accept full responsibility for your actions.

Here's a typical example of the kind of defending and justifying tactics that take couples away from where they want to go:

> Mary said to George, "You make me mad. You always try to put on a show so everybody will think you are this kind, loving husband. When nobody is around you treat me as though I'm not worth anything."
>
> He quickly remarked, "I treat you well and I would treat you better if you weren't such a nag."
>
> Just as quickly she snapped back, "Hey, I don't nag. It's that you don't have time to help me out and don't care. Besides that, I'm afraid of you and your temper."
>
> He replied, "Talk about a temper, you've really got one. Add your foul mouth and you're no jewel to be around."

Notice the way the conversation went from one subject to another, with greater attacks and justification at each turn. When I asked Mary and George to remind me of the reason they were in my office, they both said they wanted to save their marriage. I said, "With what I witnessed just now, I can't believe you two want to be with each other." Mary said, "We love each other; it's just that we don't know how to talk to each other."

One of the points I make with my clients is that in my office there is no single message. This means that when I am talking to the husband, I am also talking to the wife and vice versa. If there are single messages then it may seem there is a double standard. In marriage, there is a single standard of behavior. "What is good for the goose is good for the gander," and this is the point I made with Mary and George.

I asked George, "Is it your intention to have Mary feel like she is not worth much? And do you want her to be afraid of you?" His answer to both questions was, "No, I love her." To that I replied, "I believe those are your intentions. Has there been a time when your actions didn't match your intentions?" He said, "I am sure there has been." My next question was, "What is it that you are doing that might cause her to experience both worthlessness and fear?" He said, "Well, I'm not totally sure." I told George that I wanted him to believe in his intentions and if he believed in them he did not need to defend or justify his actions. I suggested that he was to be ready to take responsibility for his actions and that I was going to script him in an exchange with Mary. Here's how it went:

I asked Mary to state again her angry feelings and she repeated her original statement, "George, you make me mad. You always try to put on a show so everybody will think you are this kind, loving husband. When nobody is around you treat me as though I'm not worth much."

To which George was scripted to say, "That's got to be hard to live with." Then he added, "I guess I haven't paid attention to how I treat you. I'm really sorry. [Then back to the script] Tell me how I treat you when we're alone."

Mary looked into his eyes and asked if he really wanted to know and he replied he did. Tears began to well up in her eyes as she rehearsed some of his rude comments and uncaring remarks.

George then said, "I didn't realize I was being such a jerk. What do I do to make you afraid of me?"

"When you come home you are usually very impatient with me and the kids," Mary said. "If things don't go smoothly you're quick to yell and threaten. We try to keep out of your way. I'm afraid that one day you will really lose your temper and I don't know what will happen."

George looked at her, reached out, and put his hand on her shoulder and said, "How could I treat the woman I love like that? Thank you for telling me. I truly am sorry and I will work at doing better." Mary leaned over to him and they held on to each other and both shed a few tears.

What a difference in the outcome when the focus of the conversation stays with the one who starts it—when the other listens, asks questions to find out information, takes full responsibility for his or her own actions, isn't looking to defend what he did or justify anything—just ready to work at being different.

THE THREE-PRONGED APPROACH

At the next session, George and Mary reported having a much better and calmer week. They were ready for another suggestion to improve their way of resolving conflicts. The way problems are presented can have a lot to do with the way they are received. The word "you" is used too much and in a way that becomes accusatory and pushes your mate to become defensive.

BY ACKNOWLEDGING YOUR EMOTIONS YOU MAY NOT NEED TO ACT THEM OUT.

The three-pronged approach is based on taking responsibility for yourself and how you feel. Statements are made from the "I" position. This takes some practice, but it will work if applied. The three parts are: I feel <u>(an emotion)</u> about <u>(event)</u> and I need_____. Usually couples get through some semblance of the first two parts and the last part is assumed and never spoken. Let's break down each of these steps.

I FEEL _____There is generally some emotion associated with conflict and this needs to be acknowledged. Dr. Jay Lundberg, a marriage and family therapist and my brother, identified the four basic emotions as: mad, glad, sad, and afraid. Each of these has a number of other descriptive emotions; I like the simplicity of using these basic four, however. By acknowledging your emotions through descriptive words, you may not need to act them out. It is also important to know that you can experience more than one emotion at a time and you can acknowledge each. For instance, Felice was washing a beautiful china platter belonging to a set she and her husband inherited from his mother. While she was drying it, it slipped from her hands and hit the cabinet before she could catch it, causing a large chip. She described the many emotions she experienced in such a short time: sad to have damaged something that had sentimental value to both of them, but especially to her husband; mad that she had not been more careful; and glad to see that the platter was still usable.

Stop momentarily and check out the emotions you are feeling just before you speak. It is important to recognize your own feelings and to own them. By acknowledging your emotions you acknowledge and validate yourself and then you take personal responsibility for those emotions. For example, the statement "You make me mad" tries to put the responsibility on someone else and basically gives your control over to that other person. Nobody can make you feel anything so what you feel is your choice. In a roundabout way, this helps you feel more in control of yourself. If you are feeling more than one emotion, then acknowledge what you are feeling.

ABOUT _____This part of the approach is the description of the event or events that have influenced your feeling. Notice that I am talking about an event. This description determines where your mind and eyes are focused. If the word "you" is used, then you focus on a person. If the event is talked about, then your eyes or the eyes of your mind focus on what happened. For instance, the statement "You make me mad because you yelled at me" would cause the eyes to focus on the "you" or person. If the statement "I get angry when I'm yelled at" were used, then there might be a momentary glance at the person and then the attention would be focused on reviewing what happened. Better yet, use the phrase, "I am angry about being yelled at when I forgot to buy the milk." This allows your mate to understand exactly what event is upsetting you.

In attempting to resolve a problem, some couples may get to this point and that is where they stop. Spouses often think that if their mate loves them then he or she will know what they need. This assumption sets up another guessing game and often results in hurt feelings and unmet needs.

I NEED _____ The best chance of getting your needs met is to ask for what you need. You may not get everything you ask for; when you ask, however, the probability of receiving improves immensely. Trish gives a good example of clearly asking for what she needs:

> When we were first married, I felt bad that Rod didn't do much about my birthday (his family never did much when he was growing up and my family had always made it a big deal). So I finally just told him that I wanted to be taken to dinner and given a present for my birthday, and it's been fine since then. He even does a trip or something on our anniversary now every year!

Sometimes when we begin to talk out our needs they change. Our thinking clears when we put our thoughts into words in an attempt to have our mate understand what we have been thinking. What may seem clear to us may need further explanation in order for our mate to respond. When a wife is presenting her need, it is important that the husband listen completely. If you are not clear on what your wife is telling you or requesting, then ask questions. Remember you do not need to defend or justify yourself and you don't need to change your wife's perception or guide her with your questions. Your job is to do the best you can to understand from her point of view what she is feeling, thinking, and wanting. This goes for both of you.

RESPONDING

Once you understand what your mate is asking for, it is up to you to respond. This response is your commitment to meet, as best you can, his or her need. If you can meet that need, tell him or her so and do it. Suppose your spouse is asking you to do something you are unable or unwilling to do—what do you do? Each of us has boundaries and limitations. Say, a straightforward statement like, "I'm not able (willing) to do what you are asking. However, I could do . . ." Here you propose what you can do. He or she may counter with another proposal. This is a time for calm negotiations. If you love and honor each other then you can negotiate so that each can get his or her needs met. You can do this if you treat each other with kindness, gentleness, and respect.

Now it may be that the things you are asking for seem perfectly logical and right to you, but just as you have limitations, so does your mate. In order to resolve a conflict it must be a win–win situation. If either of you is forced or coerced into doing something, then there is resentment and an underlying anger that will fester and eventually boil over into another problem. Your desire is to have your need respected and responded to. You must respect your spouse's need for understanding and respect his or her limitations.

THE HERE AND NOW

One of my clients remarked to me, "My wife doesn't get hysterical, she gets historical." Many respondents to our survey and many of my clients describe how their mate continually brings up all the past problems, even if they have been resolved. One day I asked a client the reason for bringing up so much of the past and he said, "If I bring up enough evidence then I can win the argument or get my way."

I watch many clients seemingly beating their mate with all this history in an attempt to overwhelm any opposition. Yet using all of your history is really a futile exercise. How does historical battering affect you or your spouse during your discussions? Or have you observed other couples as they are in a discussion—have you watched the eyes of the one being inundated with all his past shortcomings? There are no peaceful, happy feelings or resolutions in these scenarios.

So if this happens to you what do you do? Remember that the only person you can control is yourself. So if this happens, kindly say, "Yes, that did happen in the past; what can we do about this current situation?" Or "I did that in the past; how can we work through this current problem?" Keep focused on the here and now. If you are tempted to use the past on your spouse, stop yourself and silently ask, "Would I want this done to me?" Take a deep breath and refocus your thinking on the current problem. Stop yourself from detouring. Bring a resolution to the current discussion then go to the next subject. Remember how George and Mary's discussion started and was going nowhere. When they focused on one part of the need at a time and stayed in the current feeling and need, they were able to draw close to each other and come to the beginning of a resolution.

IT TAKES TIME

Good communication doesn't just happen—you make it happen. The pressures of life expand to take over all available space. With a job, children, community involvement, schooling, church, PTA, hobbies, music lessons, and friends there is not much time left over. By the time night comes around, it seems as if all you can do is fall into bed. Sometimes one spouse will develop a late-night TV habit, which further complicates time for talking. Unless you carve out time it will not happen.

There was an interesting article based on an experiment conducted by *McCall's* magazine, titled "22 Minutes to a Better Marriage." They asked three couples who were happy together but felt that at times they were like two ships passing in the night to participate by taking twenty-two minutes a day to talk. The time was equated to watching one TV sitcom a day without the commercials. "The rules were simple: no children in the room, no radio in the background, no dinner and, please, no dinner dishes. Turn the answering machine on. Do it for one month." The report from the couples was that it was more successful "than they had ever dreamed possible."[41] They found this time to be a little awkward at first but didn't give up. These couples began to share their daily happenings from work and from home. It gave them a greater tie to each other and each other's world. One couple reported that the wife was able to sleep more peacefully and the husband was more energized. This husband also said it drew him closer to his children because of the things his wife shared.

In a previous chapter we said that "people don't fall out of love; they forget to love." You may forget to love because you don't make the time available to do the things that you used to do when you courted. So often couples tell me that they used to spend hours talking and laughing together during their courtship and early marriage and now can hardly find time to say hello to each other. Do the experiment above and you will be surprised at the results you achieve in acquiring this new habit of communication.

BEGIN TODAY

Now that you have read this chapter through once, go back and review the suggestions to improve your communication skills. Underline some of the ideas that fit the needs of your marriage and begin to use them now, little by little. Check the way you listen and see if you shift into the problem-solving mode or if you fully listen. Practice asking questions that encourage your spouse to share, knowing that you will not correct his or her perception. Improving communication needs to start with someone and it might as well be you.

Be Your Mate's Favorite Cheerleader

When love and skill work together expect a masterpiece. —JOHN RUSKIN

A TEAM MEMBER'S JOB

Picture yourself as a member of a basketball team. Your fellow teammate has been fouled and is at the free throw line. The game is tied with only three seconds left. He bounces the ball, takes a deep breath, and tosses it toward the basket. The crowd is dead silent. The ball hits the inside of the rim, rolls around, and bounces out of the basket. No score. So close, but no score. You step forward with other teammates and give him supportive fives and words of encouragement. He moves to the line for his second throw, feeling the support of his team while sweat rolls off his forehead. Another deep breath, the toss and . . . it's nothing but net! The crowd goes wild. Your teammate is a hero. And the whole team is cheering, laughing, and hugging each other.

Now consider the same scenario. Your teammate is at the line ready to make his first shot. He misses. You move in close to him and say, "You should have made that basket! You knew how the team was depending on you.

IT'S SAD WHEN A SPOUSE IS THERE CHEERING YOU ON ONLY WHEN YOU WIN.

You had your big chance and you blew it. You don't have the talent to make the next shot, so why even try." What is the likelihood of your teammate making the next shot after a comment like that? What is the likelihood of anyone with your attitude remaining on the team?

On a successful team, that kind of belittling would never happen. Teammates work together—they are each other's most valuable cheerleader. When one succeeds, the whole team succeeds and everyone is happy. That needs to happen in marriage. As a spouse, you are a member of the most important team in the world—your "home" team.

YOU WIN SOME, YOU LOSE SOME

Life is full of wins and losses and it's sad when a spouse is there cheering you on only when you win. Craig's experience provides a good example:

> I had the opportunity to buy a business with a partner who had been working with me as a fellow employee. I talked it over with my wife, Charlotte, and convinced her that it was a wonderful opportunity. Though she had some reservations, she was happy to see my excitement and gave her support. That was the beginning of one of the most difficult periods of my life. My partner and I worked feverishly for seven years, having some good years and some not-so-good years as we rode that risky roller-coaster. Then we merged with another company, and though we were still involved, they took over running the business.
>
> Within a year of the merge the business failed and we were left with a sizable debt. It was a terrible disappointment for me, and the financial loss was tremendous. The thing I remember most about that whole experience was that not once did Charlotte criticize or blame me for the business failure. She didn't say, "You

should never have gone into that business in the first place." She acknowledged my hard work and cried with me over the loss, with no pointing fingers that made *me* feel like a failure.

These things happen in life. We need to learn from them and go on. When you achieve success, you also want and need your spouse to be supportive. Sharing each other's happiness is simply having double happiness. It never takes away from yourself—it only adds. Having your spouse as your cheerleader, and being one for your mate, adds to the good times and will help you through the very rough times.

MATCH WISDOM WITH OPPORTUNITY

Some men and women have expressed sadness over the fact that their mates don't support them in venturing into new business opportunities. Fear of failure is a terrible inhibitor. Life is to be lived fully and filled with adventure. That old adage rings true: *nothing ventured, nothing gained.* I'm not suggesting foolhardiness here. Before entering any venture, ask serious questions about it. It's important that you are not taken advantage of in your desire to try new things. Investigate with full support from your mate, allow your mate to ask the hard questions, and get reliable answers before decisions are made. You need to be wise, but in your effort to be wise don't stop an important dream from coming true. If a dream turns into a nightmare, be there for each other, learn from it, and go on with even greater wisdom for the next venture. It keeps life interesting.

No one enters a career opportunity with the intent of losing or failing. Gloria Hirsch, who at the time of my internship was the clinical director of Friends of the Family, a counseling center in Van Nuys, California, said, "Believe in the good intentions of your mate." A powerful amount of cheerleading will result by putting that statement into practice.

ENJOY YOUR MATE'S TALENTS

When Billie Letts, author of the book *Where the Heart Is,* appeared on *Oprah,* she expressed her appreciation for the encouragement her husband gave her. And he did it long before she was a best-selling author. Whether or not your spouse develops a million-dollar talent is immaterial. If it happens, then enjoy the happy surprise. When it doesn't, which so often is the case, just enjoy the fulfillment your mate is experiencing as he or she develops and uses his or her talent.

At our seminars we have had some women come to us expressing sorrow that their mates would not support them in their creative ventures. One woman said, "I love writing music, but I have to do it when my husband isn't anywhere near." She said, "He'll say to me, 'Why are you wasting your time. Those songs aren't going anywhere.'" These comments have hurt her deeply. Even if she never published any of them, she finds fulfillment in creating them. How sad it is that he won't sit down in an easy chair and just listen while she plays some of them and rejoice in her accomplishments. Can you imagine the joy she would feel if he encouraged her and praised her efforts? It couldn't help but bring loving feelings into their relationship.

Darla and Wynn enjoy an entirely different relationship. He said, "After work and dinner one of my favorite things to do is lie on the couch and listen to Darla play the piano. It calms me and brings such a peaceful feeling into our home." Darla is a very talented pianist, but instead of pursuing a concert career she preferred to stay at home rearing their children. She has not regretted her decision, due in part to her husband's support of her continuing to develop her talent. He made sure she had a grand piano when they couldn't even afford other furniture for their living room. Each year he encourages her to give a "Friends and Family Concert" in their home. Their large living room is always packed with people, and her husband is there greeting the guests and introducing her at the beginning of the concert. He also supports her using her talent at church and community events.

Of course, this kind of support goes both ways. Several years ago Dorothy Blanchard was interviewed on television about her husband, Oscar Hammerstein II, of Rodgers and Hammerstein fame. *South Pacific* and *The Sound of Music* were among their many hit musicals. The TV host was commenting that music composers usually receive more accolades than the lyricists. Dorothy said, "Sadly, that is true, but you must remember that without my husband this song would only have been" (and she hummed the tune) "la, la, laa, la, la, laa. But with *his* contribution it became" (and she sang the words) "Some enchanted evening." She said, "Now, you tell me, what would that song be without those words?" Talk about a cheerleader! Here was a woman proud of her husband's talent and not afraid to say it.

Kyle and Charlotte had a similar relationship. Charlotte loved performing in musical theater. When children came along she had to give it up. As you can imagine, being a mother of ten children, ranging from age four to twenty, took every ounce of her effort. The producer of a traveling show knew of Charlotte's talent and wanted her to play the part of a mother. The part piqued her interest and, after talking it over with her husband, she accepted the role with some definite conditions. Kyle felt she needed the spark it would put into her life, and they decided that if she could take one or two children with her on each road trip, she would accept. The producer agreed, even working the children into small performing parts. For nearly four years the show toured many weekends and during summers traveled for three or four weeks at a time. She missed very few performances.

After the first year the producer spoke to Kyle and asked him how it was working out. Kyle said, "Charlotte needed this. She's so happy to be able to perform again. She has a great talent and I am happy to support her and help make this happen." It meant extra work for him whenever she was gone, but he saw it as not only an advantage for his wife, but one for each of the children since it allowed them to have this special time with their mother. They have a solid, happy marriage because they both know how to be each other's cheerleader.

Former U.S. president Jimmy Carter recognizes the talents of his wife, Rosalynn, and values her input. With their Carter Center program their "work is almost entirely among the poorest and most needy people, in this country and in foreign nations. . . . Rosalynn is a full partner with me, and she has been in charge of our efforts in the field of mental health. Under her leadership, more than sixty formerly uncooperative organizations now come together annually to share their common ideas and goals."[42] He continually praises her talents and contributions to their humanitarian efforts. They both acknowledge the work they have put into their relationship to become teammates in their projects.

ASSIST IN EDUCATIONAL OPPORTUNITIES

Stewart, an air force pilot, shared the following experience from his pilot training:

> The study required was grueling and demanding. Emergency procedures had to be memorized so completely that in a split second the appropriate action would be taken. I asked my wife, Marva, if she would help me. Every night she would quiz me on the procedures . . . over and over, night after night, until I knew them perfectly. She could have told any pilot what to do in almost any emergency situation. I was so grateful for her help.
>
> Marva told me later that many times when I would be up flying, her heart would be in her throat. Too

many student pilots had lost their lives, and it scared
her. But never once did she suggest that I should resign
or change to a less hazardous field in the service. She
said, "I just prayed for your safety instead, because I
knew you loved it." I can't begin to tell you how important that support was to me.

As we go through life our needs and desires change. Leah had
begun her studies for a bachelor's degree in English when she
and Andrew were married. Her education was put on "hold"
when their first baby arrived one year later. Andrew promised
her the day would come when she would continue her education. She was content to be at home with the children. She
said:

> That's when I began earning my "degree" in mother-
> ing. Andrew continued his education and went on to
> receive his doctoral degree, becoming head coach of a
> university baseball team. During those years three more
> children were born. Now we had four sons. When they
> were four, six, eight, and ten, Andrew encouraged me
> to return to school during the summer when he had
> more time off. He volunteered to be the DM, "desig-
> nated mother," his takeoff of baseball's term "desig-
> nated hitter." I was a little fearful of being a scholar
> again. I was, without a doubt, out of practice. He was
> so persistent that he even enrolled in a Shakespeare
> class with me—quite a stretch for a coach/P.E. instruc-
> tor, but he did it cheerfully to help me regain my aca-
> demic confidence.
>   During that first year the DM kept forgetting that he
> was the first line of contact for these four very active, of-
> ten hungry, frequently needing-a-ride somewhere sons
> of ours. The boys would seek me out first, reporting that
> Dad had sent them. I would cycle them back to him. It
> took a little time until he realized what DM really meant.

During this time we both developed an empathy for each other that we had never before known.

As my B.A. degree neared, Andrew said, "Don't stop. Go on and get your graduate degree." Again my confidence waned, but his belief in me (and the fact that he brought home the application and nudged me to complete it) gave me the incentive to apply to law school. When I was accepted, we held a family council to decide if Mom ought to actually take on the additional role of law student. Andrew's optimism and confidence in me was contagious, and I soon had five males cheering me on!

Nothing could compare to the rigors of law school. But even after the novelty wore off and patience wore thin, our commitment to one another and to this family goal would get us through any minicrisis. We tried to do the best we could, one day at a time, and when I received my degree three years later, I told the five of them—especially Andrew—they each owned part of my diploma. Without their pep talks, shoulder rubs, and unfailing conviction that I would succeed, I could never have accomplished this goal.

Leah graduated with honors and was offered a prestigious administrative position at the law school. She enjoys her work immensely and the whole venture has drawn her and Andrew even closer as they continue to work out their schedules together for the good of their marriage and their family. Leah said, "All the way along Andrew has been my personal cheerleader. I couldn't have done it without him. And as for me, I love attending his games with our boys and cheering for 'our' team."

Leah added the following postscript to her story:

One of the nicest things about being married a long time is that you usually get a chance to return a favor. I have now been a university administrator for eleven years and have learned a few things along the way. Andrew has recently had a change of job assignment that has taken him from the teaching/coaching ranks to the administrative. After twenty-eight years in one role, he is faced with the challenge of making a different contribution and learning new skills. I have absolute confidence that he is more than equal to the task and will be an unequivocal success in his new position. Currently I'm his enthusiastic tutor, introducing him to the amazing world of word processing, databases, and the Internet. Our adventure in teamwork continues!

STAND UP FOR EACH OTHER

Being your mate's cheerleader can take on many forms. There is nothing quite so comforting as having a mate who will stand up for you when the going gets tough, or nothing quite so sad when one won't. Tiffani's experience is a witness to this need. She wrote:

I was working the night shift with my friend, Fran, at a food canning company. One night, at 3:00 A.M., we were suddenly fired and asked to go home. My husband, Clark, was too embarrassed to go with us to meet with management to discuss the injustice. Fran's husband was supportive of her and went with us to the meeting. We found out that lies were being told about us by the lead lady. The company fired her and hired us back. Fran was promoted to lead lady. We worked together for three more years.

It may seem like a little thing, but even though that was several years ago, I remember how disappointed I felt that Clark would not accompany me and stand by me like Fran's husband had. He just seems too embar-

YOUR MATE DOESN'T NEED YOU THERE FOR EVERY LITTLE THING, BUT WHEN IT IS IMPORTANT TO HER OR HIM . . . BE THERE.

rassed to "be there" for me in any situation where I need a little additional support. I don't ask him any more because it's too disappointing to be turned down.

Some of you reading this account may say, "It was her job. She needed to take care of it herself." Likely there were many things she did to take care of herself; this was a time, however, when she really wanted her husband to be with her and give her that physical "in-the-flesh I'm-with-you" support. Of course, your mate doesn't need you there for every little thing, but when it's important to her or him . . . be there. It's much easier to be a cheerleader when you're within earshot.

Florence faced a similar, yet different, problem. She and Darwin moved into a brand-new home. The first time it rained, the roof leaked and the water ran down the inside of the walls, popping the circuit breakers. She had experienced a few other defects before this happened and had been given the runaround by the builders. When this new problem arose she said to Darwin, "Please go with me to the builders so we can get this fixed." He refused, saying, "You're better at that than I am . . . you can handle it fine. I'm not going." She said, "I'm getting no respect from them. I need a man to stand up to them. Please come." He refused again. Finally, out of desperation she went alone. She said, "It was so frustrating. I hate it when women are treated like second-rate citizens. I needed Darwin to be there even just to say, 'Look Buddy, don't treat my wife like that.' But he's never there helping with these things. It always ends up being my job and I'm sick of it."

Florence needed Darwin's help. This was one of those cases where she didn't need cheering from the sidelines. She needed a full-fledged team member in there playing the game with her.

THE MAGIC OF APPROVAL

Sometimes, when it's a one-person job, cheering from the sidelines is the only place we can give support. There is a moving example of this in the *Rocky II* movie. When Rocky made the decision to fight again, his wife, Adrian, was opposed to it. Of course, her opposition was based on the fear that he would receive serious injuries. Those who saw this movie will recall the disappointment and struggle he went through as he trained and prepared for the match without her support.

She finally saw how important this was to him and realized that she was being selfish. Just before the fight she said to him, "There's one thing I want you to do for me. Win! Win!" That statement empowered him to fight like he never could have without it. And he won. The interesting thing is, so did she. When your mate fulfills a dream with your support, it works magic in the marriage. If he had lost, the magic would still be there because they were together pulling for each other.

NO PLACE FOR JEALOUSY

Recently, at a large gathering of people who had come to hear a prominent lecturer give her presentation, a song was sung to pay tribute to her husband. He is always there quietly helping set up her sound equipment and doing anything else that she needs, giving her his full support. Many times he can be heard graciously accepting praise for his wife's wonderful accomplishments. Consider his feelings as the song "The Wind Beneath My Wings" was sung as a surprise to pay tribute to *him* at the conclusion of her lecture. This devoted husband could not hold back the tears. Nor could his wife, because of the gratitude she felt for him and all he does for her. He is her hero, as the song describes. He always considers it an honor to assist his wife. Those who know him are fully aware that he feels no jealousy, only delight in his wife's accomplishments.

With this kind of caring there is no place for envy or need for competition, just a feeling of genuine joy for your spouse. If one spouse does feel left out, perhaps it's time for the one feeling left out to devote some time to developing a skill or talent he or she would enjoy. Encouragement from this person's spouse can help make that happen.

BEGIN TODAY

Has your mate ever mentioned something he or she would like to do that you didn't support? Has your husband wanted to take a class or develop a musical talent and you thought it was a waste of time and money? Has your wife wanted to take watercolor lessons but you didn't think you could afford it? Has your husband wanted to change careers, but you were too afraid of a new venture? Has your wife needed you to stand with her in a hard-to-face situation?

Now is a good time to consider these questions and the many others that you may be dealing with in your marriage regarding the need to cheer each other on. Please take a few minutes together and write down a couple of dreams or wishes you have and share them with each other. Then discuss how you can "be there," cheering each other on in these areas.

Being a member of your "home" team means actively playing the game together. Teammates hang in there, pulling for each other throughout the entire game of life. When that happens, playing the game is much more fun and rewarding.

Set Your Boundaries

*Back of every noble life there are principles
that have fashioned it.*
—GEORGE HORACE LORIMAR

WHAT ARE BOUNDARIES?

Any farmer can tell you what boundaries are. To him they are
the fences that mark his fields. They show the limits of where
he can plow, plant, harvest, and graze his cattle. To a home-
owner they are basically the same. They are where the house
can be built, the grass can be planted and mowed, the children can play, and flower gardens planted. The property line
defines what belongs to that person.

Shape can also define boundaries. A house, a car, a
truck—everything you can see is defined by its boundaries.
What makes one house or car more appealing than the other?
The desirability of anything is determined by what is contained within its boundaries and what is seen by the eye of
the beholder.

Personal boundaries are much the same.
Your boundaries are what make you who you
are. You are made up of what you think and
believe; what you will do or won't do; where
you will go or won't go; what you will allow
others to do with you, to you, around you;

**BOUNDARIES
ARE YOUR
PERSONAL
PRINCIPLES
AND VALUES
IN ACTION.**

and how close you will allow others to you. Your life experiences shape all of these things and help determine the principles by which you live. And you are not stuck with these principles if you find they are not working for you. In his book, *The Power Principle,* Dr. Blaine Lee states "the principles you live by create the world you live in; if you change the principles you live by, you will change your world."[43] These principles are the personal picture you create of yourself. Boundaries, then, are your personal principles and values in action.

HOLOGRAM OR REAL?

Modern technology has developed some marvelous things. One of these is a hologram, an electronic display that projects an image into space that looks like a real person. If you go to touch the image it has no substance and cannot be felt or held on to. This is what a person without boundaries is like. Although you can touch the person, it's as if he is not there. This reminds me of some of my clients. Life in their family is going on and running right through them as though they did not exist. Abbie's experience is an excellent example:

> For years disrespect, rudeness, yelling, and harsh distasteful words were being used by both my husband and me toward each other. I have four part-time jobs, one husband, three kids, a dog, a mortgage, and I do church work. Needless to say, with this schedule I require some occasional help. I have told my husband for years, "I'm not happy with the way things are; I need your help in making my life and our family work."
>
> If we were out of milk or bread, he wouldn't stop at the store to pick some up. He'd say, "That's a wife's job." I'd say something back and we would get into a fight. If the laundry was piling up, he wouldn't start the machine. I'd yell at him to help out. If the house was a

mess he'd yell at me to get it cleaned up and I'd yell at him to clean it up. If I wore a comfortable loose outfit to lounge around the house in, he'd call me "big cow." I'd say something ugly back to him and the fighting would start again. If the bills needed to be paid, he wouldn't pay them, saying it was my job to do the budget, and we'd argue again. If he was wanting something to eat, he'd say "I'm hungry" and expect me to immediately stop what I was doing and get him food. If there was an issue with the kids, I had to deal with it so he wouldn't be upset by having to face their problems. If I was watching a TV program and it was of no interest to him, he would turn the channel without so much as a word to anyone. I either let him watch what he wanted and sit there in silent resentment or I'd start arguing with him, eventually leaving the room upset.

With rarely a mention of thanks from him for anything I did, I felt unappreciated and overwhelmed with expectations, demands, and arguments. I'd usually give in to his demands just to keep the peace. Occasionally, I'd mention to him my needs and feelings of being overwhelmed and needing some help from him and that his disrespect for me was uncalled for. We'd argue, resolving nothing. It was as if he wouldn't hear me and would continue to do things his way.

At this point, what does Abbie look like? Does she resemble the hologram? Though she could be touched, it was as if she didn't exist. Life in her home went on right through her. The next part of her story illustrates her discovery of boundaries.

"Then I realized I'd never set any *boundaries*. It was time I set my boundaries! I discovered the universal need was true: I am of worth, my feelings matter, and I care about me!

If my husband wanted food I no longer jumped up and just did it. I'd say, "Honey, if you would like a salad, I'd be happy to fix it for you. From now on please ask me kindly if you want me to make you something to eat." Then I'd go fix the salad. If there was an issue with the kids, I would have the children go talk with their dad about the situation and let him deal with it. If he sent the kids back to me to solve it, I'd walk with them back to their dad, sit down with them, state the situation, and ask dear ole dad what he thought was the best way to deal with it. I'd sit there and listen as they would discuss things.

When he'd call me "big cow," I would say, very boldly but kindly, "Do not call me that." Then I would walk away and not get into an argument. If he yelled at me, I'd look him in the eye and very kindly say, "Do not ever talk to me in that manner. Talk to me and I'll hear you; yell at me and I'm deaf."

To my surprise what happened was quite the opposite of what I expected—things got worse instead of better. He didn't quite know how to deal with my newfound boundaries. I continued to be kind, gentle, respectful, and *firm*. When it came to something I felt strongly about, I stated my case, stood my ground, and would not yell or argue (being careful to choose my battle wisely). I'd been doing this now for several weeks and I was feeling better about things, although I didn't know if I was getting through to him.

Yesterday, when I came home from church I found a bouquet of flowers and a card saying, "I'm not always so easy to get along with. I'm sorry for the things I say that I shouldn't and for not always seeing the places where my help and care are needed. I wish I could tell you that it will never happen again, but you'd smile and rightly so. But I can tell you that I'm really sorry and that

I'll be trying to be more kind, considerate, and more caring each day. I love you."

I was very touched and realized that boundaries do work and there is hope.

BOUNDARY-SETTING PROCESS

This story illustrates many of the different parts of the process of boundary setting. The first part had to do with Abbie's recognizing what she didn't like and what needed to be changed; next, that she was worth the change and her marriage was worth rescuing. Then came the recognition of her part in being someone she didn't want to be and that the only person she could change was herself. As she started to have a picture of herself, she gave substance to who she is and became comfortable with her new image. It is so important to recognize that your image of yourself does not come from others. Your self-image means just that—your image of yourself. It comes from within yourself. You choose who you want to be and set that course to make that happen one small step at a time. When you become comfortable with yourself, you can be comfortable with anyone else.

Abbie learned the lesson well that boundaries must be *kind, gentle, respectful,* and *firm.* Too often people believe that in order for boundaries to be effective they need to be mean, nasty, ugly, and firm. The difficulty with this is that we end up arguing about the mean, nasty, and ugly way we are dealing with each other, and the firm boundary is lost. Being kind, gentle, and respectful makes it possible for the "firm" to be heard and respected.

AFTER DRAWING A BOUNDARY, TREAT YOUR MATE NORMALLY— LIKE YOU WOULD WANT TO BE TREATED.

This is also an indication that you are comfortable with yourself and your boundaries. When a person has to be loud and forceful, you can't help but think of that quote from Shakespeare: "Me thinks she doth protest too much." Or put another way, "Who is she trying to convince—herself or me?"

Boundaries are like drawing a line in the sand. Some think they need to withdraw after stating their boundary. Yet when a spouse forcefully draws a line and withdraws, the other spouse may think that the two of you are now at odds, almost like enemies. There is increased tension and separateness. Personal strength comes when, after drawing the boundary, you treat your spouse normally—like you would want to be treated. Abbie only withdrew when she was being treated disrespectfully and returned treating her husband kindly, still maintaining the boundary.

IT MAY GET WORSE BEFORE IT GETS BETTER

Change is often resisted, particularly by men. They like things to be consistent while women like more changes. In behavior, however, most of us resist changes in others because we know how to deal with that person as they are. When others change we don't know how to deal with this new person. At this point, we often try to get the person who changed to "unchange" or return to her old self. Abbie found this to be true. Her husband continued to treat her the way he did and even increased the old behavior. Hence, it got worse before it got better. When the change is made for the right reason, however, the other person will eventually adjust, which is the same as changing themselves.

BOUNDARIES DEFINE WHAT THERE IS ABOUT YOU TO LOVE.

What is the right reason? The change must be a right thing to do and a right thing for you. Abbie changed because being treated that way was not the right thing for her spouse to do to her and a change of treatment was right for her. If you change in order to change your spouse, you aren't doing the right thing. And when that happens, you will end up changing again if you don't see the results you wanted. This is confusing to your spouse and to yourself. This is also known as manipulation. Because Abbie changed for the right reasons, she could be comfortable with her change. Her next challenge was to remain consistent in her boundaries. When the change is made for the right reason then you can remain constant. This gives the message that you are serious about the change. And that is the next step in creating good boundaries—consistency.

Boundaries define what there is about you to love. Pause a moment and go back to the message Abbie's husband wrote in his card. It was a message of love and respect for this new person she had become and a commitment to respond to her needs. You see, it is hard to love a hologram or a doormat. A hologram is just that—hollow, without substance. Doormats are for walking and wiping your feet on and eventually they get discarded. You cherish that which has value and desirable quality.

Nan found that out as she began to draw her boundaries with her alcoholic husband. He would drink every night after work. She didn't drink. After a number of drinks, he wanted to go for a ride and he would insist on driving. She wanted peace in her home and believed in "peace at all costs." For years she had gone on these nightly drives with him, being terrified for her safety. As she worked on her boundaries, she said he started to pay more attention to her and treat her differently. "Now he can't keep his hands off of me. This is quite a change because our intimacy had decreased greatly." Then came the time she took a stand on the nightly rides. He became very unhappy with her and after a few days told her he was leaving her and wanted a divorce. They separated and she was very sad but said she had known for a number of years this would happen because she couldn't stand his drinking.

An interesting development occurred about a week later. He called her and said he was going to commit suicide. She talked with him and the end result was that he put himself in detox. He made it through the program and they are back together with a greatly improved relationship. They still have many hills to climb with his alcoholic problem but now they are on a joint path together. It got worse before it got better.

CHILDREN PUSH THE BOUNDARIES

Children push the boundaries, too—your personal boundaries as well as the rules in your home. Remember, a child's main job is to get his or her needs met at all costs. Personal boundaries won't be important and won't mean a thing to your children unless they are real and remain constant. If children get the message that personal boundaries are not respected between their parents, then they will push those boundaries the same way their parents do to each other, plus a whole lot more. For instance, if you and your spouse curse, yell, and are disrespectful to each other they will do the same even if you tell them not to. The old adage fits: "How can I hear what you are saying when what you are doing is thundering in my ears." Couples are often shocked when their children swear at them. But if you ask the husband and wife if they swear at each other, they usually remark, "not like the kids are doing." Your children will take what you do and go at least one step further. Truly, your principles do create the world in which you live.

COUPLES NEED A PLACE THAT IS THEIRS—A HAVEN THEY CAN CALL ALL THEIR OWN.

WHAT IS YOURS?

Boundaries also consist of physical space in the home. Couples need a place that is theirs—a haven they can call all their own. Too often there is no place in the home a couple can call its own. Everything is turned into a family place. Even their bedroom doubles as another family room, TV room, or playroom. Income, size of family, and size of home may dictate how much space there is for the family, but if it is possible, you should have a private room where you can have private time. Make your bedroom be that place, no matter how small. If you are fortunate enough to have a bathroom off your bedroom, then treat this as your master bedroom suite. The threshold to your bedroom becomes your boundary to your space, as mentioned in Secret #7: Enjoy Sexual Intimacy. This doesn't mean the children can't be invited in. It means they will learn to respect the parents' area. This respect will be demonstrated by how you respect your area. Remember, this is your haven—the place you have to get away, the place where you will be making love, as well as finding peaceful solitude.

Tom and Cindy have a small home with a master bedroom. Cindy describes their bedroom:

> We barely have enough room to get on each side of the bed. He has his side of the room piled with his things and I have my side piled with mine. We can't even close the door because we even have things piled in front of the open door. The rest of the house is pretty much like our bedroom. Our children use our bed for a play area and place to watch TV.

Finding privacy in their home was very hard for Cindy and Tom. Once they cleaned up their bedroom, making it a more peaceful, private place that included boundaries, they were able to improve on their communication, lower their stress, have more control in their own and their children's lives, increase the level of respect within the family, and increase the amount of intimacy between the two of them. The children, also, started to take more pride in their own rooms and began to be respectful of the parents' room. The order continued to spread to the rest of the house and to the way the family interacted with each other.

MY FAMILY/YOUR FAMILY

Most extended families are wonderful and caring. Sometimes the caring is taken too far or is shown in the wrong way. Marta and Joseph got married and settled down in the same town as Marta's parents. Their story shows the vital need for couples to set boundaries of their own.

Every day just after Joseph left for work Marta's mother came over. She spent the whole day with Marta, telling her what to do and how to do it. She wouldn't let Marta go shopping alone. Just before Joseph would get home, her mother would leave. Part of the everyday conversation consisted of Marta's mother telling her daughter what a poor husband Joe was and how the daughter had married so far beneath herself. Marta didn't know what to do and would say things like, "Mom, Joseph is a good man" or "You just don't know Joseph."

This went on for several years until Joseph had a change of job and they moved many miles away. This didn't slow mother down—she phoned every day with many of the same messages as well as anger at Joe for taking her daughter away. All of this was very hurtful to Joseph and put a real strain on the marriage. In therapy, Marta learned about boundaries and how to set them with her mother. She even practiced the phone call she would make to her mother by role-playing the conversation.

The day came when Marta felt ready to call her mother. Marta reported she followed the script pretty well and said, "Mom, all these years of the conversations concerning Joseph have hurt me deeply. I love Joseph very much and I love you. I will no longer listen to any conversations where Joseph is put down. If that happens again, I will hang up and talk to you later when Joseph is being talked about respectfully."

She then reported that this helped her have the courage to tell her mother of some other hurts. "I remembered to be kind, gentle, respectful, and firm. To my surprise, mother listened very well, asked a few questions, acted a little hurt, and we hung up without too many tears. I also remembered: Treat her normally.

"A few days later, I had a good reason to call my mother to tell her about one of our sons who had a minor injury. I talked to her normally, as though nothing had happened. The conversation was a little strained at first, then it was good. Things have been much better with Mom and she doesn't say bad things about Joseph anymore. This is such a relief."

It is hard to understand the motivation of this mother or the reason she seemed to think what she was doing was a caring thing for her daughter, yet many couples go through similar scenarios. Some families build a fierce loyalty with blood kin to such an extent that they push out anyone who is not blood. In-laws are not blood, so the spouse is pushed out of the acceptable circle of family. Grandchildren are blood so they are drawn in. Those who are doing the drawing in believe they are showing great care for their children and don't seem to recognize the damage they are doing to their child's marriage. Often, the excluded spouse is talked about in very derogatory terms. This will go on until a boundary is set to preserve the marriage and closeness of the husband and wife. The spouse who is drawn in must set the boundary by saying something like, "I will not be coming to the family gatherings without my spouse and I will not have my spouse talked about in any derogatory

> THERE ARE NO BOUNDARIES IN A CHILD'S MIND WHEN IT COMES TO GETTING WHATEVER HE OR SHE WANTS.

way." This takes courage and follow through and must be done to preserve the marriage.

When tragedy strikes one of your parents, there may be expectations and demands placed on one of you by your extended family. In some cases, the family expects the oldest son or daughter to take over the responsibilities that formerly belonged to the deceased parent. Other siblings sometimes expect money, clothing, food, repairs, even housing for themselves. Or they expect the older sibling to take care of the surviving parent. It is amazing how much guilt siblings can apply to get these needs met and the amount of pressure it puts on a marriage. There may be a level of help you can give when there is a genuine need without putting your marriage in jeopardy. Whatever you decide to do, however, must be agreed upon by both husband and wife. If the requests exceed your ability to meet them, then boundaries must be set by the spouse whose extended family is applying the pressure. He or she may use a comment such as, "I wish we could help, but we are not able to at this time." That is the only way it will work; otherwise, there will be more animosity and further withdrawal.

In Secret #2: Keep Your Mate at the Top of Your List, there are a couple of good examples of setting boundaries when surviving parents are putting excessive demands on your time and energies. Please go back and review the section Extended Family Pressures. These examples show effective ways of setting boundaries kindly.

BOUNDARIES WITH CHILDREN

Parenting, though wonderful and worth the effort, is a challenge that puts unbelievable pressures on a marriage. To reiterate, a child's main job is "to get his or her needs met at all costs." Children will only grow up when they have to. There are no natural boundaries in a child's mind when it comes to getting whatever he or she wants. Children become very adept at playing one parent against the other and will do so until they find out it no longer works. The strange thing is that it is we who teach our children how to manipulate us. Boundaries are learned and must be taught by the parents. When these boundaries are not clear, consistent, or followed up on, then we teach our children how to get around us.

Notice when you read Secret #11: Raise Your Kids Together that unless you and your spouse draw your boundaries together they don't work. Boundaries help a child know what the real world is like and that a world without boundaries is unreal and creates expectations that cannot be met. When parents work together in setting these boundaries they grow closer and create a stable environment for themselves and their children.

SECOND MARRIAGES (BLENDED FAMILIES)

Second marriages are often successful, though almost always difficult. What makes them difficult? They have the same challenges as first marriages plus they are littered with the baggage accumulated in the first marriage. This baggage consists of unresolved problems and issues that are brought about by the divorce, along with the fact that if there are children there will always be at least one ex-spouse to deal with.

Sadly, it seems that many ex-spouses have to prove to the world that the divorce was not their fault and they are determined that their ex cannot and will not succeed at anything. The weapon they use to ensure this is the children. This sounds preachy and pessimistic, but my experience shows that, for the most part, it's true. Of course there are many divorces where the ex-spouses work out their differences and get along but these are too few and far between.

> SECOND MARRIAGES HAVE THE SAME CHALLENGES AS FIRST MARRIAGES PLUS THEY ARE LITTERED WITH THE BAGGAGE ACCUMULATED FROM THE FIRST MARRIAGE.

Why would an ex-spouse tell his or her children that they don't need to obey the rules of the other parent? I have seen cases where this and worse happens—all in the name of getting even. If the ex-spouse remarries, there is an all-out effort to make life as miserable as possible so that the new marriage will fail, proving to the world that the ex-spouse was the louse. There seems to be a fear that if the new marriage succeeds then "I might have to admit that I had a part in the failure of our marriage."

If you are divorced and are doing any of the above, not only are you messing up the lives of your children, you are messing up your own life by expending energies that could be put to use making your own new marriage successful. Or if you are being victimized by a vindictive former mate, you need to draw some boundaries and minimize the effect of his or her vindictiveness on you. Remember that peace at all costs does not work—you'll end up being a doormat to your children and your ex-spouse, unable to fully function in your current marriage. Being peaceful with the right boundaries does work. And this can happen when spouses work together in determining boundaries they both can support.

There are many emotions that accompany a divorce— anger, fear, guilt, and loss of control are only some of them. Guilt is often one of the guiding emotions. "Look at what I have put my children through—they will be scarred all their lives. If I don't make things easier for them the scarring will be deeper, and besides they may not want to live with me or visit me. Then I will not have any influence on them." Face it, the children are the real victims of a divorce and they will be scarred, even more so if the parents are at cross-purposes in raising them.

This is exemplified in the case of Walt and Suzanne: They both had been married before and had children from their first marriages. Both of their ex-spouses are determined to ruin Walt and Suzanne's marriage. They are doing everything in their power to turn the children against them and their marriage. Walt had a good relationship with all of his children until he remarried. Suzanne had a fairly good relationship with her children even though their father had been demanding and abusive. The destructive efforts of their former mates have put great pressure on the marriage and have fueled the feelings of anger, sadness, guilt, and resentment toward the ex-spouse, which are often dumped on the current spouse. Because of these problems, most of Walt and Suzanne's energy is centered on the children, which leaves little time or energy to build their marriage. They find themselves at odds with each other because they have not agreed upon their boundaries.

All couples in blended families must set effective boundaries by following these three steps:

1. Make a decision regarding how you will deal with abusive talk by your ex-spouses. Suzanne's ex would call on the telephone and tell her how terrible she is and what a poor mother she was and is. She said, "I would listen to his tirades, feel terrible, and believe what he said. After he got through, I would be angry, hurt, and bitter and would often inflict those feelings on Walt." She learned to set boundaries with her ex by saying to him when he started his abusive comments, "I will be happy to talk with you when I am spoken to respectfully. Until then, good-bye." She would say this kindly and hang up. Little by little he changed his abusive way of speaking to her because she was consistent in holding to her boundary.

2. Decide together the basic set of rules for your home. This is often difficult because each parent seems to think that his or her children are in need of exceptions. You need to ask yourselves these questions:

➤ If these children were born to us, what would we expect of them?

➤ What rules can we agree upon?

➤ How can we make this work?

➤ What do we need to do when we disagree on a certain point?

➤ What is the goal we are working toward?

To make this work, you each must be willing to do some things differently than you have in the past. Remember, this is now your home together, and when you are comfortable with the rules, the children can sense that comfort and unity.

Children of divorce are really no different than children of intact families other than they have a few more weapons to use to get their needs met as they try to adapt to two different households. Some of Walt's and Suzanne's children have become abusive to them and have physically damaged their home in fits of anger. Suzanne's feelings of guilt and fear have caused her to excuse the children's bad behavior. The children use her guilt to keep a battle going between Walt and Suzanne. Walt's children use the "You don't love me as much as Suzanne and her children" phrase. Both sets of children witnessed how divided Walt and Suzanne are over rules and boundaries.

In cases like this the challenge is to disarm or minimize the additional weapons and not give either the children or the ex-spouses more weapons. This can only be done when you both work out a mutually agreeable plan. When a child says, "You don't love me as much as Suzanne and her children," this is usually an attempt to manipulate you or to bend some rule. The answer could be, "I love you very much and the rule still stands." When there is consistency within the home this has a greater chance to work.

3. Normalize your children's experience within your household and let them be loved as children of an intact family. Do not put them in the middle of any disagreement and do not use them as messengers to your ex-spouse. Remember, the only person and place you can control is your own

self and *your* home. When your children see respect shown between their divorced parents, even though there are differences, and respect shown in the new marriage, then they have a better chance of adapting to the shift between two households, even though the boundaries may be different at each home. The ideal is for divorced parents to set similar boundaries for their children in each of their homes so that the children do not have to keep adjusting. Unfortunately, this is rarely done.

This is a long way of saying that boundaries in a divorced and blended family situation are desperately needed. There is the possibility that your child may not come visit you or may want to go live with the other parent. The danger of this happening, however, is greater when there are no boundaries. Keep in mind that boundaries need to be *kind, gentle, respectful,* and *firm.* If the first three attributes—kind, gentle, respectful—are the normal way your home is run, then when the firm is needed, it will work. It will work because you two are holding on to each other and have a united stand. A marriage and a home that are based on these principles are desirable and irresistible.

Carl and Leta found this out. Here's their story:

"We met and married after we each had had a poor marriage," said Carl. "I wanted to be as healed and emotionally healthy as I could be, so I took time to work through my issues from my first marriage before seriously dating."

"I, too, had issues to work through so I went to a therapist to help me work through them," Leta remarked.

"We met and fell in love. During our courtship we began to decide how our home would be and how we would work at blending our eight children. Respect and kindness were going to be our main principles to each other, our children, and our ex-spouses regardless of what they may do," said Carl. "We needed to work together on setting the rules of our home so there would be a consistency in our lives and our children's."

Leta said, "My ex was not very involved with my children so they bonded with Carl very quickly."

"My ex was a different story," remarked Carl, "she is in and out of our lives in a way that disrupts the family. She plays the manipulation game by attempting to buy or bribe the children to get their love and keep them away from our home."

"When the bribes and promises are not followed through with, we're the ones who have to pick up the broken hearts and fallen spirits," said Leta. "For instance, Carl's ex would call up the boys to go out for a birthday meal and time together and not even show up. There we were left with a child crying and not able to understand why their mother didn't care.

Carl frowned and said, "The child support was raised to a very high figure. My daughter came crying to us saying that her mother would not give her clothes for her last year in school. It was just like a child playing one parent against the other only at a distance. We were sympathetic but had to hold to the boundary that the clothes had to come from her mother who had the money. As difficult as this was, we knew we had to set this boundary and leave the solution in the hands of her mother."

"We decided to make our home as consistent as possible," said Leta. "Our aim is to have some things that the children can count on. Sometimes this is very hard because of the high demands of Carl's job. We have been to out-of-town games and concerts that the children were involved in even though we had to drive at excessive speeds to get there on time. We also set up a night for the children to invite their friends over for games and fun. This night is constant whether some children are bribed away by his ex or not."

"This has been extremely hard and has put a lot of strain and stress on our marriage," stated Carl. "It would be impossible if we were not working together and, for the most part, in agreement with how to handle the challenges. As a result, we are happily approaching our tenth anniversary.

It is hard enough to maintain boundaries when you are the intact natural parents. But when there are four people vying for parenthood rights, the task is extremely difficult. The need for you, as husband and wife, to draw together and to work in harmony is essential.

BEGIN TODAY

Boundaries are important to yourself and others. What boundaries do you have? Now that you have read this chapter, have you discovered any that you need to begin enforcing? This would be a good time to list the ones you think would enhance your marriage, then choose one and begin working on it today.

Boundaries are the mortar that holds you together as an individual and give you and your spouse something to hold on to. They are the building materials that make you a definable being. When they are set kindly, gently, respectfully, and firmly and for the right reasons, they work. They bring order and peace out of chaos. They are your principles and values in action. They make it possible for you to build a loving marriage relationship.

Raise Your Kids Together

*Children have more need of models
than of critics.*—JOSEPH JOUBERT

WHOSE JOB IS IT?

There you are at the concert, both of you, watching your teenage daughter play a concerto, and it's a dream come true. She gets a standing ovation, and as you jump to your feet and applaud more vigorously than anyone there, smiling from ear to ear, you look at each other and can't explain the feeling; but it's okay because you don't have to—you're both experiencing the joy equally. All the nagging and enduring of endless practices with missed notes and monotonous tunes, the less than perfect recitals, and the scraping together of money to pay for the lessons has finally rewarded you and you are exhilarated. No one else in the whole audience, not even Grandma, can feel the love and pride that the two of you feel. That's the glory of united parenting.

It is not a job for one. It takes both parents working together to be able to enjoy the happy moments of success and to cry together over the sad times when children come close to breaking your hearts. Parenting is not an easy

TOO MANY MARRIAGES ARE BROKEN OR AT LEAST WOUNDED BY PARENTING PROBLEMS.

job, even when you've got relatively easy kids. Some of you are thinking, *Does anybody ever have "relatively easy kids"? We certainly don't!* Indeed, while some parents experience the relief of having one, rarely ever do all children in a family fall into the category. And that's a good thing—the world needs a few strong-willed, bullheaded, doggedly determined types to lead noble causes. That's not a bad thing to keep in mind when you're dealing with your own little Joan of Arc. Another thing to keep in mind is that all the different types of personalities that parents bring into the world will likely make it just fine if the couples are united in their parenting. And your marriage will flourish in the process.

Too many marriages are broken or at least wounded by parenting problems. Parenting provides a fertile battleground where you can easily be sucked into an unnecessary war between you and your spouse. Parenting is not a popularity contest between the mother and father. It's a joint effort that requires your greatest skills and determination to be "one in purpose" though different in some of your approaches. When this oneness is accomplished, your marriage will be greatly enhanced.

PLAYING ONE PARENT AGAINST THE OTHER

Too often kids end up in far greater trouble because Mom and Dad can't agree on how to raise them. Couples need to remember that a child's main job is to get his needs met at all costs. If that means getting Mom upset at Dad in order to get those needs met, then junior will do just that. Children are very shortsighted. They cannot see the end from the beginning. They want a secure home, but the very thing they are doing when they play one against the other will undermine that security. All they know is that if they get Dad upset enough to yell, and maybe even spank, then Mom will come to their rescue and they're "off the hook." What they don't understand is that this very thing can drive a wedge between

Mom and Dad, and if animosity continues to fester between them then junior may no longer have the security of both parents. Divorce may occur and junior will find himself sobbing in his bed, missing one or the other of his parents.

IF YOU DON'T AGREE WITH HOW YOUR SPOUSE IS HANDLING A SITUATION, TALK IT OVER LATER OUT OF EARSHOT OF THE CHILD.

Kids can't figure that out, and they shouldn't have to. That's your job. As husband and wife you need to talk about your child-raising philosophies and support each other. It is far better for your children if the one not doing the disciplining at the moment stays out of it, even if you don't agree, than it is to jump in and defend the child. Of course, abuse of a child is the exception. A little swat on the rear is not abuse. If you don't agree with how your spouse is handling a situation, talk it over later, calmly and intelligently, out of earshot of the child. Decide what's best for the child and be willing to compromise in order to be united when dealing with the children. If you are not, it can create real problems in your marriage as well as greater discipline problems with the kids.

PLAN YOUR STRATEGIES

Imagine for a minute that two people, Conrad and Helen, are representatives of a computer company. They are partners and have been selected by their company to make a presentation to a large firm, and if they are successful in selling their product to this firm's executives, they will receive huge bonuses. How well will Conrad and Helen plan their strategies together? You can bet that a lot of time, energy, and creative planning will go into their preparation. They will go forth as a team with a united goal. What do you think would happen if, during their actual presentation, they began to be critical of each other's methods of presentation. What if, at one point, Helen said to Conrad, in front of the firm's executives, "Conrad, don't say that. You know our company can't meet that deadline." And

Conrad replied with, "Why don't you just butt out, Helen. I know what our company can and can't do!" How much confidence will the firm have in these two reps? What is the likelihood of a sale if this were to happen?

How much confidence will your children have in you as parents if you argue in front of them about a family rule, and loudly and clearly you let it be known what you think is wrong with your mate's approach to the situation that has suddenly arisen? All confidence will be lost and the children's energies will simply be turned to getting their own way by allying with whoever is pulling for the easiest way out for them. In this case a child learns that he can get whatever he wants if he can get Mom and Dad mad at each other.

Learn from the sales reps and have planning meetings, just the two of you, to discuss what you will and won't do in raising your children. Don't panic when I say "meetings." They really don't have to be long and drawn out. They can be short and to the point, but they must happen or there will be no unity. And you can't just have one meeting and think you're done. Needs change; children grow and require different curfews, responsibilities, and expectations.

DECIDE IN ADVANCE HOW YOU ARE GOING TO WORK TOGETHER AS A COUPLE.

Here are some items you need to discuss and agree upon.

➤ Supporting each other: Make a plan for those times when you will have differing opinions.

➤ Children's chores: Decide what are reasonable jobs for each child at their age level and when they need to be done.

➤ Curfews: Many parents have a weekday curfew and a weekend curfew that vary depending on the age of the child. If there is a special event you may need to consider a different curfew for that night.

➤ Homework and other activities: Decide when homework needs to be completed each day. Generally, the sooner it's done the better things go. Then they are free to participate in other activities.

➤ Punishments: Agree on what kinds of punishments you will give to your children in response to misbehavior. Will you or will you not spank your child? If you decide spanking is appropriate on some occasions, spell out exactly what those are. If you decide to use spankings, do so only on rare occasions and use it to drive a point home without bruising a bottom. Discuss other, more positive ways to discipline.

➤ Exceptions: When exceptions need to be made decide that you will excuse yourselves and go to another room to discuss and agree upon an alternative, then present it together, even if, at times, you have to take turns compromising.

Whatever the needs, do your best to decide in advance how you are going to work together as a couple. Clearly understand what the family rules are. Generally, it works well to include the children in making the rules at a separate time. They will be more willing to comply if they have input. You are the powers that be and have the final say, however. The bonus you both will receive as a result of this preparation will be far greater than anything a company could ever offer its reps.

For times when you are suddenly presented with a problem and you don't agree on the solution, here's a dialogue you could try. Let's say your son wants to go to a ball game, but he hasn't done his homework as he was told to do. Your husband says to him, "You can't go to the game until your homework is done and that's all there is to it."

Your child turns to you and says, "Mom, Dad's not being fair! This is an important game and I should be able to go. I'll catch up on my homework later."

You know how important the game is to your son and you are tempted at that moment to say to your husband, "Don't be so hard on him. This game really matters to him." Don't say it!

Instead, look your son in the eyes and kindly say, "I know that's disappointing for you. Dad has told you what needs to be done, however, and I support him in his decision. Dad and I will be happy to let you go next time if your homework is all caught up." You can say that honestly because the two of you have previously discussed and decided together on this family rule. Your child will learn responsibility and your husband will adore you for supporting him in his disciplinary efforts. When he does likewise and stays out of it when you take action, even if he doesn't agree, it will also work. Support each other. Don't let your children build a wall between you. If you are determined in doing this, your children will blossom and so will your marriage.

COMPROMISE IS NECESSARY

Usually one spouse will be more strict with the children than the other. Jillian said, "If I didn't step in and discipline the kids, they wouldn't amount to a thing. Harley is just a big softie. He let's the kids get away with murder." Harley said that Jillian is too strict and he thinks the kids need to be shown a little more understanding. When this combination of disciplinary philosophies exists it may make it difficult, but it's actually a very good thing. Two overly strict parents could create an adversarial relationship with the child. When one is more easygoing than the other it allows for a little more compassion and a different look at what might be done for the child. There has to be compromise with both husband and wife participating in the disciplining methods. If it's always "his way" or "her way" then it won't work. Neither spouse has to be right all of the time. If that happens, then one or the other will feel less valued and that, too, will drive a wedge between you.

Sylvia B. Rimm, Ph.D., director of the Family Achievement Clinic at MetroHealth Medical Center in Cleveland, said, "compromise can mean agreeing to go Dad's way for some things, Mom's way for others. . . . to achieve this requires planning." She gave an example of parents who had allowed their three-year-old daughter to sleep with them since she was a baby. The mother, Tamra, said, "Chad wants to end it now and get her to sleep in her own room, but I want to continue letting her sleep with us until she's comfortable sleeping on her own." As you might imagine, their romantic life is suffering.

Dr. Rimm suggested that "Mom compromise by spending special time with her daughter before bedtime, [and] Dad allow the child to sleep with Mom and Dad during a bad thunderstorm or if she has a nightmare." She explained that "this compromise has a threefold advantage: It offers the child a path to becoming independent from her parents; it allows Mom to maintain her closeness with her child; and it lets Dad reconnect with his wife."[44] The marriage relationship needs to be a priority in all your efforts to meet your children's needs. Had this situation continued it could have had a devastating effect on their marriage.

Many unforeseen parenting issues come along on a regular basis where you may not see eye to eye. Perhaps your husband has handled a situation in a way that you believe really is unfair to the child. He may not have had all the facts that you have, and if he had, in all likelihood he would have made a different decision. His discipline has caused your daughter to run out of the room and into hers in tears. Let her go. She'll be okay. Don't discount what he has done in front of her. Talk to your husband alone and bring him up to date on the missing facts. He may see that he has made his decision in error. At that point both of you can go to your daughter with a new decision. He needs to be the spokesperson telling the new decision because he was the one issuing the previous mandate. That's a vitally important point. He could say something like, "Mom and I talked it over and I didn't realize (whatever it was that you didn't understand). Now that I understand, I think it would be all right after all for you to go with your friends."

Your daughter will know you are united in your decision and she will likely hug you both and appreciate your understanding. And the two of you will feel like partners, not enemies defending your positions. Another plus will be that your daughter will know that married people can disagree and talk through a problem.

There is also the possibility that, after talking it over, you realize that your husband's decision was in the best interest of your daughter. Then accept it. She'll be just fine as long as you both show an increase in your love for her while supporting the discipline that was given.

SHARE THE HEAVY LOAD

When one spouse is always saddled with the difficult job of handling a problem child it can feel overwhelming. Trisha illustrates this point in her story:

> Our fifteen-year-old son, Neil, was constantly getting in fights with a certain group of boys at his school. Neil is a good kid and has some nice friends who he hangs out with most of the time, and we couldn't figure out why these other boys were beating up on him. I kept getting calls from the principal to come in to meet with him and take my expelled-for-the-day child home. After a couple of those experiences I asked my husband, Sid, to go talk to the principal. He said, "You go, I have to work. Besides, it's the mother's job to take care of this kind of thing." I said, "I'm working, too, and I went last time. It's your turn." But he wouldn't and I had to go again. My boss wasn't any more pleased about it than his boss would have been.
>
> When we talked this over with Neil, he said these boys were calling him names and he got sick of it and punched one of them. I told Neil he needed to keep his hands to himself and ignore them. My husband

said, "No. You need to defend your honor; smack him a good one so he'll think twice about calling you names again."

I was so disgusted with Sid for saying that. Now I felt like I was battling with both my son and my husband. So I ended up talking to my son privately, telling him again to keep his hands to himself, that he needed to live the golden rule, and things like that. His behavior didn't change and he went on getting into trouble several times more. Finally, I found out that Neil was provoking these fights by doing his own name calling and bullying. That's when Sid realized that his counsel to our son was not helping. He then joined me and firmly said to Neil. "Now that I know what's been happening, I have one thing to say: Stop provoking these fights! No more hitting anyone. Do you understand?" At last, we were working together. The fights stopped and there were no more calls from the principal. It seemed that once my husband and I were on the same bandwagon everything changed. And Sid and I are getting along better as an added plus.

Sherman and Gayla understood the power of parenting together. Their twelve-year-old daughter, Mia, was mentally impaired and in special education classes, along with some classes with the "normal" kids at school. Gayla, a stay-at-home mother of five, was often called by the school over problems Mia was causing or to discuss the latest "expert" opinion on all the things Mia *couldn't* do. She kept Sherman abreast of all the goings on. She was dreading one particular day when the school had scheduled extensive testing for Mia. Gayla didn't want to be there alone, so she asked Sherman to arrange his schedule so he could accompany her. He could easily have said, "You can handle it just fine. You've been doing it all along, and, anyway, I don't have time." But he didn't. He understood her need to have him there, giving her the moral support she needed, and even more than that, stepping in with his own opinion regarding their daughter's needs. They both knew the school was trying to push their daughter out of the normal school setting because having her there presented challenges for the teachers. Gayla had fought hard to get her as far as she had come. She and Sherman were united in their desire to give Mia every possible opportunity for a good life.

After the testing results were tallied, Sherman and Mia, the teachers, the psychologist, and the principal discussed the possibilities. Sherman's opinion was extremely valuable, as was Gayla's, and the school set a plan to work with Mia in a more cooperative way, even though the tests showed she would need significant help. Two standing together become a much stronger force than one standing alone.

That works in less dramatic situations as well, such as children needing help with homework. How do you work that out together? If one is continually stuck with the job while the other is enjoying a favorite TV program, it's not fair. Animosity will grow. It's no fun being the one who always has to sacrifice leisure time to help the kids. In your planning discussions, decide who will help with what. Maybe the wife is better at helping with English while the husband is good at solving math problems. Or maybe one of you will help one evening and one the next. Or maybe one will help one child and the other another child. Share the load and it won't be so heavy to carry.

That holds true with chores as well. Children respond well when a parent works with them until they get the hang of how to do the job. When both husband and wife join in teaching work skills it lightens the burden for all.

What about back-to-school nights and parent/teacher conferences? These, too, need two. When both parents are in on these events then they will be more knowledgeable about what their children are experiencing at school and what special help they may need. Of course, there are times when both may not be able to attend. The two of you need to work out a system that works with your schedules and demands. The main goal here is for both of you to be in on your children's educational struggles and successes, and to agree on your rules regarding school.

> COMPLIMENTING YOUR MATE FOR BEING A GOOD PARENT FOSTERS DEEP FEELINGS OF LOVE.

Shuttling kids to music and dance lessons, games, and other activities often ends up being the wife's job, particularly if she's a stay-at-home mom. When a husband jumps in and helps with this duty it can be very relieving. If he can't, then an acknowledgment and expression of gratitude to his wife is in order. Keep in mind the power of those simple courtesy words, "please" and "thank you." Praise your wife for her dedication to the kids. In fact, praise each other for the things you each do in the parenting process. Being complimented by your mate for being a good parent is one of the highest forms of praise you can give. It fosters deep feelings of love.

STAND BY EACH OTHER

It isn't always easy to take unpopular stands with your children—and it is crucial that you and your mate stand together, no matter how hard. Take the example of Edgar and Caroline. Their seventeen-year-old daughter, Celia, had just been asked to the prom. Not only did she want to go to the prom, but she wanted to go with Greg, a fine young man whom both parents knew and liked. Greg had asked her and Celia was ecstatic. After telling her mother the happy news, she went to her room, full of excitement. A few minutes later Caroline had a strong premonition that they shouldn't let her go with Greg. She told Edgar about her feeling and he said, "This will be hard, but you need to tell her." He didn't question his wife's premonition. Caroline went to Celia's room and told her the news. She said, "It was so hard because I didn't have any reason, except that I felt she shouldn't go. It would have been easier if I had something against Greg, but I didn't." Celia was stunned. She tried to talk her mother out of it. Then she went to her father and tried to reason with him. He was sympathetic, but supported his wife and asked his daughter to obey them and break the date with Greg. Celia cried herself to sleep and the next day reluctantly broke the date.

The night of the prom arrived and Celia spent it in her room sobbing. Greg had asked someone else, and all night long she imagined the wonderful time they must be having. Her heart was broken. The next morning she was at a church youth activity with friends and could hardly believe what she heard. She ran home and told her parents the news. Greg and his date had been in an accident on the way to the prom and both of them were killed. Crying tears of sorrow and gratitude she threw her arms around her parents and thanked them for insisting she break the date. Edgar and Caroline held each other and their precious daughter and were grateful that they had stood by each other in this unusual happening. This couple said many prayers of gratitude that night. Being willing to trust the instincts of your mate in difficult situations is very important to your marriage, to your family solidarity, and maybe even to the life of one of your children.

Strange things happen when you raise children. Rozlynn and Cramer never dreamed that their happy energetic daughter, Carla, would end up with a serious eating disorder. Added to the life-threatening nature of this condition was the sad fact that Cramer wouldn't admit that it was a real problem. Rozlynn had to carry the load herself, taking Carla to doctors, discovering that there really wasn't much help out there for her daughter. She said, "It was a sad, lonely time for me as I faced this problem on my own." The more she learned about anorexia the more frightened she became. She knew her daughter could lose her life if she didn't get the right medical help. Still Cramer refused to recognize the seriousness of the situation. Now Rozlynn's worry for her daughter was accompanied by anger toward her husband. It became a terrible strain on their marriage. Rozlynn said she couldn't understand his response to this critical problem. She said, "Had it not been for support groups, I couldn't have made it." When Carla was finally hospitalized Cramer began to grasp the depth of the situation.

Somehow their marriage survived, but barely. Now Cramer has joined in and has become active in creating a Web site to help other parents learn more about this frightening illness. Their marriage is now stronger than it's been for some time, but still has a way to go. Rozlynn said, "I'm working on putting my anger aside for all those years when he wouldn't join me in this fight for Carla's life, but things are definitely better than they have been for a long time. Now it's my job to forgive."

There are times when a mate can't seem to face reality. That's the time you simply move forward, as Rozlynn did, and do what has to be done for the child's sake, hoping your mate will join you in the tough task of helping your child. Denial of a problem is extremely difficult to deal with; however, it will only be made worse by adding divorce to the tragedy.

DRAW ON EACH OTHER'S STRENGTHS

Darci and Quinn faced the critical problem of learning that their son, Sean, was using drugs. This is a horror no parent wants to have to deal with, but unfortunately it happens. Here's Darci's account of their discovery:

> Sean began acting distant and grouchy and he wouldn't obey our family rules, especially the curfew time. This just wasn't like him—he had been a good kid. We knew his friends were not the kind we wanted him to hang out with but we didn't realize the power they had over him. We had no idea they were into drugs. When

he started to disobey us Quinn's strict disciplinary nature went into full force. I couldn't stand to see how
terribly strict he was. He took away privileges, denied
him use of the car, wouldn't give him any money, and
on it went.

It's not my nature to be strict. I felt sorry for Sean
and, at times right in front of Sean, I would tell Quinn
he was being too strict. Sean figured out that I would
give in and believe his false stories and excuses. He
knew his dad would not, so he would come to me for
sympathy and a handout. I became his ally, with Quinn
being the enemy to both of us. It was a disaster. Quinn
would get very upset with me for not supporting him
and I would get equally upset with him for being too
strict. I ended up spending nearly every night crying
myself to sleep over what was happening to our son
and to us.

Finally, I could see that what I was doing was making it possible for Sean to do whatever he darn well
pleased and his behavior was getting worse and worse.
That's when Quinn and I had a serious talk and jointly
decided what must be done. We both recognized that I
was a wimp when it came to Sean. So we decided that
whenever Sean would come to me for something or
try to get out of keeping the rules, I would send him
to his father.

The next time Sean came to me and said, "Mom,
I need ten dollars." (He would always make up some
legitimate-sounding reason for needing it, and I would
give in. But not anymore.) I said, "Go talk to your father." I stuck to our plan. Quinn made Sean tow the
line and wouldn't give in. When Sean came home past
the curfew time, Quinn locked the door and wouldn't
let him in. I could hardly stand it, but in my heart I
knew we had to do it for Sean to understand that we
meant what we said.

Sean's behavior toward me changed and he started yelling at me in a rude abusive manner. I would say, "Don't speak to me like that." Quinn would stop him and enforce the rules. It got really ugly sometimes, but it was the only way we could deal with it. When we found out he had been on drugs, we got him into a drug rehab center. It took a lot of hard, painful work and lots of tough love on our part, but he overcame the habit and found new friends.

The thing that made it work out was that Quinn and I were finally working together. I know our son would never have received the help he needed if we hadn't come together with a plan and stuck to it. That was ten years ago and he is still drug free and has a very good relationship with us; and Quinn and I have developed a much closer relationship with each other.

Husband and wife need to draw on each other's strengths. Darci knew her limitations and drew on Quinn's strength. There may be a time when the tables are turned and a gentle approach is the best approach. If you can't control your anger in certain situations with a child, decide that your spouse will do the disciplining in those cases. The key is to talk about what approach your child needs and decide together how you will handle each situation and support each other.

Telling a child to "Go talk to your father" or "Go ask your mother" works when both parents have agreed to it. If one parent sends a child to the other to get out of solving the problem, it doesn't work. That opens the door for children to play one parent against the other. Whoever is the one faced with the problem is the one who needs to handle it. If reinforcements are needed then call for help and stand together.

IF ONE PARENT SENDS A CHILD TO THE OTHER TO GET OUT OF SOLVING A PROBLEM IT OPENS THE DOOR TO PLAYING ONE PARENT AGAINST THE OTHER.

CHILDREN WANT BOTH PARENTS

Have you seen the television spot that ended with the statement: "Family—isn't it about time?" It showed the father crawling in bed late one night, and just as he was settling in to sleep after a hard day's work, his little three-year-old daughter, who had awakened, came into the room with a storybook. She went straight to her father and said, "Daddy, can you read me a story?" Exhausted he whispered, "Go ask Mommy." She went over to the other side of the bed and said, "Mommy, can Daddy read me a story?" The look on Daddy's face let everyone know that he was about to spend some time with his little girl.

Children demand time when they're young; unless we have made it a practice, however, they will scarcely allow it when they are teenagers. Yet inside they are crying for it. There is nothing that tells a child more emphatically that he is loved than spending time with him. It is like food for a starving child. The story of a young college student sharing her experience after returning from Christmas vacation is a telling illustration of this point. As she stood in front of a group of her peers, with tears running down her cheeks, she said:

My parents were divorced when I was just three years old. I lived with my mother and spent visiting time with my dad. All my life I dreamed of the day I could spend time with them together. It never happened. It was either Mom or Dad, but never both at the same time. I watched other kids with their parents and felt heartbroken that I could not have that same experience. (Her tears started flowing as she continued.)

Finally, after all these years, I got my wish. For Christmas I gave my mother a ticket to the local roller skating rink. I gave my father the same gift and bought one for myself. I told them that the only thing I wanted for Christmas was to be at the roller skating rink with

both of them there. I knew they weren't very friendly
with each other, so I didn't know if they would come.
They did! During one of the skating "dances" I asked
Mom to hold my right hand while Dad held my left.
They consented and the three of us skated around the
rink together. There I was, at last, with both of my
parents together . . . with me. It was the happiest feeling I have ever had in my entire life.

About that time everyone there was crying. What a tender
example of how important it is for children to have parents
unite in their behalf.

BLENDED FAMILY CHALLENGES

This brings up another important parenting need. If you are
in a second marriage, trying to blend your families, who does
the disciplining? Sides can easily be taken when it's "his"
child or "my" child. Bethany found herself in this situation.
Her new husband, Stan, decided it was his responsibility to be
the missing fatherly disciplinarian for her daughter, Danielle.
Danielle became defiant and resentful, and Bethany was upset at Stan for trying to take over her job. Bethany said,
"When we realized what was happening we talked it over and
decided that I would be the one to tell Danielle what the
rules were and Stan would be there to back me up." If
Danielle disobeyed when Bethany wasn't home and Stan was,
he would say, for example, "Your mother said you were not
to go, so you may not go." If Bethany chose to let Danielle
do something that Stan did not agree with, they would talk
about it privately, and the final decision would be Bethany's
and he would support her in it.

By using this method, Bethany and Stan have had much
more peace with Danielle and with each other. If you are a
blended family, your children desperately need to see you and
your current spouse working together. And you both need to

experience that cooperation and unity in order to keep your marriage strong. For more help see Secret #10: Set Your Boundaries, under the heading "Second Marriage (Blended Families)."

BOOKS TO READ

Our main focus in this chapter is to build a happier marriage relationship by helping parents discover ways to work together in raising their children. For more specific disciplining techniques and parenting ideas, we suggest these two excellent books: *How to Behave So Your Children Will, Too!* by Sal Severe, Ph.D., and *Back in Control* by Gregory Bodenhamer. These are only two of the many great books that are available to help parents raise happy, productive children.

BEGIN TODAY

Although many other parenting issues will arise, these suggestions will help you in other challenges you may face. To minimize whatever problems you are dealing with right now, refer to the beginning of this chapter and review the list of items that parents need to discuss. Talk together sometime today and decide if there is anything you two need to do to improve your parenting-together skills.

The greatest gift you can give your children *and yourselves* is parents who love each other. There is a feeling of security when children have both parents helping them, guiding them, disciplining them, playing with them, and loving them. And what a beautiful blessing it is to your marriage relationship when you share this vitally important responsibility. It will help you create a love that will last far beyond the time when your children grow up and leave home.

Manage Your Money in Harmony

Money is a terrible master but an excellent servant.—P. T. BARNUM

THE NEED FOR MONEY

We all wish we had a money tree growing in our backyards. Just imagine how easy it would be if we could go out each morning and pick off a few hundred dollar bills to meet the needs of the day. Unfortunately . . . or rather, *fortunately,* it doesn't work that way. The need for money is a driving force that gets us out of bed and moves us into action. The need to obtain it and wisely use it is a great motivating force to the human spirit. Because of this need, talents are developed, interesting careers are honed, and character is enhanced as we learn to work and sacrifice for the support and well-being of ourselves and our loved ones. It takes planning and working together as a couple to meet the family needs, and all couples face the need to obtain money. Living beyond their means is one of the biggest problems couples both young and old face, regardless of their income. It's tempting for young couples to go into debt because they look around and see all that their parents and even some contemporaries have, and they want it now. Money, or the lack of money, is one of the major problems in marriage. This chapter contains some ideas to help you create financial harmony together. Learn from these ideas and see how they might apply to your situation. This chapter does not take the place of a financial professional, but rather it offers some ideas to help you prevent some of the misery couples sometimes experience because of money issues. Many successful couples consult financial planners to keep out of difficulties or to get out of ones they've slipped into. That can be very helpful.

WHO EARNS THE MONEY?

Everything I see in my family therapy practice supports the idea that when the husband takes the responsibility of earning the living for the family, there is greater peace in the marriage and more stability in the family. Most husbands take this responsibility seriously, but when they do not there are problems in the marriage. Of course, there are some exceptions to this, such as illness or disability. And there may be other times, such as job losses, when a couple agrees that the wife will be the provider while the husband cares for the home and the children. Some statistics show that "roughly three-quarters of a million American men stay home with their children."[45] That's a hefty number, but still a very small percentage when compared with the millions of men who do take the major responsibility of providing the family income. There is often a price to be paid when we go against the natural inborn tendencies of men and women. Sometimes it may work well for a period of time and then backfire, taking a terrible toll on your marriage.

Branson and Elaine made the decision that Elaine would provide for their family because her education gave her the ability to bring in a larger income; and it seemed that Branson's efforts proved less productive. As time went on Elaine began to have bitter feelings toward Branson. Her inner need was to have him earn the living while she followed her natural desires to stay home with their young children, or at least to have him put forth sincere effort to get more training or education, so he could eventually take over the major responsibility of providing for the family. When he didn't respond to that need, she left him—a tragic decision that not only hurt both of them but deeply hurt their children. It could have been avoided if Branson had taken his responsibility and if Elaine had set a definite goal about what Branson needed to do, including an acceptable time frame. It would have required more patience on her part and more cooperation on his, but this type of cooperation and understanding can work out well for couples in this situation.

Couples need to seriously consider what course of action will be the best for their marriage and their children. If there are times when the wife needs to work out of the home, it must not mean that the husband abandons his responsibility.

WHERE SHOULD THE MONEY GO?

One of the biggest problems couples have is that they don't agree on where to spend their money once they have it. A wife may want a new outfit while a husband thinks she already has plenty of clothes and the extra money would be better spent on a new fishing rod. After all, with a fishing rod he could provide food for the family. Right? In his mind, at least his desire has a purpose. She thinks his old fishing rod works just fine. It catches all the fish she wants to eat and then some. In her mind, she needs a new outfit more than he needs a new fishing rod. So where does a couple go with this kind of differing opinion? First of all they both must avoid this statement like the plague: "Look, I earn it, so I say where it goes."

Husbands and wives need to plan together and value each other's opinion. Money is a significant factor in your marriage. It is an ever present issue. You need it to pay rent, to

HUSBANDS AND WIVES NEED TO PLAN TOGETHER AND VALUE EACH OTHER'S OPINION.

buy clothes and food. You need it to buy a car, and then you need it to provide upkeep and pay for the car insurance. Everyone needs money. It can't be ignored. When it is ignored, trouble is inevitable. It has to be earned and it has to be spent in a way that benefits the family.

Before you were married you had complete control of your own money. You made all the decisions about what to do with what you had. If you went over your head in debt, then you were the one who had to bail yourself out. When you got married, all of a sudden the question came: Who has control? Whose is what? That's usually when the trouble begins.

IMITATING YOUR PARENTS

You may have grown up with a father who was such a tight-wad that every penny earned was pinched to the point of making spending feel like a sin. Or you may have had a mother whose great pleasure was shopping, not only for herself but for the children. She just had to have the latest fashions, regardless of what the budget would allow. Or maybe one of you had a father who was a worrier, who filled your ears with a continual litany of "I don't know what we're going to do, there just isn't enough money."

These traits are usually passed along to the next generation. Out of the heat of the moment, couples need to discuss their upbringing regarding money and spending, without any accusations or insults. You can learn from the past and then, in an understanding and caring way, develop a plan that works for you. Remember, it will take time as you each learn new methods of dealing with money.

POOL YOUR RESOURCES

Making a plan is a necessity. The plan must be equitable for both—not too rigid, but enough agreed-upon structure to guide the flow of the funds. There was an extreme example of inequity in one of the marriage relationships in Amy Tan's novel *The Joy Luck Club.* Lena and Harold divided everything equally—to the penny. She had to account for every cent spent for the household and so did he. Since both were employed, they added the household expenditures all together and would split the cost 50/50 at the end of the month. This may sound just, but the inequity came in what he considered to be part of the household as opposed to what she did. He was including things that were definitely not in that category and made her delete things she had purchased that she felt definitely were household expenses.

Another inequity became apparent from the difference in their incomes. Harold made seven times more than Lena made and yet she had to pay equal portions. At one point she couldn't take it any longer and became angry, and when he asked her what was wrong, she replied, "Everything . . . the way we account for everything. What we share. What we don't share. I'm so tired of it, adding things up, subtracting, making it come out even. I'm sick of it."[46] His domineering, self-centered attitude killed the love she had had for him, and eventually all she wanted was to be out of the marriage.

IF COUPLES COULD ONLY REMEMBER THAT LOVE SHARES, THEIR LIVES WOULD BE MUCH HAPPIER.

Where is the love when two people become so selfish that they can't contribute generously for the needs of the family—especially when they have extra to give? For a marriage to work, spouses need to pool their resources and then make a plan as to how it will be used for the good of the whole, without comparing incomes or belittling each other. What about the wife, who may be working very hard as a full-time homemaker—or in many cases, working hard out of the home *and* in it? If couples could only remember that *love shares,* their lives would be much happier.

KEEPING GENEROSITY IN BALANCE

There is no question that real love is generous. However, this generosity needs to be tempered with wisdom. The world is full of tempting things that can eat up your money. The advertisements are so appealing that they make you think their product is not just a want, but a real need that you have to have. It's tempting to spend money you don't have, particularly when it's for your spouse. You love her and you want to please her, even spoil her. Basically, you want to make her happy and you think this will help. But it doesn't always work that way. See if you find a familiar ring in Ian and Jessica's story:

It was our wedding anniversary and I wanted to give Jessica a gift that would show the depth of my love for her. She had been through a lot since our marriage five years ago. She was so sick during the pregnancy of our twins. And then when they came, it was overwhelming, especially for her. She's the one who is there all day taking care of them. And she is amazing.

Money has always been tight for us. I work construction and sometimes there are lulls when I don't get many hours. Sometimes the utility bill, or some other bill, is late, but we're making it . . . barely.

It's not the way I pictured our life. I thought I would get plenty of hours and do really well at making enough money and more. She deserves more, especially for our anniversary. I found a beautiful little diamond necklace on sale for $199. I didn't really have the money for it, but I wanted her to have it; so I put it on the credit card. When I gave it to her she was so happy, she cried. She really liked it.

Then when the credit card bill came she cried again, only not because she was touched but because she was crushed. All she said was, "Ian, how are we ever going to pay for this?" I didn't have an answer. She took the necklace back . . . and *I* was crushed.

A GIFT WITH A DEBT ATTACHED IS NO GIFT AT ALL.

What could have happened in Ian and Jessica's case to prevent a good thing from resulting in a feeling of devastation? The solution seems obvious. If he had planned ahead and saved a little at a time so that the gift was purchased with cash, it would have made all the difference. Or he could have bought a much less expensive gift and given it with the same amount of loving appreciation. A gift with a debt attached is no gift at all. Too often the gift then becomes the focus of an argument or the beginning of an ulcer.

Of course, there is another way Jessica could have handled this problem. She could have kept silent about the shock of seeing the credit card bill and tried to cut back in other ways to make sure there was money to pay for it. That would have saved Ian from feeling so sad. Still, it's difficult to justify a gift that the receiver has to help pay for by some other deprivation, unless it's agreed to in advance. There will be a sore spot at some point if there isn't the money to pay for it. Just pay cash and avoid all the problems debt can bring into the marriage.

I had a client whose complaint was the opposite of Jessica's. She said, "My husband never gives me a present . . . for anything." His comment was, "We never have the money." She told him that all she ever really wanted was just a small remembrance, even just a card with a tender message, letting her know he was thinking of her. Sometimes men don't give any gift because they can't give something expensive. JoAnn, a divorced woman, expressing this same disappointment, said, "My ex never gave me a gift. When I would bring it up he'd say he didn't want to give me some cheap little thing. He was waiting until he could give me something that was really worthwhile. Well, that time never came. I think it was a

WHEN BOTH
PARTNERS
EARN THE
LIVING, THEY
NEED TO PLAN
WHERE
THE INCOME
FROM BOTH
PAYCHECKS
WILL GO.

flimsy excuse for not wanting to put forth the effort to do anything."

The giving of gifts to each other needs to be part of your financial plan. If your income is tight, decide in advance how much can be allowed for these gifts. Some couples find this works very well. Plan anniversary celebrations together and save for them, instead of blaming each other if one doesn't remember with a gift. After all, the anniversary belongs to both of you. Special occasions should not be a test of memory or love.

BUILD TRUST

Being able to trust your mate to be wise with the family money is vital to having a happy marriage. Many men work hard and then automatically turn the money over to their wives to use for the family expenses month in and month out. James commented on this practice:

> I never hesitated in doing it because I trust my wife, and she trusts me. We have discussions on where the money needs to go and I know she will follow our plan; and she knows I will, too, or we'll think of an even better one.

When both partners work to earn the living, they need to plan where the income from both paychecks will go. Sometimes women expect their husband's check to cover all the household bills while theirs goes to the things they want to buy. That's not fair. Put the money together and plan. Make a wish list. Sometimes he gets to spend some on just what he wants, and sometimes it's her turn. Be fair, but not rigid. After the household expenditures are taken care of, make a plan for the remainder. Allow for some fun now, and some preparation for the future. Investigate ways to save and invest even a few dollars a month. Over the long run, if it's never touched, it can provide a nest egg.

PERSONAL POCKET CHANGE

Both men and women need to have some "pocket change." It's a terrible feeling to not have any money in your wallet or purse. If spouses can always carry at least a few dollars with them, they don't feel so deprived. This is especially important for a man. Usually the woman has the checkbook and can rely on that. A man will feel pretty depressed if he has nothing in his wallet for all his hard work. It's important for his emotional well-being, even if it's just five dollars.

After experiencing this dead-broke feeling for too long, Blaine finally talked about it to his wife, Sally. He said, "It's very embarrassing to be out on a job and my co-workers say, 'Hey, let's stop and get a Big Gulp,' and I sit and watch, pretending I'm not thirsty because I don't have any money. I hate it." Sally saw how important this was to her husband and realized he didn't need much. "Even just five dollars of my own would be enough," he said. That day they made a decision that they would always do their best to see that he had at least twenty dollars in his wallet.

Everyone needs some money for his or her own use that has no strings attached to it, including not needing to report on how it is used. Figure out how much you can each have and still stay within your budget. Some spouses keep separate checking accounts, deciding which basics they will each pay for. If you try something and it doesn't work, don't be afraid to admit it and try something else, always respecting each other's needs without saying something like, "I knew that wouldn't work." In the end, make sure you come up with a plan that works for both of you.

DON'T SPEND YOUR FUTURE

Some couples spend every cent they have and beyond. They live from paycheck to paycheck with no backup for a problem that may arise. Face it, there will be times when employment is cut back, when medical expenses increase, when a child needs eyeglasses, when the car needs new tires, and so on. Plan for it.

Shauna and Ethan realize how important financial planning is to the stability of their family. Here's Ethan's report of what they do:

> I'm a schoolteacher and love it, but my paycheck is pathetic. Everyone we know earns more than I do. Fortunately, Shauna knows how to stretch a dollar like a magician. Boy, am I lucky I married her. We decided early on in our marriage, even while I was still in school and she was working as a dental assistant, that we should always have some money in a savings account. We decided that one thousand dollars would be our minimum. We had seen other couples struggle to keep afloat when troubles hit—like car brakes needing to be replaced. They had nowhere to go. To us it was a simple decision—save so we will have some place to go.
>
> We were determined to keep it for emergencies and we did. When we used some of it, we would build it back up, no matter how hard it was. The feeling of security was well worth it. Now we have built it well beyond the thousand dollars because I'm beginning my schooling for a master's degree and we're going to need extra to get by.
>
> We have two children and another on the way and Shauna is a stay-at-home mom. She teaches piano lessons to earn a little extra and I work a couple of hours

a day for a landscaping business after school to add more to our income. We pay cash for whatever we buy, or we don't buy it, except for our home and car. It's not easy but we work it out and still have some left for fun. We're both so glad we don't have the strain of multiple debt payments hanging over our heads.

> **WE PAY CASH FOR WHATEVER WE BUY, OR WE DON'T BUY IT.**

Shauna and Ethan have got it! They have a plan and they work their plan . . . together. Besides having money set aside for a rainy day, they have hit upon the key to financial success: Live within your means and pay cash for what you buy.

There are times when either the husband or the wife will find something they really want to buy that the other doesn't feel is necessary or that they just can't afford. A couple came to me struggling with this issue. In fact, just about any time Lillian would talk about anything that might cost money, Bruce went into a fit. Their biggest issue was over their old worn-out bedroom set. When they would go to bed she would say, "Honey, we really do need a new bedroom set." That's all it took for him and bam he was off railing, "We can't afford it! You just have to make do. What's wrong with you? You know we don't have the money."

Knowing this was an explosive issue in their relationship, I told them, after a few sessions, that we were going to talk about one of their issues: communication. "I'm going to pick the subject you two are going to talk about." And then I wrote down a few questions on a piece of paper. That's when I told them what their assigned topic was: a new bedroom set. Bruce immediately sat up stiffly and I could almost see the hair on the back of his neck bristle. I gave him the piece of paper and told him that his job was to ask her *only* the questions on the paper. I told Lillian to tell him how she feels about their bedroom set.

She began with, "Oh, it's old, it's rickety, practically falling apart and we need a new bedroom set in the worst way."

He sat up straighter and started to say, "We can't afford it."

I interrupted him and said, "Read the questions."

Squirming in his seat he obediently read the first question, "What kind of bedroom set would you like?" It was almost more than he could make himself say.

"A really pretty one—maybe French provincial style," she answered.

He started to say again that they couldn't afford it, and I interrupted, saying, "Just read the questions."

Reluctantly, he went on to the second one, "Would you like one dresser or two?"

She answered, "I think we could share one large dresser."

He paused in his pain and I said, "Read the next question."

"Would you like night stands to go with it?"

"Oh, yes," she answered quickly.

The next question came more readily, "What kind of wood?"

"Well, I'd like a cherry wood set."

Then he said, "You really do deserve a new bedroom set."

She stopped, looked at him, and said, "Thank you, honey, but right now we really can't afford it."

He could hardly believe what he heard. She wasn't stupid. She knew they couldn't afford it. All she needed to do was dream about it out loud with the one person who would share the dream with her.

When you stifle your mate's dreams about what she would like to buy, it puts her in the mode of thinking about it almost incessantly. You actually may push her into a purchase she otherwise wouldn't make, just to prove a point. Back off and enjoy the dream. If the conversation ends with "Thanks, honey. I'm going to go get it tomorrow," don't panic. Keep in mind that you love her, so you can sincerely say, "Honey, you deserve it and with all my heart I wish you could. We just don't have the money, but let's start a savings account just for the bedroom set. I want you to have it and that way we can eventually get it." That's honoring her desires without going into debt for something you can't afford right now. This works equally well with husbands. Let him dream, too. Find joy in sharing your desires, even if you can't afford the item right now. Of course, if you have the money, for goodness sakes, love each other enough to make some of your spouse's dreams come true.

THOSE KILLER CREDIT CARDS

As a marriage therapist I see the horrible effects of debt all the time. For too many couples, money becomes a monster. And I have seen how the misuse of credit cards can kill a marriage. At first it seems like a good way to buy what you need. Since you don't have the money at the moment, you put it on the credit card, thinking, *I'll just add ten dollars to the payment each month and it won't be a problem at all.* That was easy, so you charge yet another time, and then again and again. It becomes habit forming. You use up your credit limit on one card, so you get another card. And on you go until your debt is so large that it begins to press in on your marriage like a vice grip, squeezing out all the joy and fun.

> SELF-CONTROL IS REQUIRED IN ORDER TO HAVE FINANCIAL SECURITY.

Husbands and wives need to realize how much this kind of debt actually costs them in dollars and cents. The interest on credit cards is so high that by the time you pay it off, using the minimum payment, you could almost buy two of whatever it was you purchased. Here's a key fact to remember: The amount you save by simply paying cash *doubles* your spending power. It's such an obvious thing that I find it hard to understand the reason people keep using credit cards. Instant gratification seems to be the motivating cause. Self-control is required in order to have financial security.

Of course, some couples use credit cards for convenience, paying off the full amount before any interest is ever accrued. They turn their credit card into a lovable little pet instead of a ferocious killer shark. Even this can be dangerous, however. This is a pet that could bite you. Studies show that, even though they pay it off before any interest is applied, people buy more when they use a credit card than they do when they pay cash or write a check. Paying cash or writing a check shows you what you actually have left. Credit cards don't require an immediate accounting.

Dave Ramsey, author of the book *Financial Peace,* says that what people need is "plastic surgery." He suggests you ". . . have a family meeting. Let each member participate in a candlelight ceremony at which each takes part in the plastic surgery party. That's right, cut [those credit cards] up."[47]

Nina and Sterling followed this advice. They were in way over their heads with credit card debt and it was causing a problem with their marriage. They decided they had to take action. "Cutting up our credit cards was one of the smartest things we ever did," Nina said. Sterling agreed and added, "Now we pay cash or we don't buy. And every month we're paying more than the minimum payment; in fact, any extra money we have we pay on this debt to clear it off as soon as possible." They had charged so much that at one point they realized their minimum monthly payment was only covering the interest and that the actual debt would just be there forever unless they paid far more than the minimum due. Credit cards are a terrible thief that inflict cruel abuse on the financially illiterate. It seems a shame that anyone can get a credit card, whether they have the means to pay or not. Couples need to become knowledgeable about how to wisely use their money.

I WANT THAT CAR!

A few years ago Joy and I almost got caught in a financial trap. We were looking at used cars. We usually buy a one- or two-year-old car. At the car dealership the salesman showed us a brand spanking new car. Oh, was it pretty! It was loaded with every plush goody a guy could want. The dealer showed us how it would cost slightly less a month than the used one we were looking at. We were tired and hungry by the time we had reached that point, so we left him and went for a bite to eat, with the promise we would be back with our decision.

We went to a nearby Chinese restaurant, ate, and then opened our fortune cookies. Joy's said, "Beware of bad investments." We should have taken the hint. Instead, temptation overcame us, we went back and signed the lease and drove the gorgeous new vehicle home. That night I woke up in the middle of the night, got the contract out, and did the real math. Oh, my! It was incredible to discover how much we would actually pay at the end of the contract and then in three years have to pay again to buy out the contract. It would have cost us all of the equity in our previous car plus all of the lease payments, and at the end of the contract we could have either turned the car back and had *nothing,* or purchased the car back at a reduced but ridiculously high price. The cost to us was astronomical.

The next morning, Joy, who was already feeling equally miserable over the deal, and I discussed the awful reality. We promptly got in the car and drove it back to the dealer. Fortunately, in our state there is a seventy-two-hour period where a buyer has the right to change his mind and return the car. They tried with all their power to talk us out of returning it. We were immovable. We bought the two-year-old car and felt unbelievable relief.

Samantha and Igor were not so fortunate. They needed a bigger car for their growing family of four children. They, too, were lured in. A beautiful new van captivated their interest and they signed a lease. The next day they had that appalling experience of discovering what a big mistake they had made. Their state, however, did not have any think-it-over period, and no matter how hard they tried to talk the dealer out of it, they were stuck. It has been a terrible strain on their budget and their marriage. When you purchase a car make sure you look into all the financial ramifications of the "deal" you are being offered. If you're not sure, get some professional advice. If you have already made an unwise purchase, work through it in harmony and learn from the experience.

The next question may be, should we buy a new or used car? Buying a new car is not always wise. You drive it off the lot and you've just lost thousands of dollars in depreciation. Why not let someone else drive it off the lot and lose the money, then you buy their car sometime during the following two years. It will still be under warranty and will be practically new. Some people claim that they don't want the repairs that come with a used car. Before you finalize the sale, it's a good idea to take the car to a mechanic for a look-over to make sure it's in good shape. If the car you buy is much older than a couple of years, you may have more repair bills, but the cost of those repairs may not come close to what the payments for a new car would cost you.

Another thing to keep in mind when you buy a new or used car is how much the insurance premium will be. Just add that monthly premium to your monthly car payment to have an accurate amount of what your real "new" car outgo will be. Too many people wait until after the purchase to discover the jolting insurance news.

TOO MANY OF US ARE TEMPTED TO BUY A HOME BIGGER THAN WE NEED OR CAN AFFORD.

Be smart. Do the numbers so that you know what you can afford and decide together on the purchase that *easily* fits your income. Save for it. Put as much down as possible. Don't let a shiny new car take the glow out of your marriage—it will if you can't comfortably afford it.

A HOUSE OF OUR OWN

Having your own home is a dream come true, but it's another one of those dreams that can turn into a nightmare if you're not careful. Buy within your means, put as much down as possible, and sign a mortgage for as few years as possible. Many couples nowadays are wisely taking fifteen-year mortgages, instead of the typical thirty years. You can do this if you don't insist on living in a mansion. Too many of us are tempted to buy a home bigger than we need or can afford, and then we're strapped with such high payments that we really can't enjoy life. If you do choose the thirty-year loan, pay extra on the principal every month or even make a few extra payments during the year. "For example, a $100,000, thirty-year mortgage at 10 percent will pay off in 21.1 years just by paying one extra payment per year."[48] That's an incredible savings. Again, buy what you can comfortably afford and then pay it off as quickly as you can.

GOOD-BYE TO DEBT

Get out of debt as soon as possible. There are ways to do this that are very effective and take less time than you might imagine. Dave Ramsey suggests this simple doable method:

> [Make a list by putting] your debts in ascending order with the smallest remaining balance first and the largest last. Do this regardless of interest rate or payment. You will pay these off in this new order . . . this works because you get to see some success quickly and are not trying to pay off the largest balance just because it has a high rate of interest.[49]

He goes on to explain that after paying the minimum due on every debt, you put every extra dollar you can toward paying off

MAKE GETTING OUT OF DEBT A JOINT EFFORT.

that smaller debt. The result is that in no time at all you will have it paid off. Then take all you were paying on the smallest debt and apply it to the amount you pay on the next smallest one. Continue this process until you are down to your largest debt, which will likely be your home. Now the exciting thing is, you take all you were paying on these previous debts and add it to your monthly house payment. Ramsey showed how one couple paid off their house debt in just seven years.

Another couple, Rod and Maria, tried this method and were amazed at how quickly they were able to clear their debts. Maria said, "I think all my health problems, including depression, were linked to being so far in debt and feeling like there was no way out. Now that we are out of debt I feel like a new woman. I can't even begin to explain the freedom, the exhilaration both Rod and I feel—the ball and chain are gone and we are so happy!"

Whatever your debts may be, this plan can work for you. It's sensible and simple. Make getting out of debt a joint effort. Review your progress regularly and enjoy it. You might want to make a payoff chart so you can see your debts diminishing monthly. Have fun with it. If you can enjoy the process and get excited about it together it won't be a drudge. In fact, the two of you might have some fun fantasizing about some treat you're going to give yourselves when all your debts are paid. You might even divide up your goal into increments and reward yourselves, affordably, every few months or when a certain debt is paid off.

FASHION ON A SHOESTRING

Just because you don't have much money doesn't mean you can't have nice things. Mallory and Rob figured out a way that works well for them. If you saw the way they and their three children dress you would think they had plenty of money. Here's Mallory's description of what they do:

I like to dress my kids in cute clothes and some of the more expensive brand names are the ones I like. Wouldn't you know! A few years ago Rob and I decided to go garage sale shopping to see if we could find some of those cute clothes for the kids. We chose the sales in the upper-income neighborhoods and were so pleased to find exactly what we were looking for—adorable clothes for only a dollar or two.

What surprised us was not only did we find cute clothes for the kids, we found some super good buys for ourselves. Rob just recently found a very classy business suit for only five dollars! We had to have a couple of alterations done on it and that cost us twenty dollars. So he has a great-looking suit for only twenty-five dollars! I've found dresses and pants for me for under five dollars.

We also discovered secondhand stores. Many people with money donate their nearly new clothes to these thrift stores and we have found some fabulous buys there, including work boots for Rob.

Last year we bought most of our kids' Christmas toys at garage sales, and they're like new. It made for a very fun and inexpensive Christmas, without the horrible feeling of having to pay it off later.

JaNell also used this method:

I like nice things, but I'm dead set against going into debt for them. As Brandon and I struggled through our early years of schooling, then his new bottom-of-the-totem-pole career and my being home with our young children, we found ways to have some lovely things. Some say "necessity is the mother of invention"—I say "*poverty* is the mother of invention." We were rubbing shoulders, statistically, with those below the poverty level. Garage sales, estate auctions, and thrift shops were where I shopped. I have purchased some beautiful pieces of original art and signed prints at extremely low prices. We have a beautiful solid oak dining room set, including matching lighted hutch and plant stand, that we bought at a garage sale a few years ago. It would cost at least twenty-five hundred dollars in a store, but we paid only six hundred dollars for the whole set.

Now I have discovered auctions on the Internet and just purchased a beautiful Lladro piece for far below store prices and recently picked up a valuable print for only fifteen dollars! I got into the habit of finding good deals when that was the only way we would be able to have nice things.

JaNell found a way to have fun saving money while enjoying some of the finer things in life. And no matter how little they had they always paid tithes and offerings to their church. In addition, they made a habit of saving and investing some—even if it was only a few dollars—each month. Being clever with your money can be very rewarding.

LEARN FROM THE MILLIONAIRES

In the book *The Millionaire Next Door,* there is much to be learned about gaining financial security. Eighty percent of the millionaires described in the book did not inherit their wealth; they carefully accumulated it. The authors, Drs. Thomas J. Stanley and William D. Danko, uncovered interesting tips when they interviewed these millionaires. For example: "We live well below our means. We wear inexpensive suits and . . . only a minority of us drive the current-model-year automobile. Only a minority ever lease our motor vehicles. Most of our wives are meticulous budgeters. . . . We are fastidious investors. On average, we invest nearly 20 percent of our household realized income each year."[50]

You may be thinking, *Easy for them to do, they're millionaires.* The point here is that they were not always millionaires. They were ordinary people who figured out that living within their income, saving, and investing were smart strategies that would bring them financial security. Drs. Stanley and Danko gave this helpful tip:

> All too often people allow their income to define their budgets. When we tell our audiences about the budgeting and planning habits of the affluent, someone always asks a predictable question: Why would someone who is a millionaire need to budget? Our answer is always the same: They became millionaires by budgeting and controlling expenses and they maintain their affluent status the same way.[51]

KIDS NEED MOM AT HOME

We live in an era of overspenders. In a *Psychology Today* magazine article, Olivia Mellan reported that "because of our community breakdown and spiritual alienation, many people feel a core emptiness that they try to fill up with Things."[52] Perhaps it's time to focus on what matters most in life. Some couples seem more concerned with keeping up with the Joneses than keeping up with what their family really needs. There are many couples with children still at home who believe they can't make it without the wife also working and bringing in additional income. I can't make a judgment regarding who should work out of the home and who should not. Many wives deserve high praise for the financial contributions they make to the family, and in some cases their contribution is crucial in providing some of the essential needs of the family. There are times, however, when a working mother is working for luxury rather than needs.

LOVE IS WILLING TO SACRIFICE.

When possible it is best for mothers to be at home with the children. There is no way out of the fact that children suffer when they don't have a mother at home to nurture and care for them. No amount of "things" can replace this emotional and physical need of the children. In some families that may require a big sacrifice. Love is willing to sacrifice.

In his article *Live Well on One Income,* Andy Dappen made a valid point when he wrote, "The cost of having both spouses work is higher than most people think. It has been estimated that the average dual-career family needs to earn 35 percent more than a single-income family to meet the same standard of living. . . . By staying home and stretching one income, you can shave thousands from your annual expenses—the equivalent of earning a hefty amount once your tax bracket is taken into consideration."[53] Considering this, the sacrifice is not as big as one might imagine; it just takes planning and a change in spending habits. Many young couples finish their education and are excited to realize that they may now have some money to spend. The kids haven't come yet and there is some breathing room. This is the time when many begin spending their future. It's very tempting with two incomes, little or no debt, or student loans that they have years to pay off at low payments. At last they can buy a new car, new furniture for their nice apartment, and other longed-for items, with no plan to save. Dee and Joan were in this position. Here's their story as told by Dee:

> We look back with a lot of humility and gratitude for following some wise counsel at an early stage in our marriage. We both finished college and I got a good job in Aerospace. Joan began teaching and was an outstanding teacher. She has always loved children. The future was bright and we had very few debts, so we bought a car and started looking at furniture. One day Joan came home and said, "More than anything in the world I want to be a stay-at-home mom. If we keep

buying things I won't be able to do that." We reasoned that if that were the goal then we needed to be ready at any time for children.

We agreed that no financial decision would ever be made that could not be met with my salary. Joan's salary would go into savings or be used for cash purchases. The car would be our only debt until we had enough for a down payment on a home. The down payment was achieved by setting aside and protecting ten percent of all income as savings.

The ten percent savings became a lifelong habit that has provided many wonderful financial opportunities and eventually provided funds for our children's college education.

Not all couples are as wise as Dee and Joan, but that doesn't mean they can't change. Alice and Jed realized this when they found themselves up against a financial brick wall. Here's Alice's account of their challenge and decision:

Jed is a hardworking guy. He volunteers for every extra hour he can get at work and really works hard. Still, it's just not quite enough to dig us out of a financial hole we unwisely got ourselves into. We have four young children under the age of seven. I am able to add a little to our income by doing haircuts and perms in our home but it's erratic and nothing I can count on as regular income. We were to the point of desperation when a friend of mine said the company she worked for was hiring and she assured me that I could have the job. It seemed like the answer to our problem.

We talked about it and decided it was our only way out of our mess. However, neither of us felt good about it. We kept *trying* to feel good about it, but it just wasn't happening. We decided we needed some spiritual guidance. After praying and thinking about it, I asked Jed if he got an answer. He said, "Yes, did you?" I had and said, "Yes. What was yours?" He said, "That you shouldn't leave the kids and go to work. We just need to spend less." His answer was the exact answer I had received. No voice spoke to either of us but the impression was undeniably strong. I turned down the job offer.

It hasn't been easy but we both feel very peaceful about our decision. I know that no one can care for our precious children the way I can. It's well worth the sacrifice. And it's amazing what we're learning to do without that really doesn't matter much after all. We keep on praying for strength to stick to it.

Interestingly, since we made our decision Jed has been able to get even more hours and I'm getting more haircuts. It's very nice having God on our team.

GIVING, COSIGNING, AND LOANING MONEY

It's wise to decide as a couple, in advance, what your policy about giving and loaning money will be. If you discuss it, make a decision and stick to it, then you will avoid many arguments. If there is a valid exception, agree on it together or don't make the exception.

Sometimes people, especially your children, will ask you to cosign a loan. If they need a cosigner it means the bank or lending agency would not loan to them because, in the judgment of professionals, they probably won't be able to pay off the loan—they think the borrower is too great a risk. That's an enormous clue to you that the borrower is also too great a risk for you. The likelihood of your ending up paying the loan off is too great.

There may be a rare, legitimate exception to this rule. For example, Shayla and Curtis's college-student son, Josh, called at the beginning of summer with a proposal. He had an idea for a lucrative summer landscape business that could help him through school for the next three years—all he needed was for them to cosign a loan for ten thousand dollars to buy equipment to get him started. Cosigning was not their policy. Josh felt confident that his business would succeed rapidly and that he would have the loan paid off by the end of summer when he would return to being a full-time student, resuming the business again the next summer.

DECIDE AS A COUPLE, IN ADVANCE, WHAT YOUR POLICY ABOUT GIVING AND LOANING MONEY WILL BE.

Shayla and Curtis had reservations and yet they wanted to help their son. He had been a hardworking, dependable person in the past but this was a big request. They told him they would think about it, and then the two of them discussed it in depth and came up with their parameters. They told Josh they would cosign if (1) he proved to them that it was a safe thing for them by lining up several jobs in advance, and (2) if he agreed that if he had not paid off the loan by fall, he would delay his schooling until he had earned enough to pay it off. They knew he was very serious about his schooling, but he agreed to their requests. Shayla said, "He worked very hard for the next three weeks and went beyond our expectations in meeting our requirements. He lined up many jobs and even contracted with a landscaping company to do their curb jobs." They were so impressed with his dedication, they cosigned the loan.

Curtis and Shayla realized the risk involved in cosigning their son's loan so they covered their bases to ensure he could pay them back. Most important, they worked it out together and both felt good about the plan. Curtis said, "If either of us had felt it was not a good thing we wouldn't have done it."

Being united as a couple is a must. Decide early on that you will explain your reasons for the way you feel about an issue and then go along with what seems best. When it's a "tie," someone has to give in. Sometimes the husband gives in to his wife's wishes and sometimes she gives in to his. And sometimes you will be just plain miffed at each other for a while. Equal compromise is vital.

In most cases, loaning money rarely works for the borrower or the lender. When friends or grown children borrow your money and don't pay it back as agreed, it's like dropping a big boulder right in the middle of your relationship with them. And if one or the other of you didn't want to lend the money in the first place, it drops a huge one into your marriage relationship as well. If you make a loan and they don't pay it back, then you will be under stress with your own budget and that causes marital conflict.

If you want to give a gift of money to someone, that's a different story. You're not expecting anything in return so you won't be disappointed. If you give money to the same person over and over again, however, you will make him dependent upon you and he will never grow up and learn to solve his own problems. It's rarely a favor to continue such a practice. If you think you want to give someone money, talk it over as husband and wife, do it only if you both agree, and be judicious.

SECURE YOUR FUTURE

Grown children should not borrow or take money from their parents, not only because it can leave the parents in a risky position later without emergency funds, but also because the children will be the ones who may have to jump in and financially rescue their parents later at a time when they can't afford it either. Both parents and children need to protect themselves and become financially independent of each other. If the time comes, however, when your parents need help in their old age, that will not only be your duty, but your opportunity to return the loving care they gave you as a child.

Many retired couples have found themselves in trouble financially because they have given their savings to their children and have nothing to enjoy in their later years. That's very sad. Earl and Elese found themselves in this position. They couldn't resist the requests from their children when they would call and ask for money. They thought it was their responsibility to help their children out. Now they don't have enough for even a very basic living. Elese said, "It's so hard to say no to a child when they are about to lose their car." Earl added, "And to say no when a grandchild asks for a couple of thousand dollars for a down payment on a home." Interestingly, none of these children paid them back. Elese said, "And we can't ask them for it because they still don't have any money." Children become no better off when you continue to give them money. It just keeps them dependent on others.

> **CHILDREN WHO ARE CONTINUALLY BAILED OUT BY THEIR PARENTS NEVER GROW UP OR BECOME RESPONSIBLE.**

It's difficult to turn children down, but it may be the kindest thing you can do to help them take their own responsibility. As you deny your child's financial requests, use the principles of validation and boundary setting. Simply say to the child, "That's a tough spot you're in. Giving you money, however, is not an option for us. You're smart and we know you'll be able to work it out. We have confidence in you, and you will be in our prayers." He or she will find a way and will eventually become more independent and capable as a result of your taking this stand. Children who are continually bailed out by their parents never grow up or become responsible. That doesn't mean you don't give a surprise gift of money now and then—the key here is *surprise*.

Equally important are your own financial goals. You need to protect your funds in a variety of ways for your retirement needs and desires. No one knows the future. Some people in secure jobs with "guaranteed" retirement funds from their employer find themselves in the position of losing it all when a merger or downsizing takes place. No one can rely on what might be. Cover your bases to be sure that when you retire you will have a comfortable, fulfilling lifestyle. There are many ways to provide for those years; it just takes planning. A little financial restraint coupled with savings and conservative investments in your early years can make all the difference. It is quite surprising how only a few dollars wisely invested and left untouched when you are younger can provide huge benefits when you reach retirement age.

TIPS FROM THE PROS

Suze Orman's book *The 9 Steps to Financial Freedom* gives advice and information on how to insure a financially sound future, how to wisely invest your money—even when you have little to invest—how to protect yourself and your money with living trusts, what type of life insurance is best, as well as many other valuable financial suggestions.

Another book that gives an almost revolutionary look at the place of money in our lives is *Your Money or Your Life* by Joe Dominguez and Vicki Robin. Understanding and applying their steps to financial fulfillment can be very liberating and bring a great deal of peace into your marriage. Though their philosophy reaches far beyond this statement, this quote provides a peek into their wisdom:

> Having an internal yardstick for fulfillment is actually one part of what we call Financial Integrity. You learn to make your financial choices independently of what advertising and industry have decided would be good for their business. You are free of the humiliation of being manipulated into spending your life energy on things that don't bring you fulfillment.[54]

They then proceed to help readers understand the importance of aligning their expenditure of life energy (earning money) with their values and life purpose.

Both these books, along with Dave Ramsey's *Financial Peace* and *Make Your Paycheck Last* by Harold Moe, offer useful and important advice to couples of all ages. There are many other excellent books on financial planning that could also be helpful.

BEGIN TODAY

Sit down with your spouse and talk about your financial goals; write them down. Be positive and avoid any negative comments toward each other—just begin at this moment to work in harmony to achieve your goals. If you are in debt, review the plan for getting out of debt outlined in this chapter and decide to pay off that smallest debt first. Even just beginning the process of becoming debt free will give you a lift and the determination to reach your goal.

Remember, husbands and wives who work together without belittling or criticizing each other, who make a plan and work that plan, can become financially secure and enjoy the peace it will bring. This kind of security will replace the fear and worry that drive so many marriages apart. Love sacrifices. Love shares. Love conquers all—including money problems.

Nourish the Spiritual Side of Your Marriage

With God, all things are possible.
—MATTHEW 19:26

BELIEF IN GOD

Gallup polls have found that "the level of religious belief in the U.S. remains steady and high during the past decades with approximately 95% of the population professing a belief in God, 70% professing membership in a church or synagogue. . . ."[55] Many psychologists maintain that to ignore a person's religious belief is to deny an important element of that person's wholeness. To recognize and build upon religious belief gives you greater strength as a person and, as a result, deeper meaning to life. In your marriage, sharing your belief gives you and your mate increased power to strengthen and find joy in your marriage.

> WHEN PEOPLE DRAW UPON A HIGHER POWER TO SOLVE PROBLEMS THEIR SUCCESS RATE SEEMS TO INCREASE.

When people draw upon a higher power than themselves to solve problems and meet challenges their success rate seems to increase. According to Alcoholics Anonymous and other twelve-step programs for people with addictions, acknowledging that there is a higher power and calling upon that power moves people from being helpless to being helped.

Dr. Laura Schlessinger tells her radio show listeners that understanding that you are accountable to God is significantly helpful in taking the right course of action in dealing with all people. In her book *The Ten Commandments: The Significance of God's Laws in Every Day Life,* coauthored by Rabbi Stewart Vogel, she writes:

> Can the human population survive if it tolerates no standard of values for what is correct? . . . If values are not God-derived, they come from fads and favorites . . . and a personal desire to get away with anything under the protection of nonjudgmentalism (it's my life!).
>
> Values inform our conscience which influences our behavior. Our behaviors determine the quality of our lives and the meaningfulness of our personal contribution to others, to life, and to history.[56]

Her point is well taken. When children know they have parents who care about them, who follow through with certain disciplinary actions, they behave better. Adults are not a whole lot different. Knowing that God is your ultimate authority can be very motivating in bringing about appropriate loving behavior. During a visit with their pastor, Miriam and Claude, who were struggling in their marriage, had this concept clarified when their pastor said, "By being accountable to God you become more accountable to your mate, which brings about a deeper fidelity and a more compassionate relationship."

BY BEING ACCOUNTABLE TO GOD YOU BECOME MORE ACCOUNTABLE TO YOUR MATE.

A young wife from Texas shared an example of how this accountability worked in her marriage. She described how she and her husband were both exhausted after a hard day, the house was a mess, and their toddler was teasing the baby. She wrote:

> Then suddenly my husband and I had words that quickly escalated into an argument. Feelings were hurt. I soon found myself with the children in one room of the house and my husband in another room. Silence stretched across the house.
>
> I put the children to bed, and still no words had been spoken. Our home had become simply a house: empty, cold, and silent. I tried lying down but couldn't sleep. My pillow became wet with tears, and my thoughts kept turning to my wonderful husband of six years who was sitting alone in the living room.
>
> I began praying for guidance. I wanted him to make the first move and say he was sorry, yet I wanted the loving atmosphere of our home back even more. As I prayed, my mind filled with beautiful memories of my husband, our marriage, our promises made [at our wedding], and all my blessings. A thought came to me—what would the Lord have me do? My tears increased, and before I knew it I was kneeling beside my husband, gently waking him with my tears and my hugs.
>
> Hugging me back, he said, "Please don't cry." We were both saying we were sorry over and over and telling each other how much we loved each other. Immediately a sweet spirit filled our home again.[57]

Turning to God in prayer and asking "what would You have me do?" is a good formula for overcoming problems in marriage. This is not a weakness; it is a strength. Believing in a loving Father in Heaven who created you and cares passionately about you and your family, and that He has that same depth of caring for every other human being not only gives you a comforting connection with Him, but a spiritual connection with each other. The French paleontologist Teilhard de Chardin made an interesting observation when he said,

LET YOUR FAITH BE AN INTEGRAL PART OF YOUR WORK IN OVERCOMING YOUR MARITAL PROBLEMS.

"We are not human beings having a spiritual experience; we are spiritual beings having a human experience."[58] To recognize your spiritualness is to recognize your inner strength.

If you have a basic belief in God then let your faith be an integral part of your work in overcoming your marital problems. When you call upon this divine power to help you, you will notice that you will experience greater success. There is evidence supporting this idea, including a study conducted by Lauer and Lauer, which reports that "happy couples find their religious faith to be a source of nourishment as well as stability in the marriage. Kevin is a claims manager who has been married twenty-one years. [He said]:

> I think a strong and healthy relationship with God that is shared by the mate is vital. It has helped me in feeling and believing that God somehow directed our lives together and daily supports and sustains our marriage.[59]

THE NEED FOR PRAYER

Have you ever heard of the following saying: "When life seems more than you can stand . . . kneel"? Why not take that a step further and kneel before it becomes more than you can stand? When Joy and I were married, the gentle wise man of God who pronounced us husband and wife counseled us to take each other by the hand and kneel together in prayer each night. We decided to follow his counsel and it has been our practice for all the years of our marriage. We have faced a multitude of problems as we finished schooling, looked for jobs, endured illnesses, raised our family, and tried to be forgiving of each other, to mention but a few. In all of these challenges we felt we needed divine guidance to help us through them without being overcome by them.

This does not take the place of good hard work within the marriage. It simply gives couples a stronghold. There is wisdom in the statement by the sixteenth-century English bishop Jeremy Taylor: "The body of our prayer is the sum of our duty; and as we must ask of God whatsoever we need, so we must watch and labor for all that we ask."[60] You will also find that it is hard to stay mad at each other when you pray together.

There are many ways people communicate with God and I would not presume to take on the role of telling anyone how they "should" pray. It is a very private, individual matter. It is our belief that all earnest prayers are heard and answered in the way that God knows is best for those offering the prayer. Justine's experience shows the loving power of prayer.

I had not felt well for several weeks. I kept thinking that whatever was making me ill would go away and so I hadn't gone to the doctor. One day I just lay in my bed feeling ill and depressed. My parents had both died of cancer and I was beginning to have worries that I would be next. I was softly crying when my husband, Bernie, came into the bedroom to check on me.

When he asked how I was doing I burst into full-blown sobs. He sat on the edge of the bed and held me in his arms for a minute. Then he knelt by the bed, held my hand, and said to me, "I feel so helpless. I don't know what to do, except pray."

He then prayed the sweetest, most tender prayer in my behalf that I had ever heard him utter. It touched me deeply and filled me with overwhelming love for him.

When he got up he kissed me and left the room. He knew I had not felt like eating all that day. A short time later he returned with a plate. He said, "I thought you might enjoy some of 'Uncle Bernie's' delicious mashed potatoes." (He often referred to himself as "Uncle Bernie.") He knew I loved the way he buttered and seasoned mashed potatoes. They were irresistible. It was exactly what I needed. I don't know if saying the prayer had helped him think of it, or what, but the combination of the prayer and the potatoes was very healing.

(Incidentally, I finally went to the doctor and found out I had a virus that would soon be gone. What a relief.)

The tenderness in Justine and Bernie's relationship verifies another concept taught by the pastor mentioned earlier in this chapter: "A person cannot fully understand what love is until he or she experiences being loved by God. When your vertical relationship with Him is in place, then you can have a successful horizontal relationship with your mate." Dr. Schlessinger adds emphasis to this with the following thought: "When a union between a man and a woman is endowed with a godly purpose, it becomes 'holy matrimony.'"[61]

A CAUTION

Sometimes a husband or wife may use prayer as a means of getting a message across to his or her spouse when they are praying together. This could be very hurtful to your mate. Here are two hypothetical examples to illustrate this point:

➤ Your wife is somewhat lacking in her culinary skills and you want her to do something about it, so you say in your prayer, "Help my wife learn how to cook better." About this time you might get a well-deserved kick in the shins, regardless of what heavenly being may be watching. Your wife will feel criticized, and her love for you will fly out the window at that moment.

➤ You are upset about the disrespectful way your husband treated you that day and you want him to know how you feel, so you pray, "Help my husband treat me with greater respect." How's he going to feel after that?

On the other hand, it is very caring to be specific in expressing genuine thanks by saying something like, "Thank you for my wonderful husband and the kindness he showed me today when I was out of patience with the kids." That's not giving a needs-to-do message; it's acknowledging a goodness. This kind of prayer builds love and shows gratitude to your mate and to God for a blessing.

If you've got gripes, hash them out together at another time or save them for your private personal prayers when you can unload and request whatever you want. And that's not a bad idea. Sometimes just putting your heartaches and wishes into words helps you organize your thoughts and opens up a comforting link with Heaven. This can be refreshing to your spirit and give you the help you need to improve your marriage relationship. Everyone needs a friend to share private things with and having God be that friend can be very relieving.

Time and time again in our survey people reported that one of the best things they did was to pray for the ability to forgive, to endure hard times, and to find peace. They also found solace in asking for guidance with their spouse and even became very specific in their requests. For example, Ellen said:

I don't know what I would do without the ability to pray and ask for understanding and patience in dealing with my husband and his little idiosyncrasies. And I don't know what I would do without it to overcome my own.

ATTENDING RELIGIOUS SERVICES TOGETHER

Millions of people attend their church or synagogue every week seeking spiritual guidance for themselves and their families. Participating in these services and assisting in serving in these organizations has helped many couples invite a spirit of kindness and love into their marriage relationship. In presenting one of our seminars to a group of Stephen Ministers affiliated with a Christian church in southern Texas we became well acquainted with our hosts, a husband and wife who had devoted years of service to their church. As we watched them work together in this service we were impressed with the "oneness" they seemed to share. They spoke of assisting each other in different projects from time to time and finding much joy as they served. Their religious faith has deepened their love for one another and has helped them through some serious personal crises with their family.

WHEN WE LEARN OF GOD'S LOVE FOR US, WE LEARN A BETTER WAY TO LOVE EACH OTHER.

When we attended their Sunday services with them and heard their pastor teach godly principles relating to the marriage relationship we had a broader understanding of the value their church attendance had in their lives. One might surmise then that a good old-fashioned sermon can be very motivating in doing good to your mate. Perhaps it boils down to this: When we learn of God's love for us, we learn a better way to love each other.

We have witnessed how attending religious services can also help connect couples with other couples of similar faith, building friendships that enhance their own relationship as husband and wife. You can learn from the examples of others who are also working at building strong families—religious networking, as it were.

MUSIC TO SOOTHE THE SOUL

Just as music can create feelings of romance, it can foster feelings of faith. To enjoy music with sacred messages and melodies can be a powerful influence in bringing spiritual feelings into your home. Thomas Carlyle penned the words, "music is well said to be the speech of angels."[61] Who can listen to "Amazing Grace" or Handel's "Hallelujah Chorus" without feeling a little closer to Heaven? A steady diet of only this type of music would be too much of a good thing—we need variety—but there are times when sacred music can soothe tense feelings and bring solace to the soul like no other kind of music can.

Sometimes when Joy and I are feeling discouraged we'll put on a CD of Sandi Patti's rendition of "Love in Any Language," Enya's "How Can I Keep from Singing," the Mormon Tabernacle Choir's "How Great Thou Art," or any number of selections we especially enjoy. As the strains of music fill the air, both of our empty emotional buckets fill with hope and encouragement. Sometimes we listen together and sometimes alone. A musician and professor of music, Dr. Michael Ballam, encourages people to create their own musical first-aid kit— a collection of favorite music that lifts and rejuvenates them.

Listening to inspiring music together as a couple can create a spiritual bonding. Every religion has its own special music. Discover yours and enjoy it to the fullest—privately and together. If you are of different religions, become acquainted with each other's sacred music and find enjoyment in the sharing. Music has amazing power to touch the soul. When a husband and wife enjoy uplifting music together they are drawn into a oneness

LISTENING TO INSPIRING MUSIC TOGETHER CAN CREATE A SPIRITUAL BONDING.

and can be given the energy to face life's challenges hand in hand. On some occasions, I have actually prescribed specific pieces of music to my clients, many of whom report that it has had a calming and strengthening effect in their lives. It can touch the spirit within and lift people to a higher level so that their dealings with their spouse and family members are more generous and loving.

You can enjoy the renewing value of music on an even more personal level if you or your spouse play a musical instrument. TV news anchor Katie Couric, speaking of her late husband, Jay Monahan, talked about the beauty and joy his music brought into their home and their marriage. She never seemed to tire of listening to him play their Steinway grand piano, which she also plays. She said, "It's very emotional, playing the piano, playing music. It reflects your mood. And it's really therapeutic."[62]

LIGHT UP YOUR LIFE

Most people have been advised at one time or another to "lighten up," and usually that phrase suggests the need to laugh and enjoy life more. There may be another important meaning to it, however. Color consultant and therapist Suzy Chiazzari notes that "on a physical level, natural light influences the pituitary and pineal glands, both master glands of our endocrine system. These control the release of normalizing and desirable hormones into the body, which are closely linked to our moods and emotions. On a spiritual level, the soul also needs to be nurtured by living light. Not only do we need this energy, but our ability to absorb and utilize it affects our quality of life."[63]

When people are feeling down their depression can have a negative effect on their relationships. Bringing more physical light into your home can be rejuvenating to your marriage. Open the drapes and blinds, at least some of the time, and let the light shine in. Of course, when a person has clinical depression he needs medical intervention; light, however, can play an important role in augmenting the medication.

It's interesting to note that when preachers speak of guidance from God they often refer to it as "light." Consider the benefits you can enjoy by bringing light, physical and spiritual, into your home. You may be quite surprised at the positive influence it can have on your relationship with each other and your children.

SCRIPTURE READING

Some couples read scriptures together to reenforce their understanding of God's will in their lives. Lydia and Calvin, who have been married nearly five years, describe their practice:

> We're not perfect at this, but Lydia and I have been fairly consistent at reading passages of scripture every morning before I leave for work. It means getting up just a few minutes earlier than we otherwise would, but it's well worth it. It keeps us focused on what life is all about and the importance of our relationship with each other and our daughter. We take turns reading and will often discuss how we can apply what we've read that day and how it can guide us in the goals we have set for our marriage and family.
>
> One of our favorite verses is from Proverbs 3:5–6: "Trust in the Lord with all thine heart; and lean not unto thine own understanding. In all thy ways acknowledge him, and he shall direct thy paths." Sometimes when we're in a hurry and don't have time to read, we just repeat that scripture and it gives us a direction.

With so many things pulling most couples in so many directions, you may find the practice of reading scriptures together privately fortifying and stabilizing.

DISCOVER HOLINESS IN EVERYDAY THINGS

In his book *Don't Sweat the Small Stuff . . . And It's All Small Stuff,* Richard Carlson gives us the inspired suggestion to "remember that everything has God's fingerprints on it." He writes, "Rabbi Harold Kushner reminds us that everything that God has created is potentially holy. . . . When our life is filled with the desire to see the holiness in everyday things, something magical begins to happen. A feeling of peace emerges."[64] When you experience some of these "holy" discoveries with your mate the magic happens not only inside of you, but between you.

Warren and Jeanie, who are self-employed and work together in their home, reported one such moment of discovery:

> We were driving home from doing some errands to get back to work on yet another deadline. It was late afternoon, and as we drove along, a light rain began to sprinkle the windshield. The sun was still shining through the rain. Just then we noticed a beautiful double rainbow across the eastern sky. It was breathtaking. We pulled over and just looked at it for a couple of minutes. Sharing that moment of awe together seemed to have a holiness about it. It felt like a loving Father in Heaven was smiling on the world . . . and on us.

NOTICING OUR CREATOR'S HANDIWORK AND GOODNESS NURTURES OUR SPIRITS.

Noticing our Creator's handiwork and goodness nurtures our spirits. When couples enjoy these moments together they also nurture their marriage. You can feel it when you take a walk with your spouse during the gentle unfolding of a sunrise or in the warm glow of a sunset. Couples can stroll through Central Park in New York City and enjoy the "holiness" of nature in bloom, even while hundreds of taxis rush by on the bordering streets. Or a couple can sit on a porch, look past the flowers and into fields beyond, and achieve true serenity. All of these are holy moments that nurture a marriage and feed the soul.

BEGIN TODAY

Discuss the role of spirituality and how it fits into your marriage and home life. Here are some questions you might address:

➤ Do we want to attend religious services?

➤ Which church, synagogue, or temple? Together? As a family?

➤ What about prayer? Scripture reading?

➤ What are we going to teach our children about God?

➤ What values do we uphold for ourselves and our family?

In order to include God in your marriage you have to have open, accepting conversations together or it won't happen. Having this discussion can be the beginning of a deeply spiritual relationship that will bless not only your marriage but the lives of your children.

Hold On Through the Hard Times

*Weeping may endure for a night, but joy
cometh in the morning.* —PSALMS

HARD TIMES COME

When we were on our honeymoon we bought a little
wooden plaque that had a miserable, forlorn-looking fellow
drawn on it with a cloudburst pouring down on him. Beside
him were these words: "Into each life a little rain must fall,
BUT THIS IS RIDICULOUS!" At the time, we thought it
was very funny. It has taken on new meaning several times
throughout our life together. We still have it. In fact, now it
hangs in my therapy office where clients can relate to it while
pouring their hearts out to me.

There will be hard times, even tragedies, in every couple's
life. These are the times that can pull you together or break
you apart. If you will be determined that, no matter what
happens, you are committed to each other and to your marriage, then there is no way these difficult times can break you
apart. To abandon your mate when life gets tough is like
throwing away an exquisite diamond just before it has been
polished so it achieves its most brilliant sparkle. Holding on to
each other allows the stormy seasons of life to serve as a bridge

that will lead to a relationship more radiant and beautiful than you ever thought possible—a relationship that never could have had the full depth and beauty without the struggle.

ACCEPT EACH OTHER'S COMFORTING

Sometimes when a deep sorrow or a difficult time comes into a marriage, one or the other spouse may put up a barrier that destroys the closeness you have developed. Stress and sadness do strange things. When you need loving arms around you the most, you may actually reject the effort of your mate to give you comfort, and you can't even explain why you reject it. It can be very frustrating to the one who is trying to give the comfort. Even if you feel like you don't want any hugs, accept them. The very act of opening up to a loving caress can break down the barrier and start to heal the heartbreak. Hold each other in your arms and allow each other to cry. If you or your mate don't cry, don't be critical or accusing; just hold on to the embrace. It brings about healthy healing. It's as if energy from your mate infuses you with strength to go on, even when you're both suffering.

> **HOLD EACH OTHER IN YOUR ARMS AND ALLOW EACH OTHER TO CRY.**

An internationally known university professor recounts the story of his arriving home one day feeling overburdened and totally distraught. As he sat on the edge of his bed his wife asked him if he was all right. He found himself unable to reply and could only sit there and weep. His wife sat down beside him and held him in her arms without saying a word. That was the greatest thing she could have ever done for him at the moment. He said, "I needed that silent nurturing."

SERIOUS LOSSES

Stormy seasons come in all different forms. Janet grew up on a farm in eastern Oregon. She vividly remembers a difficult time her parents went through when she was a child:

My father was a hardworking farmer with a large family of nine children. My mother was supportive of his dream to have a successful farm. They had a large machine shed where two tractors, one of which was brand new, were stored, along with several tons of fertilizer and other equipment. One winter evening my father was out working on one of the tractors in the shed. He had a small oil burning stove going to help keep him warm while he worked. As he tested the tractor he accidentally knocked the stove over and the fire spread rapidly, igniting the tractor and other items. The fertilizer was aflame in seconds. He tried to get the new tractor out, but failed and barely escaped himself.

I can remember standing there by my mother's side with my brothers and sister, watching this enormous fire destroying my parents' dreams, with no way to put it out, though they tried. Tears were streaming down her cheeks when Daddy came and stood at Mother's side as they finally stepped back and watched with horror. There was nothing they could do. Fire engines finally arrived, but only after the shed had burned nearly to the ground. I remember Daddy holding Mother in his arms as they cried together. We all cried. I also vividly remember his words to her, "Heavenly Father will help us through this. We'll find a way to start over." Their faith and determination was remarkable . . . and so was their love for each other.

Neighbors rallied to help in amazing ways that year and my father had a successful crop that helped get

them started again. It took years, but they held on to
each other and their dream.

Some hard times may come as a result of an enormous financial loss. Maria and Dallin had an even more difficult time,
losing everything when their business failed. The beautiful
home that they had worked hard to improve through the
years had to be turned over to the bank, with a 50 percent
loss to them. With the help of a good attorney, they were able
to negotiate a lower amount of debt, but nonetheless they
were still left with $120,000. This debt needed to be paid off
within one year, or bankruptcy would be their only option.
They didn't want to go into bankruptcy. They decided that
their opportunity to earn the money would be better in a
larger city, so they moved. It was difficult to leave their lovely
hometown and move into a small two-bedroom apartment in
an inner-city area—the only one they could afford—where
Dallin sold advertising.

In describing how they dealt with this change, Maria said,
"We decided it was only a house. We still had each other and
a roof over our heads. The thing that kept it from being a
devastating experience was that we held on to each other and
faced the difficulties together."

Maria took care of their four children while she did
flower arranging in her home to add to their income. By facing their difficult challenge together and making significant
sacrifices they were able to pay off the $120,000 within the
year limit. It was an amazing accomplishment for them. That
was more than twenty years ago. Later they had to face yet
another far more tragic difficulty when their little daughter,
who was born with a debilitating illness, died. What their
prior adversity had taught them helped them through this far
greater heartache. Maria said, "The formula is the same—
hold on and work through the difficult times together."
Dallin said, "Our marriage is stronger than ever and life has
greater meaning as a result of all we've been through."

Was it an easy accomplishment for this couple? At times it was extremely difficult. Did it always go smoothly in their relationship? No. At times they had to just accept the pain. Did they miss their home? Yes. Did they miss their child? Of course! No one could ever completely understand that agony without going through it. They had their times when they cried together, sought professional therapy for Maria's depression, and wiped away the tears. Then they went on, each dealing with it in his or her own way, but unified in their push forward.

ALL TOO OFTEN COUPLES LET SORROWS AND HEARTACHES DRIVE THEM APART.

All too often couples let sorrows and heartaches drive them apart. Deserting a mate during such a time never brings peace to either. It only intensifies the agony. Holding on to each other can be a magnificent healer.

THE HEARTACHE OF HAVING A DISABLED CHILD

Some tragedies are short-lived while others are ongoing, challenging couples for many years and in some cases even a lifetime. Audrey and Leland, each in their second marriage, were happily married. He had a successful computer business, which allowed her to be home with their two children from their previous marriages. After a few years they decided to add to their "yours" and "mine" and have an "ours." They looked forward to the birth of their new child with great anticipation. When the baby was born, however, he came with many physical defects, which required extensive twenty-four-hour personal care. They were willing to do all that was required and made out a care schedule in which both participated.

Problems in their marriage began to manifest themselves when Audrey became overly protective and almost obsessed with the care of their son, gradually excluding Leland from helping with him or spending time alone with her. It is a wonderful thing when a mother dedicates herself to the care of an infant such as this but this dedication must not happen at the expense of her other responsibilities, especially to her husband. She eventually refused help from willing neighbors, church members, and family. Finally, there was no time or emotion left for her husband. Leland loved his family and his little child as much as Audrey did, but she would not allow him to help her and shut him out of her life. He felt unwanted and unneeded. He no longer had a place in her life. Tragically their marriage ended in divorce.

Contrast this with the experience of Ginny and Wade, whose third child, Andy, also came into the world severely impaired. He never developed mentally beyond the age of a three-month-old and lived to the age of twenty-one, needing to be spoonfed baby food. He could not walk, or even crawl, and could not speak. They took care of his every need. The key word in this sentence is "they." Andy had an infectious smile that soothed their aching hearts and filled them with the emotional energy to care for him day in and day out.

This seems like a heavy load for a couple to carry, and it was; but there was more. Their second child, Carter, began to show mental disabilities not long after Andy was born. Though he was normal physically, his problems escalated and became far more than the schools could handle. At the time there were no programs to assist them.

Ginny and Wade felt overwhelmed. As they considered the tragedy that filled their lives they cried and wondered *why?* And they cried more. "Then," Ginny said, "one day we realized we had to stop crying and we just decided this was what our life would be and we would do the best we could . . . together." When asked how they kept their marriage strong Ginny said that they insisted on spending time together away from their children at least once a week. They would go out to dinner, to a movie, or on a drive to just talk and enjoy each other's company. "It did wonders for our relationship," she said.

They accepted help from others and were especially grateful for the helping hand of Ginny's mother. At one point, after a heart-wrenching decision that had no alternative, Carter was placed in a residential school and care center for the critically disabled. He is happy and well cared for there. Many years later Ginny and Wade are still holding on to each other, enjoying a contentment and love that their tragedies could never mar. Their world is filled with an appreciation for the simplest things of life that others take for granted. They are happily bonded together by the glue of adversity because they put into practice the principles that keep love alive.

WHEN A LOVED ONE IS IN PRISON

Nedra and Austin's hearts were broken when their daughter, Janalee, was sentenced to ten years in prison for a crime she had committed. Well-respected in their community, all of the unpleasant circumstances and media hype that preceded the trial intensified their agony. But most of all they were devastated by the fact that their own daughter could actually have done what she did. Their love for their daughter did not stop because of her crime.

> WHAT SHE DID HAS NO BEARING ON WHO WE ARE AND THE VALUES WE LIVE BY.

They knew she could make a comeback and wanted to give her their support. Nedra said:

Each visit we made to the prison to see Janalee was like a stab to our hearts—a terrible reminder of the reality we were all facing. Finally, we realized that in order to survive we had to make a mental switch as soon as we left the prison. We worked on doing this together, saying to each other as we would drive away from the prison, "This happened and we will not let it damage us further. We know that what she did has no bearing on who we are and the values we live [by]." We would then change our conversation to other more pleasant subjects. It took a concentrated effort on the part of both of us. It was easier for Austin than for me. Men seem to have the capacity to set things aside a little more easily than women; however, I eventually learned how to control my thoughts.

That doesn't mean we didn't have times when we would cry about Janalee, but it meant that we would not allow it to dominate our every thought. We had a life of our own that needed to be lived and we were determined to live it. Austin and I both agree that our love for each other has deepened through this difficult time because we refused to let it drive us apart.

Fortunately, Janalee made dramatic changes while she was in prison and was paroled after serving five years. She has become the loving daughter she had been and is doing everything she can to make up for lost time with her own children. Nedra and Austin are enjoying the fruits of the care they gave to Janalee and to themselves. Their marriage is stronger and even more loving than it has ever been.

What happens if your mate breaks the law and ends up in prison? How long do you hold on in that situation? Each case has its own set of problems and implications. Clyde and Loretta, whose children were all grown, had no idea they would be facing this challenge. A partner in an East Coast business, Clyde dealt with sales while the others handled the books. Unbeknownst to Clyde, company money was being misused as a result of directions from their corporate lawyer. To further complicate the situation the lawyer tried to cover up the fraud. Clyde trusted his lawyer, thinking he would know what was legal and what was not. As a result, the lawyer, the other partners, and Clyde were convicted of fraud and ended up in prison. It was a terrible shock to him and his wife. Loretta knew Clyde was a good man who had been duped. She said, "I love him and believe in him. His only crime was being naive. This will pass, and in the meantime I choose to stand by him and give him all the loving support I can."

They lost everything they owned and she went to work full-time and is living in a small apartment while he serves out his time. She visits him whenever it's possible (he's incarcerated a few hundred miles away) and writes him regularly. He is using his time to further his education and to be ready to start a new career when he's released. They are handling their problem with grace and dignity . . . and they're holding on to each other. They have been married many years and they are not about to let this tragedy break them apart.

THE AGONY OF ADDICTION

Addiction to any kind of drug is a terrible monster, but a monster that can be beat. A midwestern couple, Jen and Elliot, faced this problem when Jen became addicted to her prescription drugs:

> I had a difficult surgery that required heavy pain medication followed by another surgery a year later. Between these two and other stresses, including serious dental work, I became more and more dependent on the medication, until I was addicted. To complicate matters I was into the menopausal stage of my life and the doctor was having some difficulty finding the right hormone treatment for me. The pain medication seemed to be my only relief from the pain and anxiety I was going through. Eliot was very concerned about my condition—almost to the point of panic. I continually denied that I was addicted to the medicine. He didn't understand how to deal with my problems and began verbally attacking me with mean accusations. All of these problems took a terrible toll on our relation-

ship. The closeness we used to enjoy was gone and El-liot began sleeping in the guest room.

The medicine kept me from thinking clearly and being able to respond as I normally would and I became very self-focused. I finally hit rock bottom. When Eliot realized what was happening he took serious action. I resisted his attempts to get me into a drug treatment center, but he was relentless. He was adamant and sought professional help in forcing me to go.

After a month in the treatment center I returned home. What a blessing this center was for me! Without it I would still be trapped, and my marriage would have been ruined.

SOMETIMES BOUNDARIES HAVE TO BE SET AND ACTION TAKEN OR ALL WILL BE LOST.

As in Jen and Elliot's case, sometimes boundaries have to be set and action taken or all will be lost. It was an extremely difficult road for them, but they are committed to each other and their marriage vows. After nearly a year since her release from the center Jen is doing exceptionally well and she and Eliot are very happy now. Both have expressed gratitude to each other for holding on through this difficult time.

UNEXPECTED BURDENS

Sometimes unexpected surprises come in life—the kind we would never choose, as in the case of Simon and Julie. They had been married eight years and had three children, ages two, four, and six years old and another on the way. Simon's parents died within a short time of each other, leaving his four younger brothers, ages seven, ten, fourteen, and eighteen orphaned. They had no place to go where they could stay together, so Simon and Julie took on the responsibility of raising them. They decided to move into Simon's parents' home to make it easier on his brothers. They knew this new life would be hard, but were filled with an idealistic hope that everything would work out. They had no idea how extremely difficult it would be. Simon's brothers were devastated over the loss of their parents and didn't want anyone trying to take their place. They were respectful to Simon, but rude and hurtful to Julie when Simon was not around. When tragedies happen, children feel the need to blame someone. When the youngest brother started calling Simon and Julie "Mom" and "Dad," the older boys threatened to beat him up because, they said, "it wasn't being loyal to Mom and Dad."

During the hard days of that first year, with her own newborn son, Julie felt overwhelmed. Feeding and caring for eight children was far more difficult than she had dreamed. She remembers that "sometimes I would stand at the kitchen sink washing all the dishes and pans that wouldn't fit into the dishwasher and I would just cry, watching my tears splash into the dishwater." Simon's brothers had not been trained to help in the house and would seldom respond to her requests. To make matters worse, "my husband seemed blind to my unhappiness. He worked later and later at the office. He said he had to in order to provide for everyone, but I sometimes felt it was to avoid coming home to all the chaos."

At times she would go into the bathroom, turn the water on full force, cry, and express her frustration in one-sided conversations to "no one." During those early years she said she just lived one day at a time—sometimes one hour at a time. Julie continually prayed for the strength and ability to make it through this difficult period of her life. She kept remembering a little saying her own father had taught her when she was a teenager with problems: "Two men looked through prison bars; one saw mud and the other saw stars." Julie would say it over and over and try to see the stars.

At one point, Julie considered divorcing Simon. She began to quietly observe other men before taking any action, but soon "realized there was not one out there that I'd rather have than Simon. And that's when I came up with my own saying, which was: It's better the devil you know than the one you don't." She realized Simon was as overwhelmed as she was and was worth holding on to.

At one point the work Simon was doing required him to do some counseling, much of it with women. As a result, one day he said to Julie, "Honey, I used to think you were a strange breed. Now, after all I've been seeing lately, I realize that women have different emotional responses. As I look at you and what we've been through together I realize what a good woman you are and how lucky I am."

Things changed and their love began to grow like it never had before. They began to learn the importance of putting each other first, and they started doing it. They became friends again. "Everything got better," Julie said. "We learned to talk and really listen to each other." Their children are all grown now and they have a sweet loving relationship. Both of them are grateful that they held on through those tough years. They only wish they had made these changes earlier.

Many divorced and remarried couples experience unexpected burdens when they are trying to blend families. The formula for success remains the same: Work together, talk and listen, and keep each other in the number one spot, regardless.

THE ILLNESS OF A SPOUSE

For Ernie and Liticia it was a work accident that changed their lives. Ernie was working in construction when a scaffolding he was on collapsed, leaving him seriously injured. This accident resulted in lifelong physical disabilities, and though he is somewhat able to get around, he can't work his former job. Workmen's Compensation helps them, but it is not enough income to live on and take care of their five children, who are all in school. Liticia assumed the role of family provider, and though it gets hard sometimes, she said, "I'm very grateful for the skills I have that allow me to have a good paying job. And I don't mind doing it because I love Ernie so much and I'm so grateful he's still with us. It could have been so much worse." Ernie has become the parent at home, giving the family stability and doing the homemaker chores, in between the dozens of surgeries that he is still undergoing. He said, "I've even become a pretty good cook." And in addition to running their home, he is taking some courses to help qualify him for a profession that will not be physically demanding. Liticia and Ernie's love and concern for each other and their ability to work together, each carrying the part of the load that they are able to, makes this marriage work.

A similar challenge occurred when Stephanie had a stroke. She was in her early fifties and had been enjoying her office job at a large university. Oliver, a professor at the same university, was terrified at the thought that he might lose her. Little by little Stephanie regained the use of the parts of her body that had been affected. Finally, she was able to walk again. Then she fell and broke her hip. It was a terrible emotional setback for both of them, but especially her. The use of crutches caused her left arm to spasm, becoming almost unusable, and the hip still had its problems.

At that same time Oliver hurt his left wrist and also required surgery. "One morning we just looked at each other and started to laugh as we struggled to get dressed, each helping the other with our remaining good hands," Stephanie said. "We discovered that two right hands don't make up for no left hands. It almost became comical." An occasional good laugh gave them the lift they needed. "The difficulties we've experienced through these problems only strengthened our love for each other," Oliver said. "It has helped us realize how precious life and our love are and that we want to hold on to every moment of it, no matter how hard the physical challenge may be."

Sandra and Edmund came face to face with mortality when the doctor told Sandra she had breast cancer. Two days later she had a mastectomy. Here's her report of their experience:

We thought that having a mastectomy was devastating but two weeks later I started chemotherapy and we began to learn what devastation really was. Edmund and I have been best friends since we were fifteen years old. We have been married for thirty-four years and have had a wonderful loving relationship. But I never dreamed that our love could reach such great heights as it has done with this terrible illness in our lives. I know from talking to others that when something tragic happens it will either build or destroy a marriage. We have had such a foundation of love, respect, and faith that our relationship just soared.

After three months of treatment I ended up in the hospital for a week. Everything seemed to crash at one time. As a side effect of the chemotherapy, I had developed a urinary infection and a blood clot in my leg. My red and white blood cell counts were dangerously low. My dear husband slept in a chair in my room for seven nights because he didn't want to be too far away from me. Now that is love. These problems were finally corrected and I am back on my chemotherapy schedule.

Early on through this difficult time we decided that the best way to handle what we were going through was with a lot of humor. One evening Edmund, our older son, Jason, and I had gone to the mall. It was the last time I was able to go in public without wearing a wig. The dreaded moment had arrived—my hair had started to fall out. It was very windy that evening. I said to my husband, "Hurry, Edmund, and open the door before all my hair blows away." Just then Jason, who was walking behind me, started gagging. I turned around and asked what was wrong. He answered, "Hair ball!" We all burst into laughter.

We have found that there are two ways to approach life. You can either be negative and feel sorry for yourself or you can laugh. We choose to laugh as much as we can.

Laughter, as mentioned in a previous chapter, can be very healing to the body and the spirit. It can shed a ray of light on a dark time.

Still, losing a breast can be a very traumatic experience for a woman . . . and a very difficult situation for her husband. Sometimes couples don't know how to talk about it. A woman may feel like she's lost her femininity. A husband may appear not to understand her loss if he says, "Honey, don't even worry about it. I love you no matter what." Inside she may be crying out to talk about how hard it is for her. It may help if he asks her how she is feeling about it and then just listens. If she's not ready to talk about it, that's okay. Don't push her. Just hold her and express your love without mentioning it. If she feels safe with you she will talk about it at some point. When she does, validate her feelings with a comment such as, "I can only imagine how hard this is for you." (Don't say "but" here; it will invalidate what you just said.) Continue with: "I love you so much and I'm so grateful you are alive and with me."

If she mentions that she must be less of a woman in your sight, you can simply say, "I'm sad it had to happen, and I will miss it, too. The most important thing is this, the woman I married—the real you—is still whole and still with me and that's all that really matters." Then hold each other. It's okay to feel the loss together instead of hiding feelings and not being able to talk about it. Talking about heartaches with each other is so very important in keeping your love strong.

Alan and his wife, Suzanne, came face to face with this reality when a crippling illness struck, making it impossible for him to perform onstage as he had done for the majority of his life. Because of the love he and Suzanne share, his illness has only strengthened their relationship. "Our marriage is a total commitment," she said as they addressed couples attending a marriage enrichment event. "This illness has only served to strengthen our love and desire to be there for each other, wherever that takes us." Alan added that "ours is a lasting love and we intend to have it endure to the end." That very statement inspired the creation of an "Endure to the End" ring, designed by their son, Doug, to help them and others have a symbol of their commitment to hold on through the adversities of life.

What happens if the spouse's mental functions are permanently affected? Sadie faced that dilemma after Hyrum was seriously injured in a farming accident. His head injuries were so severe that it left him with a different personality:

> Before the accident and throughout the many years we had been married Hyrum was the most gentle, caring husband any woman could ever want. He treated me with patience, respect, and tenderness. We had a wonderful marriage and were deeply in love. Since the accident he has never been the same. His tenderness and patience are gone. Sometimes I don't even recognize him as the same man I was married to all those years. He isn't physically abusive or anything like that, he's just short-tempered and sometimes mean in what he says to me. It breaks my heart and I yearn for the old Hyrum back.
>
> **WHEN YOU CREATE TENDER AND LOVING MEMORIES IT MAKES THE "HOLDING ON" POSSIBLE.**
>
> So often I think of the marriage vows ". . . in sickness, in health . . ." and I remember that I promised to "hang in there," even through the tough times—and that's exactly what I'm doing. The thing that helps me is the sweet memories. I go to bed some nights and wipe away my tears with the thoughts of all those wonderful years we had before the accident. Remem-

bering makes me act more lovable toward him and, at
times, helps him be more lovable to me.

Spouses whose mates have Alzheimer's know how very difficult it can be when a spouse loses his or her mental capacities.
And yet thousands hold on to each other with devotion
throughout the whole ordeal. That's what marriage is all
about—knowing that your mate will be there, no matter
what. When you create tender and loving memories it makes
the "holding on" possible and enriches your total marriage.

Another couple, Charese and Louis had no idea of the
struggles they were about to face as they sat in the doctor's office awaiting the news of Charese's latest tests. "I'm sorry to
tell you this, Charese . . . you have multiple sclerosis." They
were stunned. They had thought that the numbness in her
hands and feet was just poor circulation or some other problem that could be easily resolved—not a debilitating disease!
On their way home the tears started. In their bedroom that
night more tears flowed as they held each other. Then they
made a decision to enjoy all of the life they had left with each
other and do everything they could to keep this disease from
destroying their love. Louis would hold Charese's hand as he
drove along. They would spend time at their neighborhood
pool in the hot tub under the stars and they continued to
laugh and have fun, like they had before.

Year by year Charese became more and more crippled.
Without the help of friends and neighbors it would have
been an impossible situation for Louis. He accepted, even
asked for help at times. As time went on, however, he could
no longer lift and take care of her. Louis had to make the difficult and sad decision to put his wife in a nursing home.

All the time she was in the nursing home he remained her
devoted husband. He would take her for rides and do all he
could to make her time pleasant. Through the years, however,
he had moments when he would cry and wish with every

fiber of his being that this terrible illness had not happened to his wife. Turning to prayer seemed to provide his only solace and helped him endure. And when she died, Louis was devastated. To those seeking to console him he would say, "My sweet angel has gone to heaven. She doesn't have to suffer anymore. And I will miss her so much."

FACING THE DEATH OF YOUR SPOUSE

Though death of a beloved mate is the hardest of all deaths to bear, those who have loved each other fully are the ones who are most comforted by their sweet memories of their spouse. How sad it would be to have nothing but bitter memories of your life together. People who have loving marriages and lose their mates to death are generally more ready to marry again, probably because they know marriage can be such a wonderful experience.

We attended the funeral of a neighbor and were deeply moved by a tribute written by his surviving wife. He was an attorney and she a university professor. They were widowed when they married each other. As old age took its toll he could not longer get around like he used to. We would see them take "walks" around the block; he in his motorized wheelchair and she on his lap. It was a tender scene. With her permission we share her inspiring tribute to him.

> George and I used to talk long into the night. Sleep is for young people; older ones know that the time is short to speak of love and wonder at the joy of a good marriage. Our love for each other filled ten years of happiness I shall never know again in this life. We embraced each other's quirks and silliness as readily as we delighted in what we saw as accomplishments and triumphs. We talked about all those things that people care about: our children and their children, our own childhoods, and, of course, secrets we had never told

anyone else. Nighttime is a gentle cover in which a husband and wife can share a sweet tenderness that makes the rest of life bearable.

I often asked him what he thought it would be like to face the Lord after we died. He said he didn't know but that he didn't worry about it. Even though it was dark, I knew he was smiling when I repeatedly asked him to be my advocate during the review of my own life. I felt then, as I do now, that everyone needs a good lawyer at that point to direct conversation toward the brighter side. How often he just held my hand and told me not to worry. I knew the conversation was over when he said, "I have a suggestion." That always meant "let's go to sleep."

The ubiquitous checkerboard is folded in the old cardboard box. There are no more footsteps on the stairway at dinner time nor the smell of clam chowder—his favorite evening meal. I miss hearing him tell me to "get that yeller cat out of here" with no more real seriousness about removing Harley than when he spoke of my late poodle as the Pratt brat. His slippers and glasses will stay where they are for a while. I memorized his dear face in the last week we had together. We both knew that the end was close and I took every opportunity to stroke his forehead and remember with my fingers the shape of his cheeks and the softness of his hair.

Just before he died, I watched the light ebb slowly from his eyes and flicker a little when I thanked him for the time we had spent together. I sang to him the day before he died—all the old songs he loved: "In the Gloaming," "Just a Song at Twilight," "Let Me Call You Sweetheart," and "I Love You Truly." It calmed him when nothing else could. I whispered to him that Veda (his first wife), his mother and father, and his daughter Celia were waiting for him. I hope he could hear me and that they were all indeed just within reach. I am so happy to know that he is well now and free from pain and that I will see him again.

I wish all of you a love like ours that fills life with simple things like sharing a meal or a ride up the canyon or just reminding each other that yours is a good marriage. Those sweet memories are my solace now, until the time I can be with my darling once again. Goodbye for just a while, George. Thank you for our time together, for the wonderful husband, father, grandfather, and great-grandfather you were, and for the gentle sweet spirit you left for all of us to cherish.[66]

This is how it can be when husband and wife love and honor each other. That's how it was with another woman who wrote about her husband of thirty-two years after he passed away:

He was a hardworking man, a great provider, and very sweet and kind. If the world had more people like my husband, it would be a wonderful place.

What would your mate say if you were to leave this life today? Each of us can build a love worthy of such tribute.

BEGIN TODAY

There is a saying that "pain is inevitable, misery is an option." You may not be able to avoid pain in this life, but you can avoid the misery—the misery that comes when you don't work together as a couple. There is nothing more important than having a loving relationship with your spouse when the hard times come.

Joy and I were at a buffet dinner recently where we witnessed a very tender scene. We saw an elderly couple at the buffet tables, she in a wheelchair and he pushing it. He was bent and frail but obviously in better health than she. He would wheel the chair close to the table where she could see the display of food, then would ask her what she would like. She was holding her plate and he would then take it and put on it what she had requested. We heard him say, "Is that enough, sweetheart? Would you like more?" She would graciously thank him and they would move on to the next choice. It was a vivid display of married love in action—they were holding on through their hard time.

What hard time are you and your spouse going through right now? Are you holding on to each other or are you allowing it to drive you apart? Talk to each other about it and make a conscious decision to be there for each other, discuss what is needed from the other, and begin to work together. Two hearts holding on to each other will keep either one from breaking. Let the hard times cement your love, not destroy it.

Conclusion

Even if marriages are made in heaven, man
has to be responsible for the maintenance.
—JAMES C. DOBSON

THE LEGACY

Many of us have seen family members and friends give up on their marriages, usually resulting in a great deal of sorrow for them and their children. It seems that these couples got lost in the journey of marriage. Marriage is a journey, one that lasts throughout our lifetime. The way we handle our marriage not only affects *our* life but also affects the next generation's attitudes and behaviors regarding marriage. This can be both good and bad. Dan shared the legacy his parents passed on to him:

My parents had a traditional marriage in the sense that my dad had a job outside the home while my mom stayed home. She cooked, cleaned, took great care of Dad and us kids. As far as I could tell she never felt inferior or struggled with who she was. I think that was partly due to the way my dad looked at and appreciated her. He always told her how great she looked, how great the house was, how great the meals were, and so on. He made sure we kids did the same. She worked hard and he treated her like a queen. Consequently we never questioned her value. My parents appreciated the work the other did. They just seemed like they were a team working together. That gave us kids a great sense of security and has helped us immensely in our marriages.

As with Dan's parents, all couples can find the joy in their marriages that will leave a legacy of love for their children.

ONE STEP AT A TIME

Now that you know *The Fourteen Secrets to a Happy Marriage,* it is our hope that you are motivated to consciously work at implementing them and that you don't feel overwhelmed. Please do not expect yourself or your spouse to do them *all* immediately. The marriage journey happens one step at a time. As long as you keep working at taking the steps, these secrets will no longer be secrets—they will become a reality that brings you the marital happiness you have always wanted.

An inspired spiritual leader, Gordon B. Hinckley, ties it all together with this wise admonition to married couples:

> If there is forbearance, if there is forgiveness, if there is an anxious looking after the happiness of one's companion, then love will flourish and blossom. The prescription is simple and wonderfully effective. It is love. It is plain, simple, everyday love and respect.[67]

If you will work at living in that spirit, your home will be a haven from the world. The following lyrics, written by Joy, express the feelings of couples who have achieved that level of love. It applies to all whether you knelt at an altar, stood under a canopy, or said "I do" in a quiet courtroom, in a beautiful garden spot, or in the home of a justice of the peace. Wherever it takes place, marriage is sacred, beautiful, and can lead to these deep feelings of love for each other:

Forever I Love You

It was many years ago
Kneeling at a sacred altar
We promised that through all our days
Our love would never falter.

At times it seemed the foes of life
Would break us with the strife,
But through the pain and through the fears
We smiled and wiped away our tears.

With a gentleness you touch my cheek.
With words so soft I hear you speak,
"I love you. Forever and ever
I love you."

Those early years were hard
As we learned to live in unity.
We held on tight, would not let go—
Our love is for eternity.
We shared our feelings as we walked.
We built our bridges as we talked.
We learned to laugh and love and play,
Now peaceful joy is ours today.

With a gentleness you touch my cheek.
With words so soft I hear you speak,
"I love you. Forever and ever
I love you."

Victor Hugo said that "the supreme happiness of life is the conviction that we are loved."[68] It is our sincere desire for you to experience this supreme happiness in your marriage—a love that takes your romance, caring, respect, and compassion to the highest realm of peace and joy. These *Fourteen Secrets to a Happy Marriage* can help make that happen.

Notes

1. Lois Glenn Carlton, "D-I-V-O-R-C-E Does Not Spell Relief," *Latter-day Woman,* March 1998, p. 36, 37.
2. Barbara Kantrowitz and Pat Wingert, *Newsweek,* April 19, 1999, p. 57.
3. Dianne Hales and Doris Wild Helmering, "Marriage Counselor's Five Best Fixes" (*Reader's Digest,* www.readerdigest.com).
4. Jeanette C. Lauer and Robert H. Lauer, *Til Death Do Us Part* (New York: Harrington Park Press, Inc., 1986), p. 179.
5. Norman Vincent Peale, *The Christian Leader's Golden Treasury* (Indianapolis: Droke House, 1955), p. 195.
6. Kahlil Gibran, *The Harper Book of Quotations* (New York: HarperCollins, 1993), p. 280.
7. Dr. Carlfred Broderick, *Couples* (New York: Simon and Schuster, 1979), p. 168.
8. Ibid.
9. *Dear Abby, Daily Herald* (Provo, Utah), February 7, 2000, C6.
10. This account is his abbreviated classroom version of the story told in his book *Couples* (New York: Simon and Schuster, 1979), pp. 72–73.
11. Gary Smalley, *Hidden Keys to Loving Relationships* (Seminar workbook), (Paoli, PA: Relationships Today, Inc., 1988), p. 15.
12. Mark Starr and Martha Brant, *Newsweek,* July 19, 1999, p. 51.
13. Domenica del Corkier, *Laughter, the Best Medicine, Reader's Digest,* 1997, p. 179.
14. Joe Tanenbaum, *Male and Female Realities* (Sugar Land, Tex.: Candle Publishing, 1990), p. 112.
15. Ibid, p. 48.
16. Ibid, p. 43.
17. Ibid, p. 43.
18. Gordon B. Hinckley, *Ensign,* May 1996, p. 94.

19. Billy & Janice Hughey, *A Rainbow of Hope* (El Reno, Okla.: Rainbow Studies, Inc., 1994), p. 75.

20. William Makepeace Thackeray, *A Treasury of Wisdom and Inspiration* (New York: New American Library, 1954), p. 195.

21. Steven M. Sultanoff, Ph.D., *Therapeutic Humor* (Publication of the American Assoc. for Therapeutic Humor, Fall 1997, vol. XI, 5), p. 1.

22. Patricia Barry, "It's No Joke: Humor Heals," *AARP Bulletin,* Washington D.C., April 1999, p. 15.

23. Ibid.

24. Ibid.

25. W. M. Bova, *Reader's Digest,* March 1993, p. 144.

26. William Hoest Enterprises, Inc., *Daily Herald* (Provo, Utah), May 12, 1999.

27. Tim and Beverly LaHaye, *The Act of Marriage* (Grand Rapids, Mich.: Zondervan Publishing House, revised edition 1998), p. 152.

28. Shmuley Boteach, *Kosher Sex* (New York: Doubleday, 1999), pp. 89–90.

29. Joe Tanenbaum, *Male and Female Realities* (Sugar Land, Tex.: Candle Publishing Co., 1990), pp. 108–9.

30. Dr. Herbert J. Miles, *Sexual Happiness in Marriage* (Grand Rapids, Mich.: Zondervan, 1967), p. 78.

31. Howard W. Hunter, *Being a Righteous Husband and Father* (Salt Lake City: The Church of Jesus Christ of Latter-day Saints, 1994), p. 7.

32. Gordon B. Hinckley, *Standing for Something* (New York: Random House, 2000), p. 37.

33. Ginny Graves, *Parents,* March 2000, p. 112.

34. Robert W. Stock, "Lost and Found," *Modern Maturity,* September–October 1999, p. 50.

35. Geoffrey Cowley, "Looking Beyond Viagra," *Newsweek,* April 24, 2000, p. 77.

36. Susan Crain Bakos, "From Lib to Libido," *Modern Maturity,* September–October 1999, p. 56.

37. Ibid., p. 56.

38. Gary and Joy Lundberg, *I Don't Have to Make Everything All Better* (New York: Viking, 1999), p. 8.

39. Stephen R. Covey, *The 7 Habits of Highly Effective People* (New York: Simon & Schuster, 1990), p. 239.

40. Gary and Joy Lundberg, *I Don't Have to Make Everything All Better* (New York: Viking, 1999, pp. 51–52.

41. Carolyn Hoyt, "22 Minutes to a Better Marriage," *McCall's,* April 1997, p. 124.

42. Jimmy Carter, *Living Faith* (New York: Random House, 1996), p. 136.

43. Blaine Lee, *The Power Principle* (New York: Simon & Schuster, 1997), p. 1.

44. Leslie Lampert, "Mom vs. Dad Discipline," *Parents,* September 1999, p. 137.

45. Andy Dappen, "Live Well on One Income," *Reader's Digest,* August 1999, p. 137.

46. Amy Tan, *The Joy Luck Club* (New York: Putnam, 1989), p. 164.

47. Dave Ramsey, *Financial Peace* (New York: Viking, 1997), p. 77.

48. Ibid, p. 88.

49. Ibid, p. 90.

50. Thomas J. Stanley, Ph.D., and William D. Danko, Ph.D., *The Millionaire Next Door* (New York: Pocket Books, 1998), pp. 9–10.

51. Ibid, p. 40.

52. Olivia Mellan, "Men, Women, & Money," *Psychology Today,* January/February 1999.

53. Andy Dappen, "Live Well on One Income," *Reader's Digest,* August 1999, p. 136.

54. Joe Dominguez and Vicki Robin, *Your Money or Your Life* (New York: Penguin Books, 1999), p. 117.

55. P. Scott Richards and Allen E. Bergin, *A Spiritual Strategy for Counseling and Psychotherapy,* Washington, D.C.: American Psychological Association, 1997, p. 7.

56. Dr. Laura Schlessinger and Rabbi Stewart Vogel, *The Ten Commandments* (New York: HarperCollins, 1998), pp. 1, 2.

57. Kelly Smith, *Ensign,* March 1998, p. 31.

58. P. Scott Richards and Allen E. Bergin, *A Spiritual Strategy for Counseling and Psychotherapy,* Washington, D.C.: American Psychological Association, 1997, p. 7.

59. Jeanette C. Lauer and Robert H. Lauer, *Til Death Do Us Part* (New York: Harrington Park Press, Inc., 1986), p. 178.

60. Jeremy Taylor, *The New Dictionary of Thoughts* (Standard Book Company, 1961), p. 504.

61. Thomas Carlyle, *The Harper Book of Quotations* (New York: Harper-Collins, 1993), p. 312.

62. Joanna Powell, *Good Housekeeping,* September 1999, p. 110.

63. Suzy Chiazzari, *Body and Soul* (Watertown, Mass., 1999), p. 58.

64. Richard Carlson, *Don't Sweat the Small Stuff . . . and It's All Small Stuff* (New York: Hyperion, 1997), p. 121.

65. Dr. Laura Schlessinger and Rabbi Stewart Vogel, *The Ten Commandments* (New York: HarperCollins, 1998), p. 9.

66. Rosalie Rebollo Pratt on the occasion of the memorial service for George Harding Mortimer, February 28, 1998, used by permission.

67. Gordon B. Hinckley, *Ensign,* November 1997, p. 69.

68. Victor Hugo, *The Harper Book of Quotations* (New York: Harper-Collins, 1993), p. 273.

Index

MARRIAGE ENRICHMENT SEMINARS AND/OR WEEKEND RETREATS

Gary and Joy Lundberg help couples gain a new understanding of what makes marriage happy and fulfilling. Whether newlyweds or longtime marrieds, happily married or on the brink of divorce, these presentations will open the eyes and hearts of all couples to ideas that will reignite their love and put new life into their relationship.

These events can be sponsored by a church or other organizations wishing to help strengthen marriages and families, or business groups wanting to give a bonus to employees and spouses at a convention or other event. The length of the seminar can be adjusted to fit the needs of the sponsor.

To learn more about the Lundbergs and other addresses and seminars they present and to see their current schedule of events, visit their Web site at **www.allbetter.net** or call 1-800-224-1606.

FOR THE BEST IN PAPERBACKS, LOOK FOR THE

In every corner of the world, on every subject under the sun, Penguin represents quality and variety—the very best in publishing today.

For complete information about books available from Penguin—including Puffins, Penguin Classics, and Compass—and how to order them, write to us at the appropriate address below. Please note that for copyright reasons the selection of books varies from country to country.

In the United Kingdom: Please write to *Dept. EP, Penguin Books Ltd, Bath Road, Harmondsworth, West Drayton, Middlesex UB7 0DA.*

In the United States: Please write to *Penguin Putnam Inc., P.O. Box 12289 Dept. B, Newark, New Jersey 07101-5289* or call 1-800-788-6262.

In Canada: Please write to *Penguin Books Canada Ltd, 10 Alcorn Avenue, Suite 300, Toronto, Ontario M4V 3B2.*

In Australia: Please write to *Penguin Books Australia Ltd, P.O. Box 257, Ringwood, Victoria 3134.*

In New Zealand: Please write to *Penguin Books (NZ) Ltd, Private Bag 102902, North Shore Mail Centre, Auckland 10.*

In India: Please write to *Penguin Books India Pvt Ltd, 11 Panchsheel Shopping Centre, Panchsheel Park, New Delhi 110 017.*

In the Netherlands: Please write to *Penguin Books Netherlands bv, Postbus 3507, NL-1001 AH Amsterdam.*

In Germany: Please write to *Penguin Books Deutschland GmbH, Metzlerstrasse 26, 60594 Frankfurt am Main.*

In Spain: Please write to *Penguin Books S. A., Bravo Murillo 19, 1° B, 28015 Madrid.*

In Italy: Please write to *Penguin Italia s.r.l., Via Benedetto Croce 2, 20094 Corsico, Milano.*

In France: Please write to *Penguin France, Le Carré Wilson, 62 rue Benjamin Baillaud, 31500 Toulouse.*

In Japan: Please write to *Penguin Books Japan Ltd, Kaneko Building, 2-3-25 Koraku, Bunkyo-Ku, Tokyo 112.*

In South Africa: Please write to *Penguin Books South Africa (Pty) Ltd, Private Bag X14, Parkview, 2122 Johannesburg.*